DAVID SHEFF is
with John Lennon an
California, with his wife and son. He spent more than two
years interviewing Nintendo executives in Japan, the United
States and Europe, and his work has appeared in *Playboy,
Conde Nast Traveller* and *Rolling Stone* magazine.

Game Over

David Sheff

Nintendo's Battle to Dominate
an Industry

CORONET BOOKS
Hodder & Stoughton

Copyright © David Sheff 1993

The right of David Sheff to be identified as the Author of
the Work has been asserted by him in accordance with the
Copyright, Designs and Patents Act 1988.

First published in Great Britain 1993 by
Hodder and Stoughton Ltd

10 9 8 7 6 5 4 3 2 1

First published in paperback 1994 by Hodder and Stoughton Ltd,
A division of Hodder Headline PLC.
Abridged edition 1999.

A Coronet paperback

All rights reserved. No part of this publication may be
reproduced, stored in a retrieval system, or transmitted,
in any form or by any means without the prior written
permission of the publisher, nor be otherwise circulated
in any form of binding or cover other than that in which
it is published and without a similar condition being
imposed on the subsequent purchaser.

British Library Cataloguing in Publication Data

Sheff, David
Game Over: Nintendo's Battle to Dominate an Industry
I. Title
338.4779480952

ISBN 0 340 75193 2

Typeset by Hewer Text Ltd, Edinburgh
Printed and bound in Great Britain by
Caledonian International Book Manufacturing Ltd, Glasgow

Hodder and Stoughton Ltd
A Division of Hodder Headline PLC
338 Euston Road
London NW1 3BH

This book is dedicated to Karen Barbour, who insists that Donatello, Rafael, Leonardo, and Michelangelo are painters, not Teenage Mutant Ninja Turties, and to my son, Nicolas, who introduced me to Nintendo, but now prefers reading.

Games are popular art, collective, social *reactions* to the main drive or action of any culture. [They] . . . are extensions of social man and of the body politic . . .

As extensions of the popular response to the workaday stress, games become faithful models of a culture. They incorporate both the action and the reaction of whole populations in a single dynamic image . . . The games of a people reveal a great deal about them.

–MARSHALL MCLUHAN
Understanding Media:
The Extensions of Man

ACKNOWLEDGEMENTS

Brief portions of this book appeared in *Rolling Stone, Playboy, Men's Life*, and *San Francisco Focus*. Thanks to sources named and unnamed, the hundreds of interview subjects. Thanks particularly to the following: At NCL, Hiroshi Yamauchi, Hiroshi Imanishi, Sigeru Miyamoto, Masayuki Uemura, Genyo Takeda, Gunpei Yokoi, Reiko Wakimoto, and Yasuhiro Minagawa. At NOA, Minoru Arakawa, Howard Lincoln, Peter Main, Al Stone, Phil Rogers, Gail Tilden, Don James, John Sakaley, Toshiko Watson, Sandy Hatcher, Sherrie Mennie, Tony Harman, Blaine Phelps, and numerous others, particularly Bill White. Yoko Arakawa was especially gracious and forthcoming. At Sega, Al Nilsen. At Atari Games, Hide Nakajima, Dennis Wood, Dan Van Elderen, and Barry Kane. At Electronic Arts, Trip Hawkins, Bing Gordon, Larry Probst, Danny Brooks, and particularly Holly Hartz, who sets the standard for public relations in this industry.

At other Nintendo licensees, Henk Rogers, Sheila Boughten,

Greg Fischbach, Bruce Lowry, Gilman Louie, Les Crane, Bob Lloyd, Allyne Mills, Joe Morici, Kathleen Watson, Kathy Prall, and the many others. At Hill & Knowlton, Jeff Fox, Karen Peck, Don Varyu, and especially Lynn Gray, for support above and beyond the line of duty when she initially championed this book. At Golin/Harris, Alison Holt and Susan Iannetta, and at Manning, Selvage and Lee, Charlene Gigliotti.

Analysts, including David Leibowitz (American Securities), Manny Gerard and Sean McGowan (Gerard Kaluer Mattison & Co.), Robert F. Kleiber (Piper, Jaffray & Hopwood), and Andrew J. Kessler (Morgan Stanley), periodically contributed their expertise.

I'd also like to thank Robert M. Callagy, Vladimir Pokhilko, Vadim Gerasimov, Howard Phillips, Nolan Bushnell, Robert Stein, Ron Judy, Suzuki Eiichi, Miyuki Grace, Jim Makonochie, Steve Arnold, Elliot Luber, Deborah Brown, Phil Adam, David Ellis, Ben Myron, Mark Smotrof, Les Inanchy (Sony), Greg Zachary of *The Wall Street Journal*, Casey Corr, Tim Healy and Tom Farrey of the *Seattle Times*, Rich Karlgaard at *Forbes ASAP*, Jaron Lanier (J.P.L.), Sharon Fitzpatrick (The Learning Co.), Lynn Hale and Sue Sesserman (Lucasfilm and LucasArts), Marty Taucher (Microsoft), Linda Goetz, and Jenifer Van Horn. In Japan: Keisuke Ono, Yukio Miyazaki, Tsunekazu Ishihara, Yoshio Ito, Koh Shimizu (Sony), and Nishi Saimaru.

Special appreciation goes to Alexey Pajitnov, the creator of 'Tetris.' Also to many sources who spoke under the condition of anonymity. At Random House, I would like to acknowledge the contributions of Deborah Aiges, Carol Schneider, Lesley Oelsner, Mitchell Ivers, Gail Blackhall, Lawrence LaRose, Becky Simpson, Brian Hudgins, and designer Oksana Kushnir, Amy Edelman for pushing deadlines, and Veronica Windholz, Ed Cohen, and Sybil Pincus for tireless copy editing.

Special thanks to my editor for his insights and his devotion to books, to Binky Urban, my agent, for her counsel and commitment, and to Barry Golson for assigning the original Nintendo article from which this book grew. My thanks as well to Arthur and to Mike Moritz and Fred Bernstein for their insights and advice. Thanks also to Amy Rennert, who assigned the article on Nolan

Bushnell for *San Francisco Focus*; to Don and Nancy Barbour, as impeccable a research department as anyone could ask for, and to the rest of my family, Joan, Sumner, Debbie, Mark, and Jenny; Steve, Susan, and Don, and my extended family of friends, including Armistead, Terry, Peggy, Susan, Buddy, Nick, and Doug.

CONTENTS

Acknowledgements	vii
Introduction from Arcade	xiii
1. A New Leader of the Club	3
2. In Heaven's Hands	12
3. I, Mario	36
4. Inside the Mother Brain	55
5. Coming to America	71
6. For a Fistful of Quarters	93
7. Reversal of Fortune	113
8. Enter the Dragon	134
9. The Grinch Who Stole Christmas	160
10. From Russia with Love	170
11. The 'Tetris' Song	193
12. Sonic Boom	223
Selected Bibliography	238

INTRODUCTION FROM ARCADE

Game Over was written in 1993. Since this time the videogames industry has both grown and changed dramatically. The record-breaking popularity of PlayStation has led to Sony emerging as a force to rival Nintendo. Indeed, many business analysts conclude that Nintendo's days as the game industry's '900lb gorilla' are over.

This doesn't mean that *Game Over*'s content has dated, however. What David Sheff has written is far more than a chronicle of Nintendo's rise to glory, it is a glimpse 'behind the curtain' at how videogames are made. Furthermore, the vast majority of the personalities you'll meet in the book – Shigeru Miyamoto, Hiroshi Yamauchi, Minoru Arakawa and Howard Lincoln – are still running Ninendo today. Besides, while it may be the case that Nintendo 64 has lost in battle to PlayStation, the war between Nintendo and Sony is far from over.

Once described as 'the greatest book about videogames . . . ever!' by *Next Generation* magazine, *Game Over* is – perhaps above everything else – a damn good read for anyone into gaming. *Arcade* magazine is very pleased to be able to offer you this edited version, free of charge, with the May issue. We hope you enjoy it.

Neil West

GAME OVER

A NEW LEADER OF THE CLUB

Most people think video games are kids' stuff, and it is true that in 'Super Mario Bros. 3,' mushrooms give super strength, enemies have names such as Morton Koopa, Jr., and a pudgy, suspendered hero jumps on the heads of Little Goombas. Yet behind 'Super Mario Bros. 3,' a video game played on the Nintendo Entertainment System (NES), is a business that is very grown-up indeed. In America alone, revenues for that one game have topped $500 million; in the field of entertainment, only the movie *ET* has grossed more.

In the video-game market, where shooting and mass destruction were the norm, the first 'Super Mario Bros.' game created a revolution in 1985 by introducing elements not often associated with computer terminals and controllers: wit and humor. Mario, the main character, made an unlikely hero – a plumber who can wisely choose to avoid enemies as well as to confront them. In this whimsical world, bright green and red mushrooms make Mario grow taller and more powerful. There are bomb-hurling mice, waltzing cacti, and turtles who can use their shells as missiles. Surprises that give players more time and extra lives lurk in the most unlikely places. Children, who loved the characters and became ensnared in the maze of the game, which was replete with Pavlovian rewards and punishments and carefully programmed increases in challenge, were captivated.

When 'Super Mario Bros. 2' was released, the beloved characters from the original game trekked through new cartoon scenery. This time they confronted foes not with cannon or lasers but with turnips, carrots, and pumpkins. Thus equipped, players headed into uncharted waters, where perseverance, wit, luck, and interminable hours of practice counted for everything. 'Super Mario 2,' like its predecessor, was a great equalizer. The game gave kids the sort of power they couldn't get anywhere else. It was safe for them to make mistakes while playing, because there was always another chance. The things that ordinarily made kids popular at school were not important when they were playing. Also, they had found an arena in which they could beat the pants off their parents, not to mention confound them with an incomprehensible vernacular ('I'm in the second world of the Sub-Con, but I can't get past the miniboss').

Months before it appeared on the market, there were rumors about the next 'Super Mario Bros.' sequel, but no one saw it until, in the winter of 1989, a movie hit the nation's theaters. *The Wizard* was less a piece of art than a one-hundred-minute advertisement for Nintendo that millions of families paid to see (it grossed $14 million). The excitement in movie theaters was palpable when kids realized they were glimpsing the latest Mario game, complete with new bells and whistles: Mario could don a raccoon disguise and – best – could fly.

Kids spread the word on playgrounds and in schools. Legions of parents were strong-armed by eight-year-olds. The pressure was enormous to be among the first to own 'Super Mario Bros. 3.'

Some parents remained oblivious and others refused to bend to the pressure, but many millions succumbed. 'Super Mario Bros. 3' would sell more copies than any video game in history – 7 million in the United States and 4 million in Japan. By record-industry standards, 'SMB3' went platinum eleven times. Michael Jackson is one of the few artists to have accomplished that feat.

The money earned from its video games and the NES system that played them transformed Nintendo into one of the world's most profitable companies. By 1991 Nintendo had supplanted Toyota as Japan's most successful company, based on the indices of growth potential, profitability, penetration of foreign and domestic markets, and stock performance. Nintendo made more for its shareholders and paid higher dividends between 1988 and 1992 than almost any other company traded on the Tokyo Stock Exchange.

Nintendo's profits per employee were consistently greater than those of any other Japanese company (excluding finance, stock, and insurance companies). Fujitsu, with profits similar to Nintendo's, had 50,000 employees. Nintendo had 850. Nintendo, in 1991, earned about $1.5 million per employee. Internationally, Nintendo employed some 5,000 people. That year Sony, with 50,000 employees, earned $400 million less than Nintendo. By 1992, the company was consistently earning pre-tax profits of more than a billion dollars a year.

The multitentacled video-game business swelled to consume larger and larger segments of the entertainment and consumer-electronics industries as well as the toy industry.

In the entertainment business, Nintendo had become a force that could not be ignored. In the early 1990s, the company netted as much as *all the American movie studios* combined and profited more than any of them, and more than the three television networks combined.

The consumer-electronics industry watched as the Nintendo Entertainment System, in just five short years, was brought into more than a third of the households in the United States and Japan. Although twice as many homes had VCRs, the movie-playing machines were made by various companies, while one company alone made all the Nintendo machines. Moreover, the VCR companies sold just the machines, not the videotapes that played on them. Nintendo, on the other hand, was making hefty profits from an ever-expanding list of games in addition to the machines to play them on. Consumer-electronics giants like Sony and Matsushita Electric Industrial finally woke up to the fact that by the turn of the century, consumer-hardware companies would be archaic if they had no involvement in software. In a game of catch-up, Sony bought Columbia Pictures and Matsushita purchased MCA, the American movie-and-entertainment giant – attempts to wrest some participation in the entertainment software market.

Nintendo had completely blindsided the American computer industry, too. The founders of the personal-computer revolution had predicted in the early eighties that computers would soon be commonplace in most homes, like toasters. Yet a decade after the personal computer was launched, only 24 million American homes had them – almost 10 million fewer than had Nintendo systems. Worldwide, there were about an equal number of Nintendo systems and PCs, some 50 to 60 million. As with VCRs, the PCs were manufactured by dozens of companies; less than 10 percent were made by the number-one PC company, IBM. With the exception of a growing number of illegal pirate versions coming out of Hong Kong and Taiwan, just *one* company manufactured and sold all the Nintendo systems. The huge Japanese computer company NEC and a video-arcade-game company, Sega, tried to compete with Nintendo, but in spite of investments in the hundreds of millions of dollars, they shared less than 10 to 15 percent of the market through 1991. Companies such as Apple and IBM looked over their shoulders and saw Nintendo on their heels. When Apple Computer president Michael Spindler was asked in March 1991 which computer company Apple feared most in the 1990s, he answered, 'Nintendo.'

The computer industry understood why Nintendo had a jump on them: Nintendo had predicated its entire strategy on the control of both hardware and software. In 1991, Apple and IBM announced an alliance to take on Microsoft, the software giant. In 1992, IBM also announced an alliance with Time Warner. Like the consumer-electronics companies, the computer-hardware giants realized that to remain competitive, they needed access to and control of software. The software edge would become particularly important in the looming battle for shares in the next technological revolution – multimedia and networking. That industry, which combines computer power with home-entertainment systems, integrating television, video recorders, CD sound systems, and the telephone, was judged by the *Los Angeles Times* to be worth a mind-boggling $3.5 trillion annually by the next century. The question was which company would become the Maytag of home computers in the potentially mammoth industry.

Did Nintendo have the foresight and wherewithal – and sheer temerity – to be that ambitious? Evidence that it did was hidden in the belly of the NES unit.

On the bottom of the innocuous, gray game-playing machine was a panel. When it was removed, a computer cable connector was revealed. A two-way doorway to the main processor, this port allowed the Nintendo system to work as a terminal that could be connected to a modem, a keyboard, or auxiliary storage devices. The Nintendo system was rolled into living rooms by children who welcomed (and worshiped) it as a game, while inside it lurked the potential to be transformed into the integral component of the largest electronic network in the country. With a phone line plugged into it, the Nintendo system could be used to shop, call up movie reviews, buy pork bellies, do research, make airline reservations, and order a pizza.

The machine's greater possibilities were first tapped in Japan when Nintendo announced the Family Computer Communications Network System. A similar network planned for the United States had the potential to dwarf the Prodigy network (a joint venture of IBM and Sears Roebuck), the most-used network in the country, which had only 1.3 million subscribers by January 1992.

Nintendo's success had an enormous impact on numerous industries worldwide. Besides the competing hardware companies, more than a hundred companies that made video games rode the Nintendo wave. In 1992 they had worldwide sales of 170 million cartridges, at an average cost of $40 each – almost $7 billion worth.

Once it became clear that the huge video-game market showed no signs of disappearing, all kinds of companies began lining up to become licensed producers of Nintendo-compatible games. Companies such as Electronic Arts and Software Toolworks, which made only games on floppy disks for computers, had tried to hold out, but Nintendo became too big to ignore. They signed up, as did some entertainment companies, including Lucasfilm and Disney (through another company called Capcom). Companies that were already cleaning up with coin-operated video games set up in arcades, malls, bowling alleys, and pizza parlors entered the Nintendo business too, adapting their hit arcade titles to the home system.

Other companies affected by Nintendo's success were outside the video-game industry. Since computer chips were used in both the Nintendo hardware and software (the game cartridges contained special chips), Nintendo used more of certain kinds of semi-conductors than any other company in Japan. Nintendo products accounted for more than 3 percent of total Japanese semiconductor production in 1991.

Quietly, Nintendo sailed past stalwart American corporations such as IBM, Disney, and Apple Computer, not only in profitability but also in impact on American culture. In the last part of the twentieth century, leaps in technology ushered in a new era in which children and a substantial part of the culture as a whole would be more influenced by interactive electronic media – in their simplest form, video games – than by television, which had defined the previous generation. The signs of the first Nintendo generation appeared as early as 1989 and 1990. A study by Nielsen Media Research, the company that monitors television viewing, showed that within a particular age group more kids were playing Nintendo than were watching the major children's TV network, Nickelodeon, at certain times on certain days of the week. Kids already spent more time in electronic environments (TV, radio, records) than they did in school or talking with friends or parents. Some of them were spending an additional two hours a day on Nintendo.

Even during the hours when kids weren't playing video games, they were being showered with the culture of Nintendo. Television cartoon shows based on Nintendo games and characters were watched by more kids than any other TV programs. Other cartoon shows (including *The Simpsons, Teenage Mutant Ninja Turtles, Chip 'N Dale Rescue Rangers*, and *Duck Tales)* became Nintendo games. A record of Nintendo songs and a feature film were developed; there were Nintendo magazines, books, videos, cereals, notebooks, drinking mugs, T-shirts, board games, puzzles, dolls, wallpaper, and bed sheets. Nintendo infiltrated every conceivable market until the question was not whether Nintendo's invasion would succeed but what the invaders would leave in their wake.

What, asked parents, teachers, and sociologists, were the long-term effects of so much game playing on kids' self-images, relationships, and social skills? How did Nintendo affect learning? Did the games encourage violence? Did they empower kids or make them passive? Did the impact vary among different age groups and genders?

Some saw video games as insidious hypnotizers and mind destroyers; others viewed them as training tools for the cybernetic world of the future. One proponent claimed that children who excelled at one game, 'Tetris,' scored higher on intelligence tests.

Besides the attempts to figure out the effect of Nintendo's invasion, there was also a great deal of intellectualizing about *why* Nintendo had become so pervasive. In an essay in the *San Francisco Examiner's Image* magazine in September 1991, 'Condemned to be Mario: The Video-game Plumber as Existential Hero,' Scott Rosenberg wrote, 'Mario is a character, a dumpy fellow with a big mustache; but he is also a stand-in, your iconic representation in the video universe . . . If millions of children and adults have melded with Mario . . . it may not be simply a matter of our shortening attention spans, our craving for novelty or our susceptibility to expensive ad campaigns. It may be that in Mario's fate – stuck in a world not of his own choosing, charged with a nearly impossible mission, doomed to perish sooner or later, yet free while he lives to grow, learn, slay demons and stop to smell the Fire Flowers – people are catching a crude, bright, hypnotic reflection of their own lives.' Or maybe it *was* just the ad campaign.

One thing was inarguable, however. Nintendo had successfully entered the collective consciousness. 'Q' ratings, which indicate the popularity of politicians, movie stars, and other public figures based on controlled surveys, showed that in 1990 the Nintendo mascot, Super Mario, was more recognized by American children than Mickey Mouse. How significant was the news? Uncle Walt Disney and Mickey Mouse were as American as – well, nothing was more American than Walt and Mickey. The idea that Mario had become more popular than Mickey was to some a travesty that signaled the next phase of the Japanese invasion. Japan had already captured America's wallets. The country's minds – beginning with children's minds – were next.

Nintendo had become Japan's biggest cultural export. Indeed, whereas the rest of the world devoured Japanese hardware – cars, Walkmen, TVs – Japanese 'software,' such as movies, books, art, and music, had little impact outside Japan. The exception was video games. The most widely known Japanese cultural ambassador was Mario and with him came a new set of values.

Generations of children had been imbued with Mickey's message: *We play fair and we work hard and we're in harmony . . . M-I-C . . . See you real soon. K-E-Y . . . Why? Because we like you . . .* Mario imparted other values: *Kill or be killed. Time is running out. You are on your own.* Donald Katz, in a February 1990 *Esquire* magazine article, observed that the lesson from Mario is 'there's always somebody bigger and more powerful than you are [and] . . . even if you kill the bad guys and save the girl – eventually you will die.'

Oh no! Not again! At the end of summer 1991, the children of America heard that the sequel to 'Super Mario Bros. 3' was on its way. For their parents, this was even more terrible news than the last time, because Nintendo had also introduced an entire new video-game system more powerful and of course more expensive than the original. 'Super Mario Bros. 4' would play only on the new Super Nintendo System.

In Japan, kids swamped stores to get their Super systems as soon as it was released. Most of them went home empty-handed; the game sold out in three days. Stores illegally parceled them out, sometimes inflating the prices, other times forcing buyers to purchase additional products if they wanted a Super Nintendo System.

In the United States, in the midst of a recession, Nintendo was less confident that the $200 Super NES would sell. By 1991, some observers of the video-game industry, noting slower sales and gloomier projections, suggested (almost gleefully) that kids seemed to be cooling off to Nintendo – that this might be the beginning of

Goliath's fall. But Nintendo had no intention of going gently. To push the new system, Nintendo packaged 'Super Mario Bros. 4,' which went under the name 'Super Mario World,' together with the Super Nintendo hardware, like the prize in a box of Frosted Flakes.

Soon the playgrounds were abuzz with news about 'Super Mario World.' Even those children who had grown bored with the original Nintendo system were excited, encouraged by the company's $25 million ad campaign. Parents, who had watched with relief as their children's fanaticism for Nintendo seemed to be fading, were greeted with a new wave of fervor. 'Dad,' the children enthused, 'you won't *believe* what Mario can do now . . .' In October 1991, Nintendo issued a press release titled 'Nintendo Loyalists Put Long-term Entertainment Value Ahead of Short-term Budget Cuts,' in which it was reported that the Super NES was selling at a rate of twelve units every retail minute, or one every five seconds. In spite of the recession and all the gloom and doom, Nintendo projected that 1992 would be its biggest year yet, with sales in America topping $4.7 billion.

2

IN HEAVEN'S HANDS

In the eastern part of Kyoto, the ancient Japanese capital city, near the famous Heian shrine, is a slumbering side street now called Higashi-ogi. In the fifteenth century, it was a pathway of hard-packed dirt that led to the Shogoin Gotenso, the summer castle of the emperor. Across from the castle stood the home of the emperor's special doctor.

Centuries later, this home was bought by Fusajiro Yamauchi. The Yamauchis would live there for generations, behind an immense gate held together with large bolts and rusted diamond-shaped brackets. The huge metal hinges that hold it up are serpents, attached to beams more than a cubic foot thick. The gate, which has survived for five hundred years, locks shut with a heavy crossbar.

Fusajiro Yamauchi was an artist and craftsman during the Meiji period, at the end of the time that Western civilization describes as the nineteenth century. Yamauchi, reputed to be fair, good-humored, and skillful, made *karuta*, playing cards. The Portuguese and Dutch had brought card games to Japan as long as 350 years ago, but the cards Yamauchi made had more in common with ancient Japanese games that were played with intricately painted seashells. *Hanafuda*, or 'flower cards,' smaller and thicker than Western cards, came to replace seashells, but the elaborate, richly colored images on them remained.

The most popular *hanafuda* game, matching flowers, appeared to be a simple game of matching images in order to make packs, but it could be as complex as bridge, and it was taken as seriously.

Yamauchi founded Nintendo Koppai in Meiji 22 (1889), to produce and sell the handmade cards. The *kanji* characters he chose to make up the name of his new company – *nin-ten-do* – could be understood as 'Leave luck to heaven,' or 'Deep in the mind we have to do whatever we have to do.' The most common reading of it was 'Work hard, but in the end it is in heaven's hands.'

Yamauchi made the paper for the flower cards in the traditional way, from the bark of mulberry, or *mitsu-mata*, trees. He pounded the bark into a paste and added clay to give it more weight. Thin layers were dried and pulled and shaped. The craftsman regarded paper as a living creature with a will of its own. Yamauchi fought with it until, at the end, it succumbed to *his* will, its new form.

Several layers were pressed together until the rigid thickness of a hardback book cover was achieved. Yamauchi designed a woodblock printing system to emboss the outline of the individual cards on a large sheet of the paper. He laid a series of stencils over the paper and, using luminous inks made from flower petals and berries, filled in the drawings. Backgrounds were red. Grass was black. The full moon was left unpainted, the straw color of the paper. The pigments bled slightly together when they met, so each card seemed hand-dyed.

Nintendo's *hanafuda* cards, called *Daitoryo* (or President), became the most popular cards in the Kyoto region. They were sold in Nintendo's shops in Kyoto and Osaka. Nintendo also made cards with different symbols that were sold in other regions. Kanto's, for instance, had swords, mountains, and human beings.

So long as *hanafuda* was solely a domestic amusement, Nintendo's business remained small and only modestly profitable, but business increased when the flower cards began to be used for gambling. In the absence of horse or dog racing or sports pools, the *yakuza*, Japan's equivalent of the Mafia, operated high-stakes games of *hanafuda* in casino-like parlors. Nintendo profited handsomely, since professional players would begin each new game with a fresh deck, discarding the old one. To keep up with the demand, Fusajiro Yamauchi trained apprentices to mass-produce the cards.

He expanded his business again in 1907, when Nintendo became the first Japanese company to manufacture Western-style playing cards, which were becoming popular in Japan. Yamauchi, who had been selling his cards only in Nintendo's shops, now needed greater distribution. He negotiated a deal with Japan Tobacco and Salt Public Corporation, the tobacco monopoly, and that company began selling Nintendo *karuta* in its cigarette shops throughout the country.

It was a profitable arrangement. By the time Fusajiro was ready to retire, Nintendo was by far the largest Japanese playing-card company.

Fusajiro Yamauchi had no son. If Nintendo was to remain in the family, Japanese tradition required that his daughter, Tei, marry a man who could take over for him. A marriage was arranged with a stern, hardworking student named Sekiryo Kaneda. He agreed to take the Yamauchi family name, as was custom if he wanted to enter his bride's family's business. In 1929, Sekiryo Yamauchi became Nintendo's second president.

Although Sekiryo and Tei's home life was not easy (she stoically tolerated her husband's philandering), they prospered. Sekiryo's outside business passion was real estate, and the Yamauchis came to own a sizable portion of eastern Kyoto as Sekiryo worked to transform Nintendo.

In 1933, he established a joint-venture corporation called Yamauchi-Nintendo and moved from the original, modest *hanafuda* shop in Kyoto to a ferroconcrete building he had constructed next door. In 1947, he created a distribution company called Marufuku to sell new varieties of modern, Western-style playing cards – pinochle and poker decks – with fancy backs. He built a sales force that called on small and large shops all over Japan. To produce the cards more quickly and efficiently (with paper bought from suppliers) he developed an assembly line of workers. Nintendo became an efficiently run business with a rigid, hierarchical management structure. Industrious managers, pressured to surpass the performance of their colleagues, were notoriously tough on subordinates.

Sekiryo and Tei were the second generation of Yamauchis to have daughters but no sons. Kimi, their eldest, married Shikanojo Inaba, from a respected family of craftsmen. Like his father-in-law before him, Inaba adopted his wife's surname and thereby became the heir apparent to Nintendo. It was assumed that Shikanojo Yamauchi would take over when Sekiryo retired.

In 1927, Shikanojo and Kimi had a child, Hiroshi, the first Yamauchi male to be born in three generations. Hiroshi was five when Shikanojo ran away, abandoning his wife and son. The young boy was told that his father was worthless and deceitful. Nothing else was ever said of him.

Disgraced, Kimi began divorce proceedings and moved in with her sister, leaving Hiroshi in the care of her parents. They reared him with the same iron fist with which they ran Nintendo. They attended to his education, his grooming, and his manners with equal severity. But Hiroshi rebelled, and the older he got, the more intractable he became.

Arrogant and impudent, Hiroshi disregarded his grandparents as he grew into a balefully handsome and debonair gentleman who carried his small body with conceited sturdiness, his head jutting forward. He wore his thick hair back and his eyebrows swept downward around his dark eyes. Hiroshi dressed in expensive, well-tailored clothes. He kept his fingernails long, manicured, and polished. He was sullen and bitter, yet he disguised his moods with levity and a dust-dry wit. His temperament was the legacy of an absent father and his grandparents' scorn.

Hiroshi saw his mother on occasion, but Kimi, who never remarried, had become more like an aunt. She worked at Nintendo, where she ran a subsidiary that was involved in sales.

Hiroshi Yamauchi never saw his father again. Shikanojo had brought shame and dishonor to the family, and when he returned, aged and ailing, desperate to see his only son, Hiroshi refused to speak to him.

One day when Hiroshi was in his late twenties, his hair already graying, he heard from a half sister he didn't know he had: their father had died of a stroke. She said Hiroshi should honor his father's memory by attending the funeral.

Yamauchi sat alone for a full day before deciding he would go.

At the funeral, Hiroshi met his four half sisters, his father's second wife, and an aunt he had never known. He was overwhelmed when his aunt told him he looked exactly like his father, and he wondered what else he had inherited from Shikanojo. He also wondered what price a son would have to pay for refusing to reconcile and forgive his father.

Hiroshi grieved for months after the funeral. He cried freely; the death changed him, and a part of him never seemed to heal. Throughout the rest of his life, he made regular visits to Shikanojo's grave.

Hiroshi was sent to a preparatory school in Kyoto in 1940, and Sekiryo planned on sending him to a university to study law or engineering. But war came, and all lives in Japan were put on hold. During the war, Hiroshi's grandmother, Tei, emerged as the leader of the Yamauchi family. The rest of the family would go underground when the air-raid sirens wailed through Kyoto nights, but Tei resolutely went about her business as if nothing was out of the ordinary.

Tei would not consider allowing Hiroshi to enter the military. When the war began, he was too young to fight, and by the time he could have been called up, the tide had already turned and the Yamauchis knew that Japan would lose. To keep him safely out of the war, Tei made Hiroshi stay in school, and he was given an assignment in a military factory.

Rice and other food were scarce; most people in the area survived on little but potatoes. Yamauchi, however, carried a precious rice lunch to work each day, from the stockpile in Tei's pantry. During his lunch break, Hiroshi noticed that a supervisor was hungrily eyeing his rice. Hiroshi shared it with the man and was rewarded, that afternoon, with time off. Hiroshi went out to a field and took a nap. After that, Yamauchi brought two lunch boxes to work each day, one for himself and one for the supervisor, and each day he was excused from work.

When the war ended in 1945, Yamauchi enrolled in Waseda University to study law. He also entered into a marriage arranged by his grandfather. His bride was Michiko Inaba (no relation to Shikanojo), a descendant of a very high-ranking samurai, loyal to the *daimyo* who lorded over Shikoku Island during the early Meiji period. This powerful and wealthy samurai had moved from Shikoku to Kyoto, where he married and took the Inaba name. He opened a small business, making delicate cloisonné pieces – Inaba cloisonné would become known throughout the world.

In Japan, when a marriage was formally arranged, the couple's parents would meet to discuss the match. However, because Hiroshi's grandparents were making the match, the couple's first date was a meeting of the two clans: the matchmaker was host to Sekiryo and Tei and Kimi Yamauchi as well as Michiko's parents and four grandparents. The couple was married soon after in a traditional ceremony.

When Hiroshi was twenty-one his grandfather had a stroke. Sekiryo asked that the young man be sent in to see him. His grandfather, propped up on pillows on his bed, spoke soberly to Hiroshi. As the first Yamauchi son since Fusajiro, Hiroshi would assume the position that was supposed to have been his father's. He would have to leave school and immediately come to work at Nintendo, as president.

Hiroshi, responding without emotion, said he would take over the company, but he insisted on several conditions. The main one was that he must be the only family member at Nintendo. This meant that his cousin had to be fired. Hiroshi wanted there never to be a question that he was in charge, the sole heir.

Weak and saddened, Sekiryo had the cousin fired, and, in 1949, Hiroshi Yamauchi was appointed the third president of Nintendo. The old man died soon thereafter, never sure whether his family and the business would survive. Since Sekiryo never saw the success Hiroshi would eventually have with Nintendo, as far as Hiroshi was concerned, to Sekiryo he remained an ill-mannered, disrespectful, and spoiled child. Hiroshi lived with the knowledge that he had betrayed and disappointed the two most important men in his life, his father and grandfather.

* * *

Young President Yamauchi was not welcomed by Nintendo's employees. They resented his youth and inexperience and worried about rumors that Yamauchi planned a clean sweep of longtime employees. True to expectations, Yamauchi fired every manager, one by one, left over from his grandfather's reign, in spite of their years of dedicated service to Nintendo. Not only did he sever what he considered dead weight, but also anyone who had a stake in Nintendo's conservative past. He wanted none of the old guard around who might question his authority.

He changed the name of the distribution company to Nintendo Karuta (Nintendo Playing Cards) in 1951 and established a new corporate headquarters on a lot he bought in town, off a small street called Takamatsu-cho. He consolidated all the Kyoto manufacturing there, modernizing the card-making process.

In an attempt to compete with the modern, fashionable cards that were being imported from the West, in 1953 Nintendo began manufacturing the first plastic-coated cards in Japan (all varieties of cards until that time had been made of uncoated paper). In 1959, Nintendo made its first licensing agreement – with an American company, Walt Disney. Playing cards backed with pictures of Mickey Mouse and other Disney characters expanded Nintendo's market to include young people and families. The Disney cards were advertised on television. To reach the new market, Yamauchi structured a new distribution system that would get the cards into larger department and toy stores. The results were instantaneous: Nintendo's sales shot up. The company sold a record 600,000 packs that year.

Yamauchi was still discontented. He wanted the company to expand faster, but he encountered stumbling blocks. In spite of his efforts to improve the quality of Nintendo's Disney cards and other Western-style pinochle and poker decks, they were still inferior to the ones being imported from America. The company's bread and butter, *hanafuda*, was, by its nature, a modest business; the profits were constant, but there was little room for growth in that market.

Yamauchi dropped the word *karuta* from the company name, which now became NCL – Nintendo Company, Ltd. – as the young president planned to branch out into new businesses. To finance them, he took Nintendo public, listing the company on the second tier of the Osaka Stock Exchange and on the Kyoto Stock Exchange, and became Nintendo's chairman.

The first product launched by the new company was a line of individually portioned instant rice. Add water and – *presto!* It was a dismal failure. Yamauchi then opened a 'love hotel,' with rooms rented by the hour. The business was, for Yamauchi, a personal passion; it was said that he was one of his own best customers (his infidelities were well known – even by his wife, who ignored them).

A taxi company Yamauchi started, Daiya, thrived, although he grew tired of negotiating with powerful taxi-driver unions, which demanded high salaries and expensive benefits for their members. He soon folded that company and closed the doors of the love hotel.

He planned more changes as he moved Nintendo again, this time to a larger building, a three-story structure of beige bricks with black door and window frames and bars on the windows.

Yamauchi had concluded that he wanted new businesses that could take advantage of one of Nintendo's strongest assets, its *karuta* distribution system, which reached into toy and department stores throughout Japan. Nintendo's roots were in entertainment, and there would be no more rice or taxis or love hotels. Yamauchi set Nintendo on a new course as an entertainment company.

Hiroshi Imanishi had the demeanor and build of a Rottweiler. He gave the appearance of a highly cultivated sophisticate who was still common and accessible. Clearly he was also fiercely bright. A recent law graduate from Doshisha University, he accepted an offer from Nintendo in spite of the fact that he found the president glum, reserved, and formal. Hiroshi Imanishi was, nonetheless, intrigued by Hiroshi Yamauchi. There was an attractive cocksureness and obdurate ambition in Yamauchi's speeches about the dramatic expansion he planned for Nintendo.

He revealed the details sparingly. It sometimes seemed as if Yamauchi was obsessed by details – 'trifles,' Imanishi felt – and the worry over minutiae was tiresome. Other times there were glimpses of a calculated, secret plan. It was a frustrating process, as there was minimum communication, only commands, and meetings often turned into lectures.

As the company geared up for a series of new ventures, Imanishi worked in many departments: administration, finance, planning. He eventually became the general affairs manager. But regardless of the title he bore, he oversaw the majority of his boss's projects. The task by 1969 was to create a department that would set Nintendo on its new course. Called simply Games, it was the company's first research-and-development office, set up in a warehouse in Uji, a Kyoto suburb.

Gunpei Yokoi had grown up in Kyoto, where his father was the director of a pharmaceutical company. He graduated from college with a degree in electronics and then made the rounds of Kyoto companies, filling out applications. The short, solid, and unpretentious man who wore gray-lensed glasses was hired by Nintendo to maintain the assembly-line machines that made the playing and *hanafuda* cards. Yokoi was the entire maintenance department for several months before Hiroshi Yamauchi called him into his office.

Yokoi sat down in a large chair opposite the chairman's desk and folded his hands on his lap. Imanishi was already there, drinking coffee. Yokoi listened intently as Yamauchi assigned him to a new project in the newly founded Games division. He was to work under Hiroshi Imanishi to create a department for *komuki* – engineering – and make something for Nintendo to sell for Christmas.

'What should I make?' Yokoi asked.

Yamauchi said, 'Something great.'

Yokoi was the first of many weekend tinkerers hired by Nintendo, the sort of hobbyists who made toys, radios, and other mechanical gadgets from spare parts. For his own amusement, he had recently invented a wooden latticework connected by bolts and with a vice-grip device on one end. When the two leaves of the handle were pushed together, the crisscrossed pieces extended and the grip on the end closed. The gadget had practical, but mostly whimsical, uses as a groping, clasping extension of the hand.

The day after their meeting, Yokoi demonstrated his contraption for Yamauchi and Imanishi. It brought a trace of a smile to the chairman's face. He gave the go-ahead and assigned Imanishi and Yokoi to begin production of Nintendo's first toy, the Ultra Hand. Advertised on television, 1.2 million units of the novelty were sold, at about 800 yen (roughly $6 in 1970) each. For Nintendo in those days, it was a resounding success.

From then on, Yokoi's job was to come up with inventions and show them to the chairman. Yamauchi, although he had no engineering background, had an uncanny sense about products. He gave Yokoi suggestions and challenged the young man to improve his designs. Yamauchi, Yokoi says, instinctively knew if a new idea would sell. The chairman never sought a second opinion. If he liked it, he instructed Imanishi to begin production.

Yokoi's inventions resulted in Nintendo's Ultra series of toys. The Ultra Machine was a pitching machine that lobbed a lighter version of a baseball (that could be batted safely indoors). Seven hundred thousand units sold each year for three years through 1973. Somewhat less successful was the Ultra Scope, a periscope-like device with a lens that automatically refocused so that kids could see around corners, over fences, or behind them. It allowed kids to spy on each other, on their neighbors, or, often, on their parents. 'It was a time of great fun,' Yokoi recalls. 'I saw myself as cartoonist who understood movements in the world and created abstractions of them.'

In the evenings, Yokoi dabbled with wires and oscilloscopes and various other electronic components and applied some of his experiments to a device called the Love Tester. Yamauchi loved it. A boy and girl grabbed on to the handles of the tester and then joined their free hands. A meter read the current passing through them and determined, with scientific inaccuracy, how much 'love' they had between them. The true objective of the device had nothing to do with science and everything to do with holding hands in a culture in which holding hands was still pretty risqué. Yokoi noted that in America or Europe a love tester would have had to involve kissing. In Japan, however, a device that inspired hand holding was tantalizing enough to become a hit.

Yokoi's R&D department grew with a steady addition of young engineers. Yamauchi pushed them with his emphatic praise and scorn. He never pretended to want to foster a sense of team play; rather, he openly pitted them against each other. While many Japanese companies grew because of loyalty to the group and the corporate good, Nintendo grew because of its engineers' (and its other employees') desire to please Yamauchi. 'We lived for his praise,' one engineer says.

The next major Nintendo product, pivotal to positioning the company for its future success, came to the company by chance. Masayuki Uemura, with thick, wiry hair pushed to one side and an irrepressible ear-to-ear grin, arrived at Nintendo one day and requested a meeting with Gunpei Yokoi.

Born in 1943 in austere and beautiful Nara, Uemura had moved to Kyoto with his family to escape the wartime bombing, Kyoto then being one of the safest of Japanese cities. His father had sold kimonos but struggled to make a living (he eventually opened a record shop in Osaka). When Uemura was a child, his family's straitened finances meant he had to use his imagination to invent toys and games for himself. Masayuki learned to make radio-controlled airplanes from parts he found in junk piles. His desire to create more sophisticated devices led him to work his way through an industrial college, where he trained as an electronics technician.

By the time he graduated, Uemura could do far more than build toys, and he found a good job with an electronics manufacturer, Sharp, selling optical semiconductors used in the solar cells that might be used to power a lighthouse, or a robot that measured the amount of rainfall on the top of mountains.

The head of Sharp's Kyoto office sent Uemura on a routine sales call to Nintendo to see if he could drum up some business for the solar cells. The visit coincided with Yamauchi's most recent mandate – for Yokoi and his engineers to investigate electronic toys beyond the Love Tester. In a meeting, Yokoi and Uemura concluded that the Sharp cell had some interesting applications for entertainment products. Shortly afterward, Yokoi hired Uemura away from Sharp.

The young engineer was happy to leave sales, but he was even more thrilled to join Nintendo and return to what he had done for fun as a child: make toys. 'There was something different about Nintendo,' Uemura found. 'Here were these very serious men thinking about the content of play. Other companies were importing ideas from America and adapting them to the Japanese market, only making them cheaper and smaller. But Nintendo was interested in original ideas.'

When Yokoi saw the Sharp solar-cell battery, he envisioned a unique way to put it to use. He and Uemura experimented. Large solar cells, about the size of a silver dollar, were being used to collect and convert light into electricity. But a much smaller cell could be used as a sensor to detect light. Yokoi's idea was to adapt the technology to a shooting game, using solar cells as targets.

Yokoi and Uemura worked on a light gun that could be produced cheaply enough for the consumer market. The 'bullet' would be a thin beam of light. If the beam hit a tiny solar cell, the cell would either produce or cut off a charge, depending on the circuitry. For instance, the electricity to a magnet could be turned off so that a spring-loaded target could be let loose – and a plastic bottle of beer, pieced together as if it were puzzle, could be made to explode. A lion could roar. A stack of toy barrels could be blown apart.

Packed with light-triggered targets (the lion, the beer bottle, and the like), more than 1 million Nintendo Beam Gun games were sold for between 4,000 and 5,000 yen ($30 or so) in the early 1970s. Nintendo Co., Ltd., by then listed in the first section of the Osaka Stock Exchange, grew rapidly.

Now the company needed more space to keep up with the demand for its new products, so Yamauchi expanded once again. To build the new headquarters, Yamauchi bought out neighbors and a vacant lot alongside the company's older cement building, which was retained as the *hanafuda* factory. (Yamauchi kept the business going essentially for nostalgia's sake: cards were representing a rapidly diminishing portion of Nintendo's business.) The old building, whose front lawn held a few scattered trees, was dwarfed by the new structures (eventually three were constructed), which were high-tech slick: three floors, industrial white, huge rectangular slabs. A crisp blue NINTENDO sign in both *kanji* and roman characters could be seen by passengers on commuter trains and from the nearby hillsides, even from the gardens of the nearby Tofuku-ji Temple. A guardhouse was built, and blue-suited guards from the Kansai security firm were posted, day and night, out front.

* * *

Beam Guns were still flying off store shelves when Yokoi suggested to Yamauchi that the same technology could be used in other ways. At the time, skeet shooting was a popular sport in Japan. On a whim, Yokoid bought a rifle and went to a range to try it. When he returned, he told Yamauchi that the technology in the light gun could work in a system that would replicate the experience of shooting clay pigeons.

Yamauchi absorbed the information and came up with a commercial application for it. There had been a bowling boom in Japan in the 1960s. Alleys sprang up all over the country. Since then, enthusiasm for bowling had waned and many alleys were closed down. Yamauchi decided they could be acquired very advantageously and easily transformed into 'shooting ranges.' Simulated clay pigeons would appear at the end of a lane. A solar cell would detect when a hit was made and tally it on an electronic scoreboard. There was nothing like it anywhere. It would be the closest to real shooting most people would ever get, far more realistic than the amusement-park shooting ranges, where cork bullets sailed off course with the slightest wind.

The technology, however, was still a bit tricky. Yokoi, who was told to get the system up and running, encountered a series of problems, from the operation of moving (or apparently moving) solar collectors to the coordination of the timing of a shot with the sound of its report.

Another engineer who had joined Nintendo was assigned to work with Uemura. The young man, Genyo Takeda, had responded to a newspaper want ad for a toy designer. When he saw the ad, he says, 'some inspiration entered me.'

Takeda, who wore a polyester trench coat even indoors in midsummer, was a colorful addition to the R&D division. Born and raised in Osaka, the son of the president of a fabric-design company, he had graduated in 1970 from Shizuoka Governmental University on Honshu, where his studies often took a backseat to his involvement in the student movement. In school, Takeda studied semiconductors, but for fun he built miniature locomotives and airplanes. When Gunpei Yokoi interviewed him, he realized that Takeda would easily fit into his growing engineering team. He put Takeda to work with Uemura on Yamauchi's shooting-range project.

The press showed up to document the grand opening of the world's first Laser Clay Range in Kyoto in 1973. Just as a television news crew was getting ready, its cameras rolling, the light-shooting laser gun malfunctioned. Before anyone realized there was a problem, Takeda climbed into the box behind the targets and, keeping himself hidden, shot clay pigeons off manually, and then kicked the controller, which lit up the targets that were supposedly hit. As far as the television audience knew, the ranges were running smoothly. They were packed from the first day they opened their doors to the public.

Nintendo's Laser Clay Ranges became the hip spot for an evening's entertainment in many Japanese cities, and soon there were variations on the original theme. In 1974 came 'Wild Gunman.' A 16-mm movie projector showed actual film footage of a 'homicidal maniac' on a screen at the end of an alley. If the player blasted the wild gunman before he fired, the sensor on the screen detected it and the player scored. The image-projection-system games were sold to a trading company, which exported them to America and Europe.

The laser-gun ranges were going full tilt, but Japan had been hit by the world's first oil shortage in 1973; the country's economy went into a tailspin and, as it began to affect discretionary spending, the shooting galleries were soon empty. Orders from abroad were canceled and outstanding bills went unpaid. Nintendo's investment in the venture had been so great that the company was suddenly on the brink of collapse. Yamauchi was more desperate than ever for a breakthrough product.

The idea came from a boyhood friend of Yamauchi. The man had become an executive with one of Japan's largest electronics conglomerates. Over dinner one night in 1975, the talk was all about the latest technological breakthroughs in the electronics industry, primarily the importance of semiconductors and microprocessors. Yamauchi's interest was piqued when he realized that these technologies, as part of a revolution in office and consumer products, were becoming cheap enough to utilize in entertainment products. He researched the first traces of an industry that was emerging in America. Companies such as Atari and Magnavox were selling devices that played electronic games on home television sets.

Yamauchi negotiated a license to manufacture and sell Magnavox's video-game system in Japan. The machine played variations on the first commercial American video game, 'Pong.' A beam of light was batted back and forth between paddles that the players controlled. With plastic overlays affixed to the front of a TV screen, the light could be a football, a tennis ball, a soccer ball, or one of several other kinds of simple games.

Nintendo's operation wasn't sophisticated enough to develop and manufacture the microprocessor-based circuit boards that were the heart of the game system, so Masayuki Uemura suggested an alliance with an electronics firm. Nintendo teamed with Mitsubishi to build the video-game system and, in 1977, Nintendo entered the home market in Japan with the dramatic unveiling of Color TV Game 6, which played six versions of light tennis. It was followed by a more powerful sequel, Color TV Game 15. A million units of each were sold. The engineering team also came up with systems that played a more complex game, called 'Blockbuster,' as well as a racing game. Half a million units of these were sold. Nintendo had quietly entered the world of audio-visual entertainment and consumer electronics.

The successful TV game systems allowed Nintendo to tread water a while longer, but they were neither novel enough nor versatile enough to be the revolutionary product Yamauchi was searching for. He kept the pressure on his engineers, directing them to explore new ways of making video games. 'We must look in different directions,' Yamauchi said. 'Throw away all your old ideas in order to come up with something new.'

The electronic-calculator market was then booming. There were so many types available that the prices were shrinking almost as fast as their size – credit-card-size calculators were selling for a thousand yen, under $10. What else could be done with that miniaturized technology? 'The Nintendo way of adapting technology is not to look for the state of the art but to utilize mature technology that can be mass-produced cheaply,' says Gunpei Yokoi. He sought to make something smaller, thinner, and lighter than anything ever seen – something that was also fun.

It turned out to be Game & Watch, a video game the size of a calculator, with a tiny digital clock in the corner. With his engineers, he chose components from Uemura's old company, Sharp, and developed the smallest computer games ever seen. They weren't the easiest things to play – the controls were tiny – but they were a novelty. Nintendo shipped them all over the world by the tens, and then hundreds, of thousands. Many of the Game & Watches in circulation were illegal bootlegs – Nintendo lost potential millions because of all the non-Nintendo units made in various Asian cities – but the company nevertheless made many millions from the phenomenal number of Game & Watches they sold.

While Yokoi was 'thinking small,' Yamauchi had other engineers thinking big. After 'Wild Gunman' and his first taste of the arcade business, he wanted more of the 100-yen pieces (and quarters) that were pouring into video games from the pockets of teenagers around the world. Popular games such as 'Space Invaders' were behind a boom in the coin-op video-game business. Yamauchi wanted Nintendo to become a major player in arcades, and so his team came up with games like 'Hellfire,' 'Sheriff,' 'Sky Skipper,' and a battle game called 'Radarscope.'

Yamauchi, meanwhile, held endless meetings at Nintendo's growing R&D center with a group of designers under Masayuki Uemura. Uemura's team was working on what was emerging as the most significant new venture for Nintendo. It was a video-game system, but one that was much more sophisticated than Color TV Game 6 and 15. In America, systems had been released that played many games on interchangeable cartridges. The technology insured that the system would never become 'old and stale,' as Yamauchi put it – as long as 'new and interesting' games would be available for it.

As Yamauchi learned about the technology – knowledge gained from late-night talks with Uemura and other engineers – he realized that the machine under development could do far more than just play games. 'He had no concept that he was building a computer, but he nonetheless had his first glimpse of the incredible potential of a home-computer system disguised as a toy,' says Uemura. 'He saw far more than he let on to us.' In the short term, Yamauchi saw a system that could be the basis of a profoundly expanded company if kids loved it enough and if they wanted more and more games to play on it and if Nintendo was the only maker of all those games.

There were many obstacles, including a number of competitors in the field. By 1983, systems had already been released in Japan by companies from the United States (the Atari 2600 and Commodore Max Machine) and from Japan (Epoch's Cassette Vision, Bandai's Intellivision, Takara's Game Personal Computer M5, Tomy's Pyuta, and Casio's and Sharp's small game-playing computer, the MSX). Yamauchi told Uemura he must 'develop something that other companies cannot copy for at least one year. It must be so much better that there will be no question which system the customers will want.'

For Uemura, the greatest challenge was not the technology; price was the crucial factor. Yamauchi wanted the system in many, many homes, so it had to be cheap enough so that almost everyone could buy it. All the machines currently on the market, except for the Epoch system, were selling for 30,000 to 50,000 yen ($200 to $350). Yamauchi set a goal of 9,800 yen, less than $75. At the same time, the system had to do what other systems, whether Japanese or American, could do, but more and better.

Uemura examined the competitors' machines. They were impressive in some ways. Built mostly by engineers with expertise in office computers, they could generate still pictures and alphanumerics, as well as perform complex calculations. But game play, Uemura believed, had essentially different requirements. The movement of characters and backgrounds on the screen had to be far more active, more believable, than on the other systems; it would have to approach the quality of fast-speed animation. A 16-bit processor could have done it all with ease, but Nintendo would have to make do with a less powerful 8-bit processor if the price was going to be kept low.

For ideas, Uemura picked the brains of the engineers who worked on Nintendo's arcade games. The arcade games had bigger, more expensive processors, but Uemura was most interested in the *thinking* behind the games, not the hardware. For a coin-operated game to make money, players had to become immersed in it as soon as the first coin was inserted. Many senses had to be taken over almost instantly to make the game play 'hot,' to use Uemura's term. The entire consciousness of a player had to be captured. There seemed to be two keys to accomplishing this: fast action, or a combination of fast action and intellectual challenge. The headier stuff was up to the game designers, but fast action required complex and expensive circuitry.

Uemura spent eighteen-hour days with the arcade engineers trying to determine the essence of the key components to the circuitry in the best coin-operated games. Only that essence could be carried over to the central processing unit of the new system. Finally he chose a relatively standard microprocessor called a 6502, but the one low-cost chip couldn't power all the aspects of a complex video game. One chip could control the information required for character movement and the interaction between the machine and the player, but if it had to do more than that, it would bog down. A second chip was needed to control the television screen itself – to generate bright colors, process pictures, and move them at a very high speed.

Other companies' game machines used an integrated circuit made for old-model personal computers, Texas Instruments' T19918, which allowed six to eight colors. Nintendo's machine had to have more colors for the better graphics Uemura sought (it ended up with fifty-two colors). Uemura, together with his growing stable of engineers and programmers, slaved over calculations and experiments to determine the maximum number of sprites (similar to the dots of a television picture) that could be generated on the screen in almost no time. The first calculation gave a number that was unsatisfactory; more sprites were needed if game play was going to feel noticeably more realistic than on the competitors' machines. The circuitry was modified. More experiments were conducted to determine how big an object and how many objects could move at a time, and how many changing functions could be built into one semiconductor. 'We had to accomplish this exactly,' Uemura says. 'It was the order from the president. So much was riding on these experiments.'

Nintendo's engineers could take the design of the two key chips only so far. They had to get the expertise of an outside company.

To determine who that would be, Uemura and Yokoi met with semiconductor-company representatives. It had been determined that the two custom chips that were needed were the basic central processing unit (CPU) and the picture processing unit (PPU). A supplier had to be able to help design and then produce them both, Yamauchi insisted, for a rock-bottom price.

It was not easy to be a supplier for Nintendo. The company's demands were rigid and exacting. Designs would change overnight and suppliers would have to be ready to change specifications on demand. 'The most important thing we looked for in a supplier was the brain to cope with us,' Yokoi says. 'Unfortunately, we found that most companies are not flexible. Most companies move too slowly. That was not acceptable.'

Given the prices Yamauchi would pay, the only way a partnership with Nintendo could pay off was in volume of sales – an *enormous* number of chips would have to be sold. Many major companies wouldn't gamble on Nintendo. 'Now they wish they had,' Uemura says.

Uemura went to Ricoh, the electronics giant, with his preliminary circuit diagrams. The chips he needed, he said, had to cost no more than 2,000 yen, which is why they had been scaled down to perform only essential functions. It happened to be a slow time for Ricoh's semiconductor division, so the company was willing to work with Nintendo, but they regarded the 2,000-yen price point as absurd.

Yamauchi was informed of Ricoh's stand and he made a proposal. 'Guarantee them a three-million-chip order within two years,' he said. 'They will give us the price then.'

Others inside Nintendo thought Yamauchi's tack was preposterous; leading manufacturers in Japan were selling 20,000 to 30,000 video-game systems, and the most Nintendo had ever sold of the TV Game 6 and 15 was 1 million. There was no way they would ever use anywhere near 3 million chips.

Yamauchi demanded that the proposal be made, and as he expected, Ricoh agreed. When an agreement was signed by Uemura and approved by Yamauchi, the head of Ricoh's five-man team in charge of the Nintendo project remarked politely that he was looking forward to bringing the new Nintendo system home to his children. He accomplished more than that: by the end of 1986, Nintendo would become Ricoh's largest customer, representing 60 to 70 percent of the company's semiconductor division's sales.

Ricoh was not Nintendo's only supplier. The larger companies that worked with Nintendo included Sharp, Mitsumi, Fuji, and Hoshi. There were, eventually, thirty subcontractors. Contracts with Nintendo would become among the most lucrative in the semiconductor and electronics industries. Ricoh and Sharp would form divisions that did nothing but supply Nintendo.

Keeping Hiroshi Yamauchi and his company happy, suppliers found, was difficult: Yamauchi insisted on lower defect rates than any other customer. But it was also rewarding. A 1991–92 survey indicated that Nintendo was spending $1 billion on semiconductors each year.

As development of the new video-game system continued, the engineers brought some of their questions to Yamauchi. What had to be included in the game console? Since the system was actually a small computer, it could have all the extras that computers could have. Should there be a disk drive which could read and write information? Should it have a keyboard? Should it have a data port, through which information could be sent and received to the system? The system could have a modem that would hook up, via telephone lines, to other game players or a central Nintendo terminal. It could have large amounts of memory that would accommodate more complicated programs.

Yamauchi was looking far down the road when he cautiously answered the engineers' questions. Although he eliminated anything that would add too much cost, he built in future expansion that went far beyond video games.

In the Japanese edition of *The Japan That Can Say No*, the book's coauthor (with Shintaro Ishihara), Sony's founder and chairman, Akio Morita, slaps American corporate wrists for short-sightedness. 'We Japanese plan and develop our business strategies ten years ahead of time,' he wrote. When he asked an American businessman if U.S. companies plan so much as a week ahead of time, he was told, 'No, ten minutes.' Nowhere is the repercussion of that difference more obvious than in the game system Hiroshi Yamauchi created. It anticipated a future that would not be revealed for a decade but which had the potential to propel Nintendo into the forefront of electronics and entertainment companies.

Yamauchi instructed Uemura to leave off the frills. No keyboard – it might scare off customers. No modem or disk drive. The system would play games on cartridges, not disks. Floppy disks were threatening to computerphobes and, more important, they were copiable.

The system would have minimum memory, since memory was so expensive, but it would have more than its competitors'. Atari's system had 256 bytes of RAM (random access memory, the amount of instructions a central processing unit can refer to at one time); the Nintendo system would have 2,000 bytes of RAM. In addition, games for the new Nintendo machine could be far more complex than the most powerful Atari games; a Nintendo cartridge could contain thirty-two times more computer code than an Atari cartridge.

Yamauchi cut out all extraneous devices to save money, but he told the engineers to include, for a trivial added cost, circuitry and a connector that could send or receive an unmodified signal to the central processor. The connector could pave the way for expansion – the addition of anything from a modem to a keyboard. It was why the machine would later be called Yamauchi's Trojan Horse: it slipped into living rooms with nothing but a pair of controllers, innocently toylike, yet it included the capability to do far more than play games. Nintendo boasted about it much later. 'In the initial stages of [the system's] development, we foresaw these possibilities,' reads a 1989 corporate report. 'As such, we built a data communications function into the system and provided it with a connection terminal for an adaptor.' Uemura modestly says that the plan worked so well because 'we were lucky.' But Genyo Takeda, a friend of Uemura, says, 'He was so much an amateur that when Yamauchi told him to make this thing, he didn't know that it could not be done.'

There were more practical and aesthetic decisions along the way. Steve Jobs's obsession to design the perfect mouse for the original Macintosh was no greater than Yamauchi's attention to the details of the controllers. Should there be one or two or more buttons?

Should the system's casing have round or square edges? What color should the system be – a computer-like gray or beige, or a more playful color? Should the system box look more like a computer or a toy? (The answers they came up with were: two buttons on the right controller plus a directional pad and, on the left controller, a simple microphone through which one could 'talk' to the system; softer, less threatening, rounded edges; and red and white plastic, to make the unit as toylike as possible.)

The year 1983 was a significant one for Nintendo. Yamauchi had the new Uji plant expanded to increase the company's production capacity. His stock became listed in the most respected first tier of the Tokyo Stock Exchange. And he began selling the system his men, after months of marathon work, shrouded in secrecy, had created.

The system was selling for more than Yamauchi had planned (about $100), but it was still less than half the price of the competition. In May, he addressed the Shoshin-kai Group, a wholesalers' group. He conceded that his new video-game player was priced so low that wholesalers wouldn't make much profit on it. 'But,' he said, 'I guarantee that it will sell a lot because of the great games.' He implored them to back the machine in spite of the low margin. 'Forgo the big profits on the hardware,' he said, 'because it is really just a tool to sell software. That is where we shall make our money.' At the meeting, Yamauchi announced the name of his new system. Here, he said, was Japan's first Family Computer. He dubbed it, for short, the Famicom.

Pushed by a barrage of advertising, 500,000 Famicoms flew off the shelves in the first two months. Six months later, however, a catastrophe occurred before the Japanese New Year, the toy industry's busiest season. There were at first a few calls from retailers. Then a few more. Masayuki Uemura and Gunpei Yokoi were called into Yamauchi's office. They were told that certain games for the Famicom caused the system to freeze.

The engineers nervously returned to their labs and worked on replicating the malfunction. Finally, there it was, trouble with one of the integrated circuits that got locked when certain information traveled on certain pathways, like a multicar pile-up on a badly designed freeway.

They trudged back to Yamauchi's office and explained the problem and the required solution. The circuitry on the chip had to be corrected. They expected Yamauchi to go into an explosive tirade. This was extremely *expensive* news.

Yokoi suggested that the company could replace units when customers complained. Hiroshi Imanishi, who was working on the marketing of the new machine, said that the problem could be more severe than whatever number of units had the defective chips; it could cost more than the hundreds of thousands, maybe millions, it would cost to fix or replace machines. Imanishi said it would hurt customers' opinion of Nintendo. Worse, much of Yamauchi's window of a year – the year that it would take competitors to try to copy the Nintendo machine and get it out the door – would be lost. A delay would allow competitors to swoop in and capture the customers that Nintendo had worked so hard, and spent so much money, to win.

Yamauchi listened to the opinions of his staff but ignored them. 'Recall them all,' he said.

Systems in stores and warehouses were pulled off the shelves, returned to the plant in Uji, and retooled (the bad chips replaced). In the end, Nintendo lost millions of dollars by missing the prime sales season, but Yamauchi's gamble paid off.

After the first million Famicom systems had been sold, there was still no sign of a slowdown. Once several million families had a Famicom and desperately wanted games, Nintendo could sell all it could produce. Yamauchi saw how Nintendo's emphasis would conceivably switch from hardware, with its limited market, to software, whose market was without limits.

Desperate retailers called Nintendo, frantically demanding product. New games were anticipated with a fervor that shocked store owners, distributors, and parents. Kids camped out in front of department stores and toy shops to snap up copies before the games sold out. Nintendomania was beginning, and Yamauchi, raking in more money than he had ever seen before, couldn't feed the frenzy quickly enough.

The success of the Famicom was unprecedented. Eventually, the fourteen competing home video-game machine companies withdrew from the market. The MSX was put in its place as a personal computer, not a game machine. Sega, a small arcade-game company, released a competitor called the SG-1000 the same year Nintendo released the Famicom, but it fizzled. And in spite of updated systems released by Atari, Nintendo had no competition to speak of. What had begun as the Yamauchi family business was inconspicuously on its way to becoming one of the most successful enterprises in the history of Japan – or, indeed, the world.

I, MARIO

3

'What if you walk along and everything that you see is more than what you see – the person in the T-shirt and slacks is a warrior, the space that appears empty is a secret door to an alternate world? What if, on a crowded street, you look up and see something appear that should not, given what we know, be there? You either shake your head and dismiss it or you accept that there is much more to the world than we think. Perhaps it really is a doorway to another place. If you choose to go inside you might find many unexpected things.'
– Sigeru Miyamoto

Yamauchi's Famicoms were selling as fast as Nintendo built them. The success brought with it an unexpected, although not unwelcome, problem. A video-game system, like any other computer, could be elegant and powerful, yet it was only as useful as the software it showcased. The Famicom could have been as powerful as a mainframe computer, but no one would have noticed if the games were ordinary. Now the problem was that there were not enough good games.

Yamauchi had wisely anticipated the importance of software and prepared for it. One of the instructions he had issued to Uemura was that the Famicom must 'be appreciated by software engineers.' It had to be easy to program and able to do the kinds of things that game designers dreamed of doing. Any company, given the time, could copy the Famicom hardware. The key to staying ahead was software. By the time a competitor came out with a game that was as good as a successful Nintendo game,

Nintendo had to be releasing a game that left the others in the dust.

Nintendo would, Yamauchi decided, become a haven for video-game artists, for it was artists, not technicians, who made great games. 'An ordinary man,' Yamauchi said, 'cannot develop good games no matter how hard he tries. A handful of people in this world can develop games that everybody wants. Those are the people we want at Nintendo.' He was interested only in the one genius, as he put it, who would drive Nintendo. He wanted to turn Nintendo into the single place the hottest game designers wanted to be associated with. Since, in Japan, most employees stayed with one company for their entire career, it was generally impossible to seduce good designers from other companies. That meant that they would have to come to Nintendo on their own, fresh from college.

Yamauchi wanted to create a place where his geniuses would be encouraged and inspired. But how? He was used to badgering and cajoling, or simply demanding – and that was certainly not the same thing as inspiring people, nurturing them. His reputation for aloofness and cockiness had grown with Nintendo. He luxuriated in his position as the merciless Goliath of his industry. He was already infamous for squashing people – or companies – that crossed him. He made up his own rules as he went along and he refused to play politics (which enraged government officials, who were used to being catered to). But could he *inspire*? 'Research and development is the most difficult department to control,' he observed. 'It is difficult to control artists because they do not want to compromise.'

The chairman had no engineering background, but he discovered how to stimulate innovative design. Isolated from the rest of Japan's industrial hubs in Osaka and Nagoya, and from the financial capital of Tokyo, Yamauchi ignored the textbook corporate examples. He had hand-picked his three chief engineers – Yokoi, Uemura, and Takeda – a long time ago, and they had done good work for him. In order to push them (and to learn more about how the engineers and designers worked), in 1984 Yamauchi made himself the supervisor of all R&D at Nintendo, 'the heart of this company.' He supported them with significantly more staff and resources.

Yamauchi arrayed his chiefs directly below him, each of them in charge of his own group: R&D 1, 2, and 3. Within an R&D group were many teams, which were pitted against each other. The teams in the groups working mostly on hardware tried to outdo the others in the virtual miracles they came up with, and the software teams competed to make the greatest games that had ever been seen.

Yamauchi has never played a video game in his life and he had little interest in them. Still, he alone was the judge and jury when it came to deciding which games Nintendo would release. It was audacious, and he was either remarkably intuitive or terrifically lucky. Yamauchi was criticized for being ruthless when it came to many of his business practices – manipulating the market, *terrorizing* employees – but no one questioned his genius when it came to choosing Famicom games. A Nintendo manager criticized Yamauchi for his obstinacy but praised his instinct: 'It's like a sense for the fashion business, knowing what will become hot and popular next season. He can read a few years in advance. He is so certain that he is right that he listens to no one.'

His R&D groups competed among themselves for Yamauchi's attention and praise, but there was no doubt about their collective place in the company. They were his stars. While most companies directed input from market research and from their sales force to their R&D sections, Yamauchi in those days insisted that R&D was sacrosanct: no one told his creative people what to create. The marketing department saw games only when they were completed. 'He believes the marketing people will only look at what's popular right now,' Hiroshi Imanishi says. 'And if we make the game based on what's popular right now, the game will not be new and fresh.'

The personal attention their leader lavished on his inventors was a mixed blessing. A nod from Yamauchi could make a designer's day – or week, or month. Engineers were ecstatic when they came up with a game that delighted him. On the other hand, an admonishment could be devastating. 'Months of work can be disposed of with a scowl,' says an engineer who left Nintendo. The project is dead, instantly. His victims suggested that Yamauchi's judgements were capricious or the product of his moods, and that his callousness caused a great deal of frustration and anger. Engineers occasionally left, and others, exhausted and disappointed, were sent on sabbatical. They were told, 'The company is making money; don't worry. Spend the time, relax. Come back fresh.' Most commonly, designers whose work was rejected would only redouble their efforts, determined to have *their* game chosen the next time. Yamauchi's autocratic, often brutal system worked.

The R&D groups worked in spacious, private laboratories in the development wing of the main Nintendo building. In these whitewalled, white-ceilinged rooms, rows of computer monitors were set up on tables. Their screens shone with blow-ups of circuit boards that looked like magnified city maps. Other screens, stacked as if in a television showroom, displayed details of game characters – the left cartoon hand of a boxer, for example. Still other screens were filled with column after column of fluorescent, sallow-yellow numerals.

Here and there were drafting tables, covered with schematic blueprints for games or scribbled calculations. Laser printers, networked to dozens of terminals, spewed book-length programs, and Xerox machines churned out copies of sectional drawings of game worlds.

In the design rooms, the men (no women) worked methodically as they competed to make products that would become *the* product. The goal was excellence – anything less would wind up on the scrap heap. Yamauchi believed that it was far better to put all his resources into the production of one or two hit games a year rather than several minor successes. When he released new games, he only had to manufacture, package, market, and advertise those few, but that meant that the stakes for each Nintendo game were extremely high. The games had to warrant all the costs of development (up to $1 million per game) and marketing (up to several million more).

The high stakes meant there wasn't always *wa* (harmony) within the company. Yet in spite of the competitiveness, the three chief designers respected each other and, when they were called on to do so, worked together well. Part of the reason the competition didn't turn them against one another was that Yamauchi parceled out his praise. On the other hand, if any one team had too much success, it could be expected to be slapped down. The result was that each team came to excel in different areas and at different moments. In the end it was difficult if not impossible to determine which of the three design teams contributed more to Nintendo's growth.

Takeda says Yokoi, his mentor, was 'the sharpest designer.' Besides all the work they had done for Yamauchi in the past, Yokoi's R&D 1 designed Game Boy, which would become another extraordinary Nintendo success. His team of thirty engineers were 'a band of samurai,' says a colleague outside of Japan. They operated quietly, with less recognition than the others. Their leader was *nazonoyona*, an enigma.

Yokoi was the oldest of the top engineers (though still only in his forties) and the most like traditional, old-school engineers at other companies throughout Japan. He wore simple short-sleeved shirts, and his hair was cut so that there was a neat, clean line around his ears and neck. He was dedicated to the company over everything else; he was a Nintendo man.

The games from R&D 1 would be some of Nintendo's best. One was the phenomenal game 'Metroid.' In the video-game world of macho stereotypes, the game's hero was a surprise. Samus, the warrior, on the quest to destroy the Mother Brain, went to battle with a nifty array of weapons and slick moves, dressed in a space suit and helmet. At the end of the game, after the Mother Brain died a screaming, light-spewing death, Samus could finally relax and take off his helmet. Long blond hair fell out. Samus, the great warrior, was a woman.

The greatest contribution of Uemura's team, R&D 2, was the Nintendo hardware itself. R&D 2 also came up with peripherals, including the Communications Adapter for the Nintendo Network. Sixty-five people worked with Uemura, whose face wore a constant expression of astonishment. He spoke in a raspy, hushed tone – Tom Waits after a few bourbons – as if what he had to say was clandestine and dangerous, which it sometimes was. (Yamauchi had tapped Uemura's team for a top-secret project that was kept under wraps for years.)

Takeda ran R&D 3, which would design games such as 'Star Tropics.' More significant, however, was some of the technical magic the team performed. R&D 3 came up with technology that allowed the other groups to make games that the original Famicom hardware could never have powered on its own. The first Famicom cartridges used what were called NROM chips (N for Nintendo and ROM for Read Only Memory). Unlike computer programs on floppy or hard disks, these programs were not changeable. A game program was reproduced onto an actual integrated microcircuit. Using a photographic process, the circuit was duplicated onto thin silicon wafers that were sandwiched together and attached to connectors. Through them the information – the game program – was transmitted to other components in the system. The amount of information in a game was limited by the size of the ROM.

Each game cartridge had two main chips, one for the program itself, which could be up to 256K (kilobytes) and one for the on-screen characters, which could be 64K. Programs for games and characters had to fit within those chips until R&D 3 designed new kinds of cartridges.

R&D 3 created a cartridge called UNROM, which allowed greater memory size and bank switching. A RAM (Random Access Memory) chip was a place to store information until it was needed by the computer's processor. Bank switching was a process for grabbing, from that stored information, whatever was needed whenever it was needed. A new game screen, complete with new kinds of enemies and waterfalls and creatures (and the programs to make them work) could be retrieved from RAM when the player arrived in that 'room.'

There were still severe limits on the cartridges, however. The amount of information that could be switched was scant and the process was slow. Takeda's gang tackled the limits with new kinds of chips called MMCs (Memory Map Controllers). They made the system do things that the Famicom's 8-bit processor could never have approached on its own. Years after the Famicom was introduced, games seemed to get more and more complex. It was as if the old Apple II were suddenly powering Hypercard. Takeda's chips, by taking on some of the Famicom's processing power, essentially added RAM and other specific powers to the machine.

The Famicom could do things it was never designed to do: images could scroll diagonally, objects could move quicker, and far more could happen at one time. The system itself still had only 2 kilobytes of RAM, but this was supplemented by the custom-designed sets of circuits with specialized functions in the MMCs.

Some of the circuits, called Logic Gates, increased the speed and efficiency of the background computing that made everything happen. Others directed the program to specific locations in the memory, traffic cop style. They were smaller and cheaper than the chips in the UNROM, and they allowed larger program and character memory size. With the addition of the first MMC chip, the potential for more complex and sophisticated games had arrived. The first examples were 'The Legend of Zelda,' 'Metroid,' and 'Kid Icarus,' three breakthrough games, all huge sellers.

Subsequent MMC chips allowed the Famicom to do even more. With MMC3, the screen could split into two parts, each moving independently. With MMC5, there could be more images on the screen at a time. Unaided, the Famicom could project pictures of 960 tiny square pieces, called tiles, but only 290 could be unique, which is why there were so many walls full of bricks or other repeated patterns in early games. MMC5 made it possible for all 960 tiles to be different. It also processed math problems on its own, freeing up the main processor. Memory size for games with an MMC5 shot up to 8 megabytes, thirty-two times more than the original cartridges.

R&D 3 also figured out a way to include a battery backup system in cartridges that allowed some games to store information independently – to keep track of where a player had left off, or to track high scores. The new battery system could store the data for the life of the battery (about five years).

Takeda's group obsessed over the highly technical and the obscure. The fruits of their labors were dramatic – most of the best Nintendo games would not have been possible without them – but they were not always obvious. R&D 3, nicknamed 'Rumania,' was isolated from the other groups. Its motto was grand: 'There are no limitations, no boundaries; since we are on our own, there is nothing we cannot do; when you start with nothing you can do everything.' Their leader, with his quizzical glances under heavy arching eyebrows and his arcane, light-bulb brain, boasts, 'We *have* to have more talented people because we are given unthinkable tasks.'

Takeda's twenty-person staff was a band of *otaku* – computer hackers and nerds. They were the consummate eggheads and dweebs. 'Becoming maniacs,' Takeda said, 'is the idea.'

The three R&D groups were immersed in their respective projects one day when Yamauchi required the talents of a designer. The project was not important enough for him to pull one of the key members from their work, so he called in the apprentice in the planning department.

Sigeru Miyamoto remembers the maze of rooms in the paper-and-cedar home of his childhood. Sliding shoji screens opened up onto hallways, from which there seemed to be a medieval castle's supply of hidden rooms. The tiny home was in the countryside near Kyoto, in the town of Sonebe, where his parents and grandparents had been born before him. The surrounding landscape was Miyamoto's playground: he fished in the river, ran along the banks of sodden rice fields, and rolled down hillsides.

Across the sand-and-stone street from his home was a rice field. After the yearly harvest, when the field was dry, it became a park for baseball and other games. He played there with neighborhood children in the afternoons, and in the evenings he attended Noh plays, heroic dance dramas, or puppet shows, or he gathered with his family at one of the neighbors' homes for festive dinners.

The Miyamoto family had no television and no car. Every few months they traveled by train to Kyoto to shop and see movies: *Peter Pan, Snow White*. At home, Miyamoto lived in books, and he drew and painted and made elaborate puppets, which he presented in fanciful shows.

After school, he often lit out into the countryside for adventure. He had to pass a neighbor's house where a bulldog lay in wait for him. The dog charged every time, barking and snapping, and Miyamoto froze. At the last second, the dog's chain reached its limit and jerked it back. Miyamoto stood just out of the reach of its salivating jaws.

Investigating hillsides and creek beds and small canyons, Miyamoto once discovered the opening of a cave. He returned to it several times before he worked up the courage to go in. Lugging a homemade lantern, he went deep inside until he came to a small hole that led to another cave. Breathing deeply, his heart pounding, he climbed through. He never forgot the exhilaration he felt at this discovery.

The family moved to Kyoto, where Miyamoto and his new friends had secret meetings in the family's attic at which codes and passwords were traded. There were dares to explore forbidden places – a neighbor's yard guarded by an Akita; another neighbor's basement, which held a treasure trove of trunks stuffed with ancient costumes.

Miyamoto wanted to be a performer, a puppeteer, or a painter when he grew up. He carried pads of paper and pencils and drew nature scenes in parks and along the river that divided the city. In school, while his teachers lectured, Miyamoto daydreamed. At night, he constructed plastic models and wood-and-metal contraptions until his father sent him to his room to study. Math and grammar were put aside for drawing.

Miyamoto took cartoon-making seriously. He drew a figure and then invented its life and personality. The figures wound up in intricately drawn flip books. At school he organized a cartoon club that met regularly and had yearly exhibitions.

In 1970, Miyamoto entered Kanazawa Munici College of Industrial Arts and Crafts. It took him five years to graduate because he only attended class about half the time. Instead of studying, he spent his time sketching in his notebooks and listening to records. He loved the Nitty Gritty Dirt Band, the Country Gentlemen, and David Grisman. He taught himself how to play the guitar – American bluegrass music, of all things. It wasn't easy to find a banjo player in Kyoto, but he did, and the duo performed at coffeehouses and parties. His friends were artists and musicians. They hunted in record shops for hard-to-find (in Kyoto!) Kentucky Colonels LPs and traveled to Tokyo to see Doc Watson perform live.

When he finally graduated, Miyamoto agonized over what kind of job he should get. He had no interest in traditional business, and he knew he would never survive the monotony of a rigidly structured corporation.

Then a revelation came to young Miyamoto. He asked his father to contact an old friend, Hiroshi Yamauchi, who ran Nintendo. The elder Miyamoto asked Yamauchi to meet with his son, a recent graduate with a degree in industrial design, who was looking for a job. 'We need engineers, not painters,' Yamauchi said, but he agreed to a meeting as a favor to his friend.

Miyamoto was twenty-four in 1977, when he entered the office of the Nintendo chairman. He had shaggy hair, boyish freckles, and a cat-who-swallowed-the-canary smile. He dressed nicely, and he behaved in accordance with traditional etiquette, yet there was mischief and wonder in his eyes. Yamauchi liked the young man and asked him to return for another meeting, this time with some ideas for toys.

Miyamoto returned with a portfolio and a large sack from which he produced a recent invention. It was a clothes hanger designed for children. Nursery schools could have a row of them along the wall, he explained. Or parents could put them in children's rooms. Regular metal hangers, he told Yamauchi, were dangerous for children; the pointed hook could hurt them, even poke out an eye. His hanger, carved out of soft wood and covered with cheerful acrylic paint, was in the shape of an elephant's head. Clothes were hung on the ears and turned-up trunk. The elephant's neck fit snugly like a puzzle piece onto a knob that attached to a wall.

Miyamoto had other hangers as well: a bird and a chicken. Then he showed Yamauchi some drawings for more elaborate toys – a whimsical clock for an amusement park; a swing within a seesaw on which three children could play at once.

Yamauchi saw ingenuity and resourcefulness in the work, and he hired Miyamoto to be the company's first staff artist, even though the company had no specific need for one at the time. Miyamoto was assigned to be an apprentice in the planning department.

When Yamauchi called Miyamoto into his office in 1980 the young man looked down at his hands, his long fingers folded on the smooth table in front of him. He listened intently as Yamauchi told him that he was looking for a video game. Miyamoto had played many video games at college in Kanazawa. He loved them. In video games, cartoons came to life. He boldly told the Nintendo chairman that he would enjoy creating a game. However, he said, the shoot-'em-up and tennis-like games that were in the arcades at that time were unimaginative, simply uninteresting to many people. He had always wondered why video games were not treated more like books or movies. Why couldn't they draw on the great stories: some of his favorite legends, fairy tales, and fiction – *King Kong, Jason and the Argonauts*, even *Macbeth*?

Nodding impatiently, Yamauchi rushed to the point: A Nintendo coin-operated video game called 'Radarscope' was a disaster. There was no one else available to come up with a new game design. Miyamoto had to try to convert 'Radarscope' to something that would sell. Yokoi would oversee the project, but Miyamoto was on his own.

After consulting with the R&D 1 chief, Miyamoto returned to his desk with the schematic drawings of 'Radarscope,' which he found simplistic and banal. Enemy planes approached and players had to shoot them down. Miyamoto threw it away. He asked questions of technicians about the kinds of movements characters could make, the possibilities for different-size characters, and the variations of action and reaction that were possible. Nintendo was negotiating with King Features for the rights to use the *Popeye the Sailor Man* comic as a video game, and Miyamoto was told he could work with those characters. The Popeye license from King Features fell through (although the license was later renegotiated and the Popeye game was made), so he tried other ideas.

He thought about *Beauty and the Beast*, but simplified the story. He came up with his own beast, a King Kong-like ape, a humorous bad guy, 'nothing too evil or repulsive,' Miyamoto recalls. The ape would be the pet of the main character, 'a funny, hang-loose kind of guy' who was not especially nice to the gorilla. 'It was humiliating! How miserable it was to belong to such a mean, small man!' says Miyamoto. At his first opportunity, the gorilla escaped and kidnapped the guy's beautiful girlfriend.

The gorilla didn't take the woman to hurt her – an important point in Miyamoto's mind – but to get back at the little man. The man, of course, then had to try to save the girl.

Miyamoto wanted the main character to be goofy and awkward. He chose an ordinary carpenter, neither handsome nor heroic. He wanted him to be Walter Mittyesque, someone anyone could relate to. On a large sketch pad he drew a nose. 'Having a nose or not having a nose is completely different,' he says. 'Noses say a great deal.' The nose Miyamoto created was a distinctive bulbous orb made even more noticeable because of the exaggerated bushy mustache beneath it. From one of his old notebooks filled with characters, he chose a pair of large, pathetic eyes.

The engineers had taught Miyamoto that it was important to distinguish the body so it would be visible on a video-game screen. Therefore he clothed his chubby character in bright-colored carpenter's overalls. In order to make the movement obvious in the simple animation of video games, it was important that characters' arms moved, so he drew stocky arms that swung back and forth. The engineers said it was difficult to accurately represent hair in a video game because of inertia: when a character fell, logically his hair would have to fly up. To avoid the problem, Miyamoto added a red cap. 'Also,' he adds, 'I cannot come up with hairstyles so good.'

Many of his ideas for the game were rejected by Yokoi; Miyamoto's characters had to do simpler things than he wanted them to. He ended up having the carpenter maneuvering up the unfinished foundation of a building in order to reach the gorilla, who had climbed to the top with the girl. To get there the little man ran up ramps, climbed ladders, rode conveyor belts, and jumped on elevators while trying to avoid the objects the gorilla hurled at him – cement tubs, barrels, and beams.

Miyamoto was nearly finished, but the game needed background music. He wrote it himself, on an electronic keyboard attached to a computer and stereo cassette deck. When the game was complete, Miyamoto had to name it. He consulted the company's export manager, and together they mulled over some possibilities. They decided that *kong* would be understood to suggest a gorilla. And since this fierce but cute kong was donkey-stubborn and wily (*donkey*, according to their Japanese/English dictionary, was the translation of the Japanese word for stupid or goofy), they combined the words and named the game 'Donkey Kong.'

Later, when the American sales managers who would sell the game outside Japan heard the name, they looked at one another in disbelief, thinking Yamauchi had flipped. 'Donkey *Hong*?' 'Konkey *Dong*?' 'Honkey *Dong*?' It made no sense. Games that were selling had titles that contained words such as *mutilation, destroy, assassinate, annihilate*. When they played 'Donkey Kong,' they were even more horrified. The salesmen were used to battle games with space invaders, and heroes shooting lasers at aliens. One hated 'Donkey Kong' so much that he began looking for a new job.

Yamauchi heard all the feedback but ignored it. 'Donkey Kong,' released in 1981, became Nintendo's first super-smash hit.

When Yokoi later needed help with games for Game & Watch, Yamauchi told him to use Miyamoto, since his other designers were busy with their own projects. 'I asked him to do creation and I would supervise,' Yokoi says.

The computer chips that were affordable and tiny enough to fit into a Game & Watch could store few characters and even fewer movements, so Miyamoto was limited to telling simplistic stories. He adapted a simpler form of 'Donkey Kong' for Game & Watch, and after the agreement for the Popeye license was hammered out, he made a mini 'Popeye the Sailor Man' game. The latter game has Popeye attempting to save Olive Oyl from Brutus. When Popeye is weakened by too much of Brutus's abuse, he gains strength by downing cans of spinach. Millions of 'Donkey Kong' and 'Popeye' Game & Watches were sold.

In 1984, Miyamoto was again summoned to the chairman's office. Yamauchi explained that he needed more games, this time for the Famicom. Miyamoto was to head up a new division, R&D 4. The group, Joho Kaihatsu, or the entertainment division, had one assignment: to come up with the most imaginative video games ever. The decision was one of the smartest Yamauchi would ever make. Miyamoto, it was soon apparent, had the same talent for video games as the Beatles had for popular music. It is impossible to calculate Miyamoto's value to Nintendo, and it is not unreasonable to question whether Nintendo would have succeeded without him.

After meeting with Yamauchi, Miyamoto returned to his desk. He took a pencil and began sketching the suspendered hero from 'Donkey Kong,' who had been given the name Mario. Someone had mentioned that Mario looked more like a plumber than a carpenter, so he made the new Mario into one. Since plumbers spend their time working on pipes, large, radiant-green sewer pipes became obstacles and doorways to secret worlds in his next game, 'Super Mario Bros.'

The brother Miyamoto created for Mario was Luigi, as tall and string-bean thin as Mario was short and fat. That attribute, as well as the color chosen for his overalls (green to Mario's red), was to distinguish the two characters on the fast-moving game screen.

'Super Mario Bros.' and the sequels Miyamoto designed soon became the most loved video games ever. The 'Mario' games were more interesting because there were always new worlds to conquer, each one more magnificent than the last. There are walking plants, fish that Dr. Seuss might have created, dragons, serpents, flying turtles, fire-spitting daisies, and angel wings upon which Mario and Luigi can hitch a ride.

Humor was subtly introduced into the adventure. Miyamoto's mind bent around corners; players' minds follow, delighted. Eventually they figure out that the princess has to ride atop a ladybug if she is going to get to the boss of one level in 'Super Mario Bros. 2.' (The ladybug looks up her skirt as they head there.) The miniboss of that world – the chief bad guy – spits out lethal eggs larger than his head. In one sequel to 'Super Mario Bros.,' players have to figure out how to get through a seemingly unreachable door. Mario has to remove some of the coins that are floating in front of the door and take them back to another room to trip a 'switch block' that changes the coins into stones. The stones can then be used as steps up to the door. Kids spend hours compulsively trying to figure it out.

Adults enjoy Mario too. They respond, Miyamoto feels, because the games bring them back to their childhoods. 'It is a trigger to again become primitive, primal, as a way of thinking and remembering,' Miyamoto says. 'An adult is a child who has more ethics and morals. That's all. When I am a child, creating, I am not creating a game. I am in the game. The game is not for children, it is for me. It is for the adult that still has a character of a child.'

Miyamoto borrowed freely from folklore, literature, and pop culture – warp zones from *Star Trek*, empowering mushrooms from *Alice in Wonderland* – but his most captivating ideas came from his unique way of experiencing the world and from his memories. When Mario jumps up in space at certain locations, nothing ought to happen because nothing is there, but Mario finds secret, powerful mushrooms and invisible doorways to new worlds. 'I exaggerate what I experience and what I see,' Miyamoto says.

In the 'Mario' games and in some of Miyamoto's other popular games, such as 'The Legend of Zelda' and its sequel, part of the adventure is wandering into new places without a map. 'When I was a child, I went hiking and found a lake,' he says. 'It was quite a surprise for me to stumble upon it. When I traveled around the country without a map, trying to find my way, stumbling on amazing things as I went, I realized how it felt to go on an adventure like this.' In the games, it often is quite a surprise to come upon a lake amid a forest, a rocket ship hidden beneath the sands of a desert.

'When I went to the university at Kanazawa, it was a totally strange city for me,' Miyamoto says. 'I liked walking very much, and whenever I did, something would happen. I would pass through a tunnel and the scene was quite changed when I came out.' Tunnels in his games are doorways to unexpected things. At the other end of a tunnel the fog may be so thick that it is impossible to see what is ahead. In order to explore the new place, the player must return through the tunnel to search for a hidden torch. Armed with the torch, the player is able to go back through the tunnel and face what is hidden in the fog. In 'Super Mario Bros. 3' and 'Super Mario World,' Mario can fly. However, as in Miyamoto's (and many people's) dreams, he often cannot fly high enough or long enough before he comes crashing down to earth.

There are often great risks attached to exploring the worlds in Miyamoto's games. 'I was living in an apartment in Kyoto, and nearby was a building that had a small manhole cover mounted in the wall,' Miyamoto remembers. 'I walked by it every day and I noticed it. I wondered, Why is a manhole on the wall? Where does it lead?' Miyamoto never found out, but in 'Super Mario Bros.,' when the player encounters a manhole, he can choose to do what Miyamoto never did: open it and go inside. To do so is worthwhile.

Miyamoto as a child had worked up the courage to go beyond the periphery of the forbidding cave he had discovered. 'The spirit, the state of mind of a kid when he enters a cave alone must be realized in the game,' he says. 'Going in, he must feel the cold air around him. He must discover a branch off to one side and decide whether to explore it or not. Sometimes he loses his way.' Not just the experiences but the *feelings* connected to those events were essential to make the game meaningful. 'If you go to the cave now, as an adult, it might be silly, trivial, a small cave,' Miyamoto says. 'But as a child, in spite of being banned to go, you could not resist the temptation. It was not a small moment then.'

In Sonebe, Miyamoto had once climbed a tree and gotten high enough to see far-off mountains before he realized that he was stuck; there was no way he could get down. Super Mario gets himself into similar fixes all the time. Once while fishing when he was a young boy, Miyamoto reeled in a bony, grotesque little fish with snapping jaws. Mario encounters the fish that Miyamoto as a child *imagined* he had hooked: a monstrous creature that would happily devour him.

The memory of being lost amid the maze of sliding doors in his family's home in Sonebe was re-created in the labyrinths of the 'Zelda' games, while in the Mario series Miyamoto made safe places that felt like the haven of his parents' attic. The dog that had terrorized him when he was a child attacks Mario. 'I am especially proud of the dastardly, repulsive characters,' he says. Miyamoto's dream was to make games that created worlds in which game characters could be more like players' companions, seemingly independent. 'Perhaps they can even be ourselves at other times in our lives,' he explains obliquely.

Older and more sophisticated players often miss much of the magic in the games. Young children, who do more leisurely exploring, and quiet and thoughtful children, who are more contemplative, have a better chance of finding hidden secrets than the kids who blast through, charging toward the goal. 'The players must be thinking, "Well, I don't see anything here, but it can be, it's possible." Then the player is curious enough to visit that place. When he finds something he never expected, he feels, "Ah, I did it. I made it." It's a great kind of satisfaction.'

The most wondrous surprises are timed to occur at intervals that keep things hopping. It is worth going forward because something good is waiting around the next corner, or in the next world. Some of the secrets are so well hidden that it is a miracle kids find them at all. Each level of each game ends with a flagpole, but a secret whistle in 'Super Mario 3' is hidden *beyond* and above the flagpole – in a place that seems to be outside the game, or at least outside the part of the game that can be seen on a television screen. It is as if Mario has to fly out of the television set for a while until he reaches the entrance to a secret room. Who would ever think of trying it? Those who do are amply rewarded. The whistle gives Mario the power to travel to any world in the game at any time.

Many of Miyamoto's subsequent games not only had the same characters and roughly the same goals, but built on the skills that were learned in the preceding games. There were many new lands and new tricks, and with them the sense of accomplishing new things, yet there was also the comfort of not having to learn a game from scratch.

At Nintendo, Miyamoto's stature increased. After being made the director of his first games, he earned the title of producer. It meant a great deal to him: he had the same title as his idol, George Lucas (*Raiders of the Lost Ark* was Miyamoto's favorite movie). Now, instead of working on one game at a time, he oversaw the production of several, each budgeted at more than $1 million. From six to twenty people worked on each game for a period of twelve to eighteen months.

Technology eventually progressed to make some of the production stages easier. Originally Miyamoto had to paint each character. The colors in the painting were given numbers and the numbers were inputted into a computer, dot by dot. He showed programmers not only how the character looked but how it moved and what special traits it had (a bee, when hit, lost its wings but continued to stalk Mario; boats made out of skulls sank into a fire pit). The characters and their movements were written, line by line, as instructions in a computer program.

Tools were developed to eliminate much of the tedious work. Diagrams and drawings were translated into computer graphics with technology called Character Generator Computer Aided Design (CGCAD). 'Character banks' of images were stored along with the codes that described them. Movement, too, was now programmable from a bank of choices.

Miyamoto was a terrible manager of his division; he needed an assistant to keep everything and everyone organized. Nonetheless, he oversaw all aspects of the creation of the games. He wrote the scripts and then worked with editors, artists, and programmers. When a game was nearly completed, he spread out its blueprint across a room full of tables that had been pushed together. The blueprint was the map of a game's pathways, corridors, rooms, secret worlds, trapdoors, and myriad surprises. Miyamoto lived with it for days, traveling through the game in his mind. As he went along, he determined which points were too frustrating or too easy. He added mushrooms or a star to make Mario invincible. He made certain that the moments that gave the greatest delight – a dinosaur that hatched from an egg, a feather that let Mario fly – came at sufficiently frequent intervals.

When he had edited a game to his satisfaction, Miyamoto went back to his director and technicians and had them incorporate his revisions. They worked for many days and nights on the changes, testing idea after idea, until Miyamoto was happy with the pacing.

When the game was ready, it was scored. Music was just as important for a game as for a movie: the same world could seem scary or lighthearted, depending on the music.

Miyamoto worked with a professional, in-house composer, most often with a brilliant young musician named Koji Kondo, who wrote the music for all the 'Super Mario' games. Kondo's music became so popular that recordings of his Nintendo music were successful CDs and records. (In Tokyo, a symphony performed Kondo's 'Mario' music, and the Jamaican reggae singer Shinehead borrowed the 'Mario' theme for the chorus of a rap song.)

After the music was added and the final edit completed, Miyamoto's games were ready. Kids were waiting. Between 1985 and 1991 he produced eight 'Mario' games. An astounding 60 to 70 million were sold – either individually or packaged with hardware as an incentive to buy Nintendo systems – making Miyamoto the most successful game designer in the world. One designer suggests it is because he is left-handed. Miyamoto shrugs: 'I think it is nothing more than destiny.'

As his games' popularity grew, Miyamoto became well known in Japan and beyond. Westerners who made the pilgrimage to Kyoto to meet him included Paul McCartney, who, during a Japanese tour, said he wanted to see Miyamoto, not Mount Fuji. As a fan of the Beatles, especially *Abbey Road*, Miyamoto was thrilled, although he was never quite able to fathom the attention he received.

Meanwhile, Miyamoto had met a woman named Yasuko, who worked in Nintendo's general administration department. They dated and soon married. He had been living in a nearby Nintendo dormitory, and he and Yasuko moved into a small house near Nintendo's office. From there he walked or rode a bicycle to work. Yasuko stopped working when the first of their two babies was born. The family would walk down the street in Kyoto, and his fans, who reverently call him Dr. Miyamoto, often stopped him to pay homage. Miyamoto didn't change much. Even when he was approaching forty and started cutting his hair shorter (although no one would ever call it neat), he remained unassuming and shy. His mind never stopped wandering to new places – places that were recreated in his newest games.

In spite of a string of hits made by Miyamoto and by the other R&D groups, Yamauchi still was unable to meet the demand for games. Retailers were turning away hordes of customers, which distressed them. Yamauchi himself feared that customers who couldn't get enough games would move on to other forms of entertainment, perhaps a competitor's video game system. How, he wondered, could he increase the number of games available?

Many companies, mostly producers of video-arcade or floppy-disk computer games, had approached him, but Yamauchi hadn't wanted to relinquish any control over the games. If games of poor quality were released, his customers would become disappointed with the Famicom. But the real reason he didn't want other companies to produce games for his machine was that they would make piles of money, and Yamauchi wanted it all for Nintendo.

4
INSIDE THE MOTHER BRAIN

Across the river that divided Kyoto, it was quiet. Light emanated from the ribbon of windows that wound around the Nintendo compound. At the entrance of the main building was a large waiting area that had all the intimacy of an airport terminal. There were rows of uncomfortable molded-plastic chairs and couches and Formica-topped end tables. Behind a marble-topped reception desk were women in powder-blue skirts and smocks, some with tiny pillbox hats. The walls were devoid of all decoration. A maze of hallways with shiny waxed floors lay beyond the waiting room. Behind one anonymous door was Hiroshi Yamauchi's office, called by one employee, 'the realm of the Mother Brain.' In the game 'Metroid' the Mother Brain was the pulsing, laser-spewing creature that hurled bolts of crimson electricity and survived by sucking the universe of all of its energy.

Inside Nintendo's Mother Brain was a substantial wooden desk that faced a small coffee table with couches on either side. The carpet was industrial gray, speckled with beige. There was a small television on a shelf.

A little after nine in the evening, Yamauchi concluded his final meeting of the day. Emerging from a conference room, he padded down the hallway in rubber sandals, his tie loosened, and headed back to the seclusion of his office.

Employees filed out – a succession of men and women wearing Nintendo-blue (hospital-blue) smocks or jackets, or else white shirts with dark business suits. They headed to their cars or to the train or simply walked down the road to their nearby corporate living quarters.

Gunpei Yokoi and Hiroshi Imanishi were huddled together in a conference. Some of Sigeru Miyamoto's R&D team, in the corner of a huge room under parallel rows of fluorescent lights, were playing a test version of a new game, searching for an irksome bug that had been detected earlier that day. (A bug is a flaw in a program that causes malfunctions.) From a cubicle in one corner of a large open office, the tearful voice of a female Japanese pop singer crooned desperately to the man who had betrayed her.

There were no sounds or voices along the corridor that led to the Mother Brain. Inside, another man had joined Yamauchi. They greeted each other and sat on the couches on opposite sides of the low table. Before leaving for the day, Reiko Wakimoto, Yamauchi's secretary, delivered a silver tray upon which was a bottle of fine Scotch, two heavy crystal tumblers, and a small bucket filled with ice. She poured drinks for the two men before departing, bowing respectfully.

Yamauchi's hair had thinned, but he still combed it straight back. The silver was more pronounced, more distinguished. As he spoke, he rubbed his hands on the wooden arms of his chair. He sat with his head jutting forward, which made it seem out of proportion to his small frame. He talked through clenched teeth, his chin taut and drawn.

'Your move,' he said.

Yamauchi always wore dark suits with plum or navy ties and yellow-tinted glasses that gave his face a pronounced pallor. Without the jacket and with his tie removed, he seemed frail, his body shrunken in the oversized armchair. He leaned his head back and narrowed his eyes.

The two men clasped their drinks – Yamauchi's companion shook his in a circling motion; ice skated around the glass – and stared at the square board resting on the table between them. The board, made of blond wood, was covered with a grid of thin black lines, nineteen vertical and nineteen horizontal. The 361 intersections on the board represented the world. Smooth white 'stones' (made of clamshells) and black ones (made of slate) were positioned strategically on the board. They represented the two forces in conflict, both trying to control the game board – the universe.

The game they played, *go*, is a Japanese game sometimes compared to chess, although it is really the antithesis. The object in chess is to whittle away at one's opponent's forces until the playing field is desolate and the king is hunted down. *Go*, on the other hand, is about building and balance – balancing aggression and caution, influence and restraint, friendliness and disharmony. The rules are much simpler than chess, yet the game is more complex. David Weimer, a professor at the University of Rochester who teaches *go*, says that Western games such as chess take 'the Clausewitzean view of conflict – go for the capital and destroy everything along the way.' But in *go* 'you have to be patient; early moves may not have full consequences until much later.'

Go is a difficult game to learn to play and takes a lifetime to master. A neophyte *go* player is rated as a Q 10. As he progresses, he works his way up through the Q levels, eventually making first Q. That is followed by first *dan*, which is the equivalent of a black belt in judo or karate. A player then goes up the scale of *dan* – second, third, fourth *dan*, and so on until tenth *dan*. Hiroshi Yamauchi was sixth *dan*, a sixth-degree black belt.

Yamauchi's opponent was one of Nintendo's licensees – his company developed and sold approved Nintendo games. Licensees were in a precarious position, for Nintendo gave away little and one had to play by Yamauchi's rules.

Because of this, Yamauchi's opponent felt it was prudent to learn all he could about the Nintendo chairman. An astute man could learn volumes about an opponent by his *go* game. 'Yamauchi's game is obvious and clear. Nothing is hidden,' the man observed. 'It is very forceful when it has to be, yet there is give and take. But when he becomes strong, he does not look back. He takes advantage of weakness. He knows far in advance what will happen and he never loses his composure.'

When Yamauchi decided to allow outside companies to create games for the Famicom, he initiated a licensing program. To become a Nintendo licensee, a company had to agree to unprecedented restrictions. Companies that were 'invited' to become licensees were appalled at the terms of the agreement, but Nintendo's position was immovable. No one was forced to become a licensee, Yamauchi noted, and in spite of the complaints, companies signed up, because millions of customers were clamoring for games. The vastness of the Famicom market was enough to silence the complaints, and many companies made fortunes. Nintendo, of course, made the biggest fortune of all.

Two companies, Namco, the reigning arcade-game company, and Hudson, a computer-software maker, became the first two licensees. Hudson released a game called 'Roadrunner.' Before that, Hudson had sold a maximum of 10,000 copies of any computer game. 'Roadrunner' sold 1 million units and was responsible for the quadrupling of Hudson's annual profits in 1984. Namco sold 1.5 million copies of a game called 'Xevious.' A new Namco building was nicknamed the Xevious Building because the game had paid for its construction costs.

Another company, Taito, founded in the 1950s as a jukebox manufacturer, was a large pinball-machine and coin-operated video-game company. Taito had made the game behind a surge in interest in video arcades. In 'Space Invaders,' rows of aliens descended in formation, unremittingly, on the black-and-white TV screen of a large console. The player controlled a mobile cannon at the bottom of the screen that fired shots at the invaders, which came faster and faster until they were entirely destroyed or their opponent – the player – succumbed.

While most companies sold arcade-game machines to distributors or licensees, Taito, in Japan, also owned and operated more than 100,000 coin-op games in arcades, which meant there was no middleman participating in 'Space Invaders' earnings. Taito raked in so much cash that the company was in a strong position to diversify, and its chairman signed an agreement with Hiroshi Yamauchi. Taito and the other initial licensees (Konami, Capcom, Bandai, Namco, and Hudson) had the right to produce their own cartridges for the Famicom, a right no future developers or producers would get for many years. They paid Nintendo a large royalty on every game cartridge they sold (about 20 percent).

Konami, which was based in Kobe, had been successful at selling computer games, dedicated hand-held games (plastic Walkmansize games that had been programmed to be 'dedicated' to play one game only), and coin-op games, but it grew enormously as a result of its Nintendo license. In five years, its earnings shot up from $10 million in 1987 to $300 million in 1991; there was a 2,500 percent increase in sales between 1989 and 1991 alone.

After the six licensees had begun selling games, Hiroshi Yamauchi realized that he had not only given away his ability to control the quality of cartridges (some defective games had reached the market), but some potential profits as well, because he had allowed the companies to manufacture their own games. Henceforth Nintendo would be the sole manufacturer of games for the Famicom. The licensees would develop them and then place an order with Nintendo for a minimum of 10,000 cartridges. The terms were elegantly simple: Nintendo insisted on cash, in advance.

In the new contract, Nintendo was paid about 2,000 yen per cartridge by the licensees, about twice what it took to produce them. Whether a company ordered 10,000 or 500,000 cartridges, Nintendo profited handsomely, even if the games didn't sell.

Licensees might have operated with caution and placed small 10,000-piece orders, but those could be as risky as large orders. Companies were in business for hits, 'grand slams,' as one game maker called them. If a company cautiously ordered a small number of games and found it had a big seller on its hands, Nintendo could take its time filling the order. The game's popularity might pass by the time the games were back in the stores. Companies, particularly small licensees without deep cash reserves, had to risk perilous amounts of capital on large orders if they wanted to gamble on big successes. They shouldered all the risk while Nintendo collected obscene profits, which came with almost no additional investment. (Nintendo subcontracted licensees' orders to outside manufacturers.)

It was common for a game to sell 300,000 copies, and the number was often three or four times that many. At the low end of such sales figures, Nintendo collected $2.2 million. For a million-seller, Nintendo's take was over $7 million. It was easy money, risk-free, and the licensing agreements accounted for a growing proportion of Nintendo's profits as more companies signed on. In 1985 there were seventeen licensees. A year later there were thirty. By 1988 there were fifty.

Sitting across the table from Hiroshi Yamauchi, staring fixedly at the smooth stones on the *go* board, Henk Rogers broke into a wide smile. He had found a hole in Yamauchi's defenses and had placed a stone on the board in position for an attack.

Yamauchi's expression remained impassive. He looked up for a moment, eyeing Rogers, a generation younger and as different a man as imaginable from himself. Rogers had a wolfish, pointed beard and longish ebony hair parted in the middle and swept back over his forehead. Above coffee-colored eyes hung lavish cuneiform eyebrows.

Both men drank the Scotch from their glasses and examined the board in front of them. Rogers, as a three-*dan* player, three levels below Yamauchi, enjoyed a handicap of three. He thus got to place three stones at the start of the game, the equivalent of three free moves. This meant that Yamauchi could win only if Rogers made three mistakes.

Rogers now made his third mistake. Yamauchi had seen in his opponent a broad streak of recklessness, so the move came as no surprise. He took advantage of the error and added a stone that determined the remainder of the game. Rogers was helpless.

The younger man shrugged. 'Good move,' he whispered. There was nothing he could do to save himself.

Henk Rogers lived with his parents in Amsterdam for eleven years before his father's gem business took the family to New York City in 1964. After Henk graduated from high school, the family moved to Oahu, where he enrolled at the University of Hawaii.

Most mornings, before class, he surfed on the island's northern beaches.

Rogers spent most of his time on the U.H. campus in the computer-science building, playing games on terminals connected to mainframes. Game playing led to programming. 'For a gamer, programming is the ultimate game,' he says.

After graduating, he found a job in California at a software company that had a contract with the U.S. military. After a summer, he quit. 'I didn't want to spend my life finding better ways to kill people.'

In the meantime, Rogers's family had moved to Japan, and he joined them in 1976. He lived in Yokohama, a Tokyo suburb, and studied Japanese. He had connections that could have landed him a job at one of the major Japanese computer companies, but he felt that, as a foreigner, it would be a dead end. 'The fact is,' he says, 'if you're not Japanese, you're not going to be president of NEC. It's just not going to happen.'

He taught English and then accepted an offer to work with his father. The gem business was thriving. The Rogerses bought rough stones and had them cut in Bangkok and Hong Kong. They sold the finished gems throughout Asia and in a shop near Tokyo. Henk worked in the family business for seven years. He also learned to play *go* from his father, a six-*dan* player.

Personal computers had proliferated by then. A gamer no longer needed access to a mainframe to play and create games. Messing around with a PC, Rogers created an electronic version of 'Dungeons and Dragons,' the popular role-playing game that was an obsession on high school and college campuses back in the United States. The game, 'Black Onyx,' was, he believed, his ticket to freedom. He planned to sell it for a small fortune.

Rogers took the game to a number of computer-software companies until he found one that was interested. He shook hands on a verbal agreement with the company's president. When it came time to collect his advance and sign the contract, however, the man tried to pay less than he had promised. Computer games in those days were often created by struggling college students or unemployed hackers who were ecstatic if someone wanted to publish their game; they commonly signed contracts for almost nothing. Rogers, however, refused to sign, even when the publisher threatened to keep Rogers from publishing his game elsewhere.

Rogers decided to market 'Black Onyx' himself. He placed advertisements in computer magazines throughout Japan and, his wife manning the telephones, waited for the calls to pour in. There were three phone calls in three months.

The problem, he diagnosed, was that there was no understanding of role-playing games in Japan; 'Dungeons and Dragons' was not popular there. The solution, he concluded, was to educate Japanese gamers.

He talked his way into the editorial offices of computer magazines and convinced editors and writers to try his game. He set it up on their computers as they watched over his shoulder. After calling up an array of bodies and heads on the computer screen, he told the players to choose ones that looked like them, and he typed in their names below the figures they had created. The characters, he explained, *were them*. The essence of a role-playing game was to accept that premise. The player was not watching the character; he *was* the character.

Rogers was nothing if not enthusiastic, and his enthusiasm was contagious. He guided the editors and writers into the first of his game's dungeons, where they were shown how to explore and fight. When they won a battle, they gained experience and strength enough to venture into the next dungeon. He left the offices with the editors and writers enraptured; they continued playing for weeks. The magazines reviewed 'Black Onyx,' showering it with raves. Rogers sold 100,000 copies in 1980.

By the time he released a sequel to 'Black Onyx,' Rogers had formed a company, Bullet-Proof Software, BPS. It was a frustrating, uphill struggle to get BPS games into software shops. Rogers spoke Japanese and was accessible and respectful, but he was a *gaijin*, a foreigner. It was a formidable barrier, but he learned to use it to his advantage. He allowed the arrogance he encountered to placate business adversaries and catch them off guard. 'I walked through the wall as if it didn't exist,' he says.

With the success of his second game, 'Fire Crystal,' Rogers expanded BPS. He couldn't create all the games himself, so he went out in search of games to license. The Japanese game companies were the ones at a disadvantage at the international trade shows where designers hawked their games. Rogers had connections around the globe, spoke several languages, and had a remarkable ease with businessmen, who found him a willful negotiator, as well as with young gamers, who realized that he was one of them. When he could get away with it, Rogers wore colorful Hawaiian shirts in place of drab business suits and bestowed bear hugs instead of handshakes. From the moment he opened his mouth it was evident that he loved games. It led to licenses from all over the world.

Rogers wanted to release a computer *go* game. Although there was a proliferation of chess programs, *go* didn't lend itself as well to programming. In chess there are a limited number of good responses to any move, whereas in *go* the number is astronomical.

Go programs frustrated good players. Human opponents learned from their mistakes, but computers made the same moves over and over again. Artificial intelligence – later technology – would give computers the ability to analyze a game and 'learn' from its mistakes, but even the best *go* programs were not yet capable of highly sophisticated play.

Rogers decided to release a *go* program for novice players. If nothing else, the computer was a tireless, patient teacher. He searched for *go* programs around the world and finally came up with one he considered appropriate for beginners. It was written by a man who had won the world computer *go* championship in Beijing, and who happened to be from Rogers's native Holland. A deal was struck and BPS released the game, which sold modestly well.

BPS grew, but the computer-game business was shrinking. The largest number of people playing the games were not using computers anymore; they were using Nintendo's new Famicom videogame system. People who owned computers might buy one game a year. Famicom owners bought many.

Some computer games could be converted to run on the Famicom, which was designed to have better graphics and faster action than computers. The Famicom wasn't as powerful as computers, however, so many of the games had to be simplified. Yet the trade-off was worthwhile because of the size of the market. By 1988, there were ten million Famicom systems in Japanese homes.

Though many computer-game companies had become early Nintendo licensees, others couldn't afford to. For an entrepreneurial company as small as BPS, becoming a Nintendo licensee was almost impossible, although that didn't stop Rogers.

An ordinary attempt to reach Hiroshi Yamauchi would be unsuccessful, Rogers knew. The man was unavailable to all but his biggest customers and suppliers, and they saw him rarely. They most often met with Nintendo managers, often referred to as 'Yamauchi's generals,' who operated like guard dogs, trained to menace and intimidate.

However, Rogers did learn something about Yamauchi that might give him an entree. Rogers could appeal to him as part of the elite circle of men who played *go*.

In a letter, written on the stationery of his American office, Rogers said that his company sold the best *go* computer program in the world and that he was interested in releasing it for the Famicom. He said he was in Japan for only a few days and he would make time to visit Nintendo if Yamauchi was available.

The day after Rogers messengered the letter from Yokohama to Kyoto, he was contacted by Yamauchi's office and invited to a meeting. Rogers rushed to Kyoto on the bullet train and caught a taxi to Nintendo headquarters. A guard directed him to the lobby, where a receptionist told him to have a seat. An electronic version of a Beethoven cantata signaled that the lunch break was over. Reiko Wakimoto met him and instructed him to follow her to the chairman's office.

Yamauchi, sitting behind his large desk, gave a quick nod when Rogers bowed respectfully. He did not rise when the young man approached him to shake hands but gestured toward one of the chairs opposite the desk. Wakimoto placed glasses of green tea in front of the men.

Yamauchi listened as Rogers talked not about the *go* program or BPS but video games in general. Rogers sat up in the low-backed chair and spoke passionately. He knew what was hot in arcades and he theorized why. He revealed a keen understanding of the young people who played the games. Yamauchi let on nothing, but was impressed by both the young man's insights and his enthusiasm.

Rogers finally repeated what he had said in his letter: he wanted to create a *go* game for the Famicom. To do so, he would need more than just a license to work with Nintendo, since his small company didn't have the capital to pay for cartridges. He asked Yamauchi to back him.

Without fanfare, Yamauchi said he would work with Rogers. He could spare no programmers, only cash. Rogers said cash would be fine.

Yamauchi asked Rogers how much money he needed. Rogers had calculated how much it would cost him to develop the game and added a small profit. He threw out the figure. Yamauchi nodded. 'Good,' he said. 'Done.' Yamauchi had been so quick to agree that Rogers wondered if he had asked for too little.

Before Rogers left the meeting, he challenged Yamauchi to a game of *go*. Yamauchi nodded his acceptance. The game would follow their next meeting, he said. He would schedule it at the conclusion of a workday.

Rogers needed a new version of *go* that was simpler than his computer version. He contacted a programmer in England who had made a *go* program for the Commodore 64 computer, which had a variation of the same central processing unit as the Famicom. Rogers bought the rights.

By the time it was ready, Yamauchi had decided that the market for a *go* video game was too small. The whole point of *go* was the serenity of play, the feel of the stones, the patience, and he felt it was incompatible with the Famicom – not many people would want to play the ancient game on what he still viewed primarily as a toy. Yamauchi told Rogers he could keep the money, but that he should come up with another idea for a Famicom game.

Henk Rogers had too much invested in the *go* game not to see it released, and he asked Yamauchi if BPS could publish it. He said he would pay back the advance if Yamauchi would front him the manufacturing costs.

Yamauchi liked Rogers enough to agree. Nintendo manufactured the cartridges and sent the first order to BPS in Yokohama. Rogers brought a cartridge with him on his next visit to Nintendo, inserted it into a Famicom, turned on the television monitor, and invited Yamauchi to sit down in front of it. Yamauchi had never played a Nintendo game before. He held the controller awkwardly and became frustrated as he tried to follow Rogers's instructions. He put down the controller and refused to try again.

Rogers's *go* game sold 150,000 copies – unspectacular for a Nintendo game, but a huge number for BPS. Rogers easily paid Yamauchi back the money he had been advanced and found himself in a particularly enviable position. Not only did his company have a license to work with Nintendo, but he had something even rarer: a coveted relationship with NCL's chairman.

BPS released other Famicom games, including 'Super Black Onyx,' a newer version of Rogers's game. BPS thrived, and the relationship Rogers had with Nintendo proved valuable to both companies. When Nintendo, years later, sent an emissary to the U.S.S.R. to negotiate with the Soviets for the rights to a brilliant game called 'Tetris,' Rogers was the man the company dispatched.

The Famicom's popularity grew as licensees released their games. Another small company that signed on was Enix, a start-up formed specifically to create Nintendo games. Founded with a capital investment of 5 million yen, the company attained the status of video-game giant through a game called 'Dragon Quest' and its sequels. The original 'Dragon Quest' was a combination of two PC games. It was developed by a team of game designers, programmers, composers, and a well-known illustrator. Because Enix had so much confidence in its game, it put all its start-up money on the line and placed an order for 760,000 cartridges.

'Dragon Quest' was released in February 1986. The Enix team panicked when the game hardly sold. It began advertising in *Shukan Shonen Jump*, a weekly boys' magazine with a circulation of 4.5 million copies. The magazine's editors agreed to publish an article about the role-playing game's lore and mythology. It sparked 'Dragon Quest' sales; a groundswell followed. So many players called and wrote in with questions about the game that the magazine's editors decided to publish an ongoing series of articles about 'Dragon Quest.' Both Enix and the publisher benefited: Enix ordered more games from Nintendo – 1.4 million – and the magazine's circulation skyrocketed. Because of 'Dragon Quest' sales, Enix's management that year gave its employees a bonus equivalent to twelve months' salary.

A sequel, released the next year, sold 2.3 million cartridges, and 'Dragon Quest 3' sold 3.4 million. The degree of anticipation for the games was unprecedented. On its first day in stores, 1.3 million copies of 'Dragon Quest 4' sold out in an hour, despite a price tag of 11,050 ($75) yen, higher than for any other Nintendo game.

The readership of *Shukan Shonen Jump* shot up to 18 million, and circulation grew to 6 million. For both magazine and licensee, the tie-in was a marketing coup that would not be lost on Nintendo (which, meanwhile, profited from the sales of the 'Dragon Quest' games and from the publicity). Seven other publishers launched magazines that provided game tips, profiles of designers, and glimpses of upcoming Famicom games.

By 1990, there were seventy licensees selling millions of copies of hundreds of games, almost all manufactured by Nintendo. In turn, the licensees' games helped sell more Famicom systems, so that almost every household in Japan with children had one. Certain licensees made fortunes. The 'Dragon Quest' sequels grossed several hundred million dollars apiece.

During those days, the only companies that still complained about Nintendo's strict licensing agreement and control of the industry were, for the most part, the ones that couldn't get in. As long as their games were selling, companies were happy to give Nintendo its large cut of the fortunes they were making. There was a slightly manic sense in the industry that anything would sell.

But with the proliferation of licensees – over ninety in 1991 – something had to give. Although Nintendo spent a year or more and upward of $1 million to develop each of its games, smaller companies couldn't afford that. They used their limited resources to buy cartridges from Nintendo and for marketing and packaging. Not much was left for development. The result was an increasing number of boring games.

To curtail this disastrous flood of the market, Hiroshi Yamauchi modified the agreements with third-party licensees to limit the number of games they could release each year. Companies, he figured, would spend more to develop better games, since more would be riding on each one. Licensees, however, were incensed. Who was Nintendo to tell them how many games they could release? There were rumblings of discontent – out of earshot of Nintendo's executives – about unfair restraint of trade.

Tensions among licensees grew because of the increased competition. For part of 1990, Enix's 'Dragon Quest 4' accounted for 25 percent of the entire Famicom software business in Japan. Amid the success stories there was a growing number of disasters.

When the licensees fought one another, it played into Hiroshi Yamauchi's hands. In the industry, he said, there was room for 'one strong company and the rest weak,' and he manipulated the industry to make certain that Nintendo remained the one that was strong.

The licensees were in fear that any criticism of Nintendo would get back to Yamauchi. 'They feared him like a marionette fears the puppeteer,' says one distributor. 'If a company upset Nintendo, he could cut the strings.'

The chips that were the heart of the Famicom cartridges were in short supply during the years when consumer demand was soaring (from 1988 through late 1989) and Nintendo was obliged to ration cartridges. The company claimed to do the allotting fairly and without bias, but licensees knew better. 'Nintendo has succeeded by monopolistic practices and intimidation,' said one company executive. 'We *all* were intimidated. Like a god, Yamauchi wielded power.'

Nintendo anticipated that renegade companies unwilling (or unable) to become licensees would figure out ways to manufacture Famicom games on their own. To stop them, Masayuki Uemura's engineers had incorporated circuitry inside the Famicom that would reject non-Nintendo games. Periodically they modified the code inside new Famicoms so that only Nintendo-approved games could play.

Nintendo also deterred companies from releasing unapproved games through its control of the distribution channels. It was almost impossible for an outsider, against Nintendo's wishes, to get distribution. Wholesalers refused to carry unauthorized products for fear of being cut off by Nintendo. No distributor would risk alienating Hiroshi Yamauchi. A tacit threat pervaded: Yamauchi would crush any company that opposed him.

A small Japanese software company called Hacker International didn't have the capital to become a licensee. Moreover, Hacker made video games that included nudity and sex. Hiroshi Yamauchi allowed brutal violence in his games but forbade pornographic content. He felt that 'unclean, dirty' games would tarnish Nintendo's reputation.

Hacker's engineers dismantled Famicoms and figured out ways to make games that would work on them. When Nintendo changed the circuitry, Hacker's techies found ways to get around the changes. Further, the company circumvented Nintendo's lock on the distribution chain by selling its games by mail. It didn't pay royalties or manufacturing costs to Nintendo, so it could make a healthy profit on relatively small sales. It sold 30,000 to 50,000 copies of many of its games, hardly enough to threaten Nintendo. Nonetheless, Yamauchi decided to wage war on Hacker.

The magazines devoted to Nintendo games, Nintendo bibles for millions of kids, sold more than any other magazines targeted to young readers. They were published by independent companies, but they were in fact completely dependent on Nintendo. NCL provided much of the editorial content of the magazines in the form of tips from game designers (where to find the whistle in 'Super Mario 3'; how to fight Ganon in 'The Legend of Zelda'), so the publishers did whatever Nintendo asked. NCL was allowed to review articles before publication, and it dictated when the magazines could write about games. The magazines gave Nintendo editorial control because it was the source of the insider information for the games; without it, the magazines were sunk.

To reach avid Nintendo players, Hacker placed ads in *Family Computer* magazine, the largest publication devoted to Famicom games. A day after the first ad appeared, Hacker received notice that its ads would no longer run. Even ads that had been paid for in advance were canceled. In the subsequent issue of *Family Computer*, the magazine's editors issued an apology to Nintendo. Unusual as this was, it wasn't enough to appease Hiroshi Yamauchi. Five top managers of Takuma Shoten, the company that published *Family Computer*, rushed to Nintendo to personally apologize. Yamauchi gave them a brief audience, during which the five men, heads bowed, vowed that no such breach of Nintendo's trust would occur again.

The message was unambiguous: Hiroshi Yamauchi had a complete lock on Japan's multibillion-dollar video-game industry. It was felt by retailers, publishers, distributors, wholesalers, licensees, subcontractors, suppliers, and many others in businesses that were both integral and peripheral to Nintendo.

Throughout the 1980s, the number-one Japanese corporations, according to an independent rating by the *Japan Economic Journal*, were, alternately, Toyota and Honda. They were the best run, they performed best on the stock market, and they made the most money per employee and the highest overall profits. For 1989, however, the magazine announced that the number-one company was Nintendo. The company's ascension to this pinnacle was no abberation; the early 1990s continued to see Nintendo's economic dominance in Japan – with no slowdown in sight. And Japan was only the beginning.

COMING TO AMERICA

5

Minoru Arakawa's respected Kyoto family had been in the textile business for four generations. The company imported quality silk from China and cotton from the West and sold them to producers of linens, kimonos, *yukata*, and Western-style garments. The business had grown steadily into one of the largest in Japan and the Arakawas had invested in prime real estate throughout the most expensive section of Kyoto.

Waichiro, Minoru Arakawa's father, managed Arakawa Textiles diligently. Though not the shrewdest of businessmen, he ran his thousand-employee company with steadiness and efficiency and was satisfied with modest but consistent profits – in the neighborhood of $5 million to $6 million each year. Waichiro Arakawa didn't believe in debt or rapid growth. Instead, he was concerned with the fine quality of Arakawa products and with maintaining his good relationships with his suppliers and customers.

The family was aristocratic and deeply grounded in tradition.

The tea ceremony was important in the Arakawa home. Neighbors and friends came by for formal visits. Waichiro did make a few accommodations to Western influence – he often wore a suit and tie – but the ancient home was in most ways as it had been for the past hundred years.

The Arakawas had high expectations for their three children, who were constantly reminded that their position – and their family name – came with responsibility. The children were raised to be soft-spoken, conscientious, and impeccably mannered.

Tradition determined the paths of two of the Arakawa children. As the eldest son, Shoichi was to take over the family business. He joined Arakawa Textiles after he graduated from college. His sister, too, did as she was expected – she got married (to a professor of medicine).

There was, however, no preordained course for Minoru. Sometimes second sons followed their elder brothers into the family business, but there was no rule. Counseled by his parents to do what would make him happiest, Minoru anguished over a career choice. His father offered simplistic advice: 'Be unselfish, do something for others.' Looking back, Minoru laughs. 'I don't think I am that good,' he says.

He entered Kyoto University in 1964 and took general courses until his third year, when he settled on a major in civil engineering, in which he went on to earn a master's degree. He graduated high in his class, but with no idea what to do next.

Minoru's family wealth put him in a privileged position. 'It is difficult when you do not have to work,' he says. 'You have to think. It sounds easy, but sometimes it is not. I struggled to know why we are here and how we should best spend our lives.'

Arakawa decided to look for answers abroad, away from the protected, insular world of Japan. He was accepted into the graduate civil engineering program at MIT, and headed to Boston several months before the school year began. There he bought an old Volkswagen bus and set out on a journey through America, choosing local roads as he crisscrossed the country. Allotting himself five dollars a day for expenses, he camped in state parks, national forests, and parking lots. 'Each state is a different country,' he says. 'The people were like nothing I knew.'

Arakawa found a place to live in Cambridge with a Harvard student who became his best friend. He continued his study of civil engineering, although he still had not determined how he would use his expensive education. After a year and a half, he earned a second master's degree in 1972.

Arakawa returned to Kyoto to see his family at Christmastime, bringing along his old roommate from Cambridge, who happened to be visiting Tokyo. The two men accompanied Minoru's parents to an annual society ball, where the elite of Kyoto high society turned out each season. Everyone knew everyone else in that small, select circle. Before they arrived, Minoru warned his friend that the ball would probably be a bore. He didn't count on meeting Yoko Yamauchi, an elegant and exceptionally pretty woman. Her face was self-assured and her eyes calm. Her satiny black hair was pulled back. When she smiled, her left eyebrow arched magnificently. She said she didn't like dancing, but she danced a great deal that night.

As a child Yoko butted heads with her family. Her great-grandmother Tei, who ran the household, scolded Yoko for playing under the eaves of the old house and called her down from the high branches of the trees. Tei, who was opinionated and overbearing, made most of the decisions about Yoko's education and discipline.

Yoko's mother was invisible during those years. Michiko had had a series of miscarriages after Yoko was born and she was often ill in bed. It was seven years before she had other children, a daughter named Fujiko and then a son, Katsuhito. Once she had regained her health, Michiko was more involved with her children, and she and Yoko sat together and talked for hours at a time. Much of the talk was about Hiroshi Yamauchi.

Yamauchi terrified his children. They hated Nintendo, for they saw how it consumed him. The only attention he paid to his daughters and son was to exercise his strong will and issue edicts. He laid down the law at home, enforcing a strict curfew. Yoko had to be home at the dinner table at six, although Yamauchi himself was absent on many of those evenings.

In 1970, on her twentieth birthday, Yamauchi shocked Yoko when he announced that she was going out on the town with him. She dressed up and accompanied him to a cabaret, a *sikikake*, where five geishas attended them, serving drinks. The women obviously knew him very well. Hiroshi toasted Yoko's coming of age, but when it got late, he sent her home in a taxi. He didn't come home until dawn.

Yamauchi was especially tough on his daughters. Young women, he felt, could not be trusted. He saw what they did when they were out on their own late at night; many of the girls he met were Yoko's age. Likewise, his promiscuity, his temper, and his absences made Yoko wary of men. She decided that if she ever settled down, it would be with a man who had nothing in common with her father.

After Yoko's twentieth birthday, her parents considered arranging a marriage for her, as was still sometimes done in Japan. Michiko tried a modern approach. She and other parents conspired and planned dates for their children. Yoko agreed to go because it was a chance to get out of the house, but she had no intention of becoming involved with anyone.

During Yoko's senior year at college, where she was studying English history, a friend asked her to a society Christmas ball. Her father, contemptuous of Kyoto's old monied families, would probably have forbidden her to attend, but he was out of town. Michiko gave her consent.

The ballroom was festive with decorations and the music of a small orchestra. Yoko watched from a hallway, where she sipped from a cup of punch.

A man approached her and asked her to dance. She could tell he was tipsy and she wanted to refuse, but it would have been rude. It was difficult to maneuver in the tight dress, particularly in the high heels she had chosen.

Doing her best to keep up with the man as he guided her awkwardly around the dance floor, she tried to catch the eye of a friend of her mother's, who was dancing nearby. The woman glanced in her direction, caught Yoko's SOS, and cut in, dancing off with Yoko's partner and leaving Yoko in the arms of the young man she had been dancing with.

Mino Arakawa was dressed in a wide-lapelled tuxedo. He was tall and thin yet athletic. He wore his shiny black hair, which swept and rolled, wavelike, to one side, slightly longer than most. He and Yoko had never met, although they knew about one another.

Yoko's school friend was Minoru's cousin; she had raved about him, saying he was handsome and very bright. It struck Yoko immediately that he was different from the Kyoto men she usually met. He was cosmopolitan, educated in America, sophisticated, and funny.

Minoru and Yoko talked and danced through the evening. They laughed about the fact that they had almost become cousins; her aunt had been engaged to his uncle in an arranged marriage. The wedding never happened because, scandalously, his uncle had broken off the engagement. It was an unforgivable embarrassment to both families, who had gone so far as to exchange gifts, the traditional way of validating an engagement. The Arakawas' gift was a treasured family heirloom, a family crest intricately embroidered onto silk. Tei Yamauchi, furious because of the humiliating breach of etiquette, cut the Arakawa crest in half, returning it in pieces.

Following the Christmas ball, Mino traveled by train back and forth between Tokyo and Kyoto so he could see Yoko. They took walks together and met for lunch. Soon Mino informed his girlfriend in Tokyo that she had better move out; he was becoming seriously involved with someone else.

Yoko and Minoru enjoyed each other immensely, but they were apprehensive about their families' opinion of the match. The Yamauchis may have been almost as wealthy as the Arakawas, yet there was a wall between their families. It had already stopped one marriage; the mutilated Arakawa crest was a reminder.

Michiko had Yoko invite Minoru to dinner at the Yamauchi home. Because of the terrifying portrait Yoko had painted of her father, Arakawa felt as if he were preparing to visit Don Corleone.

Dressed in a conservative suit, he arrived at the Yamauchis'. After the introductions were made, he joined the family at the low dining table, where Michiko and Yoko served the meal. Hiroshi sat back in his chair and studied his daughter's suitor.

The evening wore on and Yamauchi fired questions at Minoru as if he were conducting a job interview. He had to be convinced that Minoru was not a heavy drinker or a playboy.

'You went to Harvard, eh?' Yamauchi asked. 'That is a good school.'

Mino politely explained that he had gone to MIT.

'I have never heard of it,' Yamauchi said.

Yoko and Mino had to convince him that MIT was okay too.

After the meal, the family withdrew to the living room for tea. There, Yamauchi looked at Arakawa and said, without emotion, 'If you are going to marry my daughter, you should marry quickly.'

Yoko and Minoru exchanged glances, and the young man nodded politely. 'Yes, sir,' he said.

Hiroshi ribbed Arakawa, saying he was a good choice because a woman shouldn't marry a man who was too good-looking. 'If you have a nice-looking man, the girls won't leave him alone,' he told his daughter.

Soon afterward, in March, Minoru officially asked Yoko to marry him. She was in love with him but worried that she should wait. Ultimately there was something about Minoru that convinced her. His sense of humor and contemplative nature were part of it. She was comforted that he was a second son who would never have to enter a family business. Nervously, she finally told him that she would marry him, and a wedding was planned.

The wedding, in November, was grand. There was a ceremony under the massive, red-orange Heian Shrine in the park near the Yamauchi home. There were 350 guests, friends of both large families (although the Arakawas' guest list was longer; Mino alone invited about fifty friends). An opulent dinner and champagne toasts in the luxurious ballroom of the Miyako Hotel followed the ceremony.

The couple moved into a small house in the Ogikubo district of Tokyo, near Shinjuku, close to Marubeni's headquarters. For Yoko, it was thrilling to be in Tokyo, away from her parents. She and her new husband were happy newlyweds, romantic. She imagined that their marriage would be like that of Mino's parents, who were still obviously in love after many decades together, taking walks together in the evenings and treating each other with affection and respect.

Yoko loved the tender and romantic attention she received from Minoru and believed that she had chosen wisely – he was as different from Hiroshi Yamauchi as imaginable. 'It was like living with a boyfriend,' she says.

By the end of the idyllic first year, Arakawa's new job was taking more and more of his time. After a training period, he became involved in some of Marubeni's foreign ventures. During his second year he was placed in charge of some small projects that took him away from Japan for ten months out of the year. He flew off to Caracas, Toulouse, Düsseldorf, and Vancouver. He was excited by the travel and the experience he was gaining, but Yoko felt deserted. 'No one prepared me for this,' she complained to her mother.

When Mino was in Tokyo it was better, but there was little time for the couple to be alone. He worked long hours, and Yoko was often dragged to business-related dinners and cocktail parties. She found the obligations of a Japanese businessman's wife appalling. Wives, Yoko Arakawa found, had no identity; their place in the unofficial hierarchy depended on their husbands' position in the company. The first time she went to a wives' luncheon, Yoko sat down next to the assistant general manager's wife and was bluntly asked to move. 'They all looked at me,' she says. 'They were thinking that Arakawa married the wrong person.'

When her complaints to her mother filtered back to Yamauchi, he called from Kyoto, fuming, berating her for having chosen Arakawa in the first place. He said she should divorce him. Yoko considered it, particularly when she had their first child, a daughter, and Arakawa was thousands of miles away. It struck her how bad things had gotten when, one time, she went to Narita International Airport to pick him up after a long absence and he passed right by her – they didn't recognize each other.

Minoru came home one evening in 1977 and announced that the family would be moving to Vancouver for at least a year. His firm had challenged him to develop a large condominium complex there. With a $1 million development budget, he would be in charge of everything from negotiating for the land to working with architects to selling the units. He told Yoko that Vancouver was a great place to live. It was cold, foggy, and rustically beautiful. The move scared her, but Yoko thought they might have more time together if they left Tokyo and the competitive company headquarters and settled into a new place together. They talked excitedly about the move.

The next night, Arakawa came home from work and told Yoko he had some bad news. Things had changed: he was going to Canada, but alone. The company was not allowing wives to go. He assured her he would send for her if it seemed the work in Canada would last, and in the meantime, he would be back and forth between Japan and Vancouver all the time.

Yoko spent a sleepless night. In the morning, she dressed up and headed to Marubeni. She stormed into the office of her husband's boss. 'If I don't go, our marriage is over,' she said flatly. The man listened and then shook his head. He said emphatically that she should not go. She would be a drain on Arakawa; she would hate living outside Japan. But Yoko told him that she would file for divorce if Arakawa went without her; it would be the company's fault that their marriage had fallen apart. The manager argued some more, but he finally shrugged and capitulated. 'But,' he said, 'I wouldn't bother bringing anything with you. You'll be back very soon.'

Yoko and Minoru left Japan with only their daughter, Maki, then three years old, and two suitcases. They arrived in Vancouver and checked into a hotel next door to a Denny's restaurant, where they ate greasy hamburgers and ice cream sundaes. 'If this is America, I have made a big mistake,' she said after one of these meals. She had smoked occasionally at home, but in Vancouver she acquired a three-pack-a-day habit. Frequently, she considered using the credit card her father had given her for emergencies to buy tickets home for herself and her daughter.

Saving his budget for real estate and construction, Arakawa, insisting that he and Yoko make it on their own, with no financial help from their families, felt he couldn't afford furniture or an exorbitant rent, so he relied on a trick he had learned when he was at MIT; he sublet the furnished home of a University of British Columbia professor who was on sabbatical. He bought a Honda Civic and drove to the new office every morning. He worked fourteen or more hours a day while Yoko, stuck at home, tried to begin a life in Canada.

She had thought that she spoke adequate English but found she could barely understand most people she met. She studied the language by watching television and developed an accent decidedly reminiscent of Peter Falk's Columbo. She wanted to enroll in English classes, but $10 an hour, the going rate, was too expensive. She hired an elderly Canadian woman to baby-sit for her daughter for $1.50 an hour and asked the woman to correct her English when she said anything wrong.

Her English improved, but she complained to Mino that she was stuck at home. He surprised her one day with an old Chevy he had picked up for $700. He opened a bank account for her with a modest deposit and gave her a map of Vancouver. 'You have money, transportation, and a map,' he said. 'You are on your way.'

Yoko was still miserable. Her first driving expedition resulted in a confrontation with the police. The Canadians in their neighborhood were impatient and rude. She had no friends, and she never saw her husband. Other than the baby-sitter, she spent time only with her daughter.

A year went by. A second daughter, Masayo, was born. The professor whose home they had rented returned, so the Arakawas had to move. Mino didn't want to spend money on movers, so Yoko did all the packing and the two of them did the lifting and carrying. It was the first of eight moves they would make, from one professor's house to another, before buying their own home in West Vancouver.

Arakawa's single goal at that time was to build the condos. Marubeni was having financial trouble, and his successful execution of the project could help. It would also establish him as an important asset to the company. He portioned out his budget and began the development on prime land he had bought near Vancouver. He directed the clearing of the land, assisted in the designing and engineering of the complex, and oversaw the construction. When the first units were ready to be shown, Arakawa himself, occasionally with Yoko's help, worked as the agent. In order to sell one condominium he spent forty-eight hours applying a fresh coat of peach-hued paint for a prospective buyer. The exhausting efforts paid off when Arakawa began to bring in a healthy profit on his company's investment.

At the same time, Arakawa was trying to extricate Marubeni from another Vancouver venture that was losing money. In a joint venture with a Canadian real estate company, a Marubeni subsidiary had built a high-rise suburban condominium complex called Central Park Place. The 434-unit project was just completed when the real estate market in that area was falling off. The condos weren't selling, so Arakawa met with the Canadian partners to figure out ways to minimize the loss.

It was a grim business for Arakawa, although one good thing came out of the experience. He met a man who would become a good friend – Phil Rogers, a tall Englishman with thinning blond hair and attentive blue eyes, who worked for the Canadian developers.

Hiroshi Yamauchi wanted to enter the American market, and he needed someone to manage the operation. Yoko had kept Michiko apprised of her husband's progress, and she, in turn, reported to Hiroshi. Hiroshi Yamauchi was impressed, not only by Arakawa's managerial and organizational skills, but by his perseverance and dedication. Yamauchi's son, Katsuhito, was too young and inexperienced to be given much responsibility at Nintendo, and he had gone off to work for Dentsu, an advertising agency. That left only Arakawa, and the international experience he had gained through his job with Marubeni was invaluable. It was imperative that Yamauchi convince his son-in-law to run the American subsidiary.

Minoru and Yoko Arakawa visited Kyoto again in early 1980. One night, the family had retired to the living room after a simple dinner at the Yamauchi home. As they settled into some wicker chairs, Michiko served glasses of Scotch. Yoko stared out the window that overlooked the garden, where she had played in her youth. Now it looked like a painting behind glass.

Hiroshi Yamauchi ran one of his delicate hands through his hair. Ignoring his wife and daughter, he turned to Minoru and began speaking softly, hesitantly. But soon he was ardent and emphatic, focusing his stare directly on his son-in-law. It took two hours for Yamauchi to outline his plan.

Though he was expecting it, it nonetheless jarred the younger man when Yamauchi told Arakawa that the plan depended on him. Arakawa sipped his drink and looked over at his wife, whose jaw was firmly set.

None of Yoko's misgiving about her father, none of her distrust or her fears about losing Mino to him, had disappeared, and she was worried because she could see that Mino was intrigued.

Arakawa didn't doubt that Nintendo was doing well in Japan, but he wondered if Yamauchi was overestimating the company's potential for expansion. Now that Arakawa had helped strengthen Marubeni, it was difficult to consider leaving the company. On the other hand, Yamauchi insisted that Nintendo was the uncontested leader of an industry that was still in its infancy.

He looked over at Yoko, who had finally come to enjoy life in Vancouver. She would fight him if he decided to do it. He looked at his father-in-law, who was pouring more Scotch into his glass. Yamauchi tugged at his soft trousers and leaned forward in his chair.

The video-game business had potentials that no one had yet been able to exploit fully, he said. His substantial investments in research and development had paid off, as his engineers were learning to adapt proven, inexpensive semiconductor technologies for new kinds of products. 'I don't see any limitations,' he said.

The offer was straightforward: Arakawa would not have to leave North America; Yamauchi now required the experience Mino had gained working there. And, he continued, Arakawa would be on his own, president of an independent subsidiary, generously backed by NCL. If he replicated in America even a small portion of NCL's growth in Japan, Arakawa would be the president of a substantial company.

'Yoko and I will discuss it,' Arakawa told his father-in-law as he and his wife wished Hiroshi and Michiko good night.

Yoko saw that Minoru was becoming excited. Her independence from her father was suddenly in jeopardy; she envisioned herself in the middle of the inevitable battles that would arise between her father and Minoru. She was afraid the tension between the two men would strain her marriage.

For Mino, the idea of starting a new company in an industry he knew nothing about was intriguing. 'Yoko and I were both from rich families,' he says. 'We could have lived our lives without working, so money wasn't a motivation. When it isn't, something else must compel you.' He tried to reassure Yoko, but she did not relent. 'No matter how much you accomplish, it will be viewed as mediocre, because you will be thought of as the son-in-law,' she said. She looked longingly at the view from their Vancouver home. She had made friends there. She had begun painting and taking art classes. Vancouver was a good community in which to raise her two daughters. Minoru, however, wanted to take the job and she finally gave in. 'Okay,' she said. 'We will see.'

New York, the center of American finance and commerce, seemed to be the logical base for Nintendo of America. Yoko gritted her teeth when the Arakawas left Vancouver in May 1980.

In order to lessen the blow, Minoru decided to make the trip east a family adventure. The day they left, the four of them driving south in a car packed with suitcases and toys (the small amount of furniture they had gathered was shipped by truck), Mount Saint Helens erupted.

Volcanic fallout filled the sky with an eerie orange dust, destroying the paint job on the car. The family retreated back into Canada and circled east, through the Canadian Rockies. Yoko thought this an inauspicious beginning.

They arrived in New Jersey, where they rented a home in Englewood Cliffs. They carefully budgeted money earned from the condominium project; it was a matter of great pride to them that neither had ever asked for money from their families. Yoko had never used the credit card her father had slipped her, and she had never accepted money from her mother in spite of the phone calls from Kyoto in which Michiko pleaded, 'Can't I at least send you a little something? Your father would never know.'

Yoko was Nintendo of America's first employee, helping Arakawa choose a location for an office in Manhattan. They rented a small suite in a high-rise at Twenty-fifth Street and Broadway, on the seventeenth floor. Mornings, the two of them drove into the city together, dropping the children at a babysitter's on the way.

Nintendo of America's first task was to break into the coin-op arcade business, which at $8 billion per year was, at that time, the largest entertainment industry in the United States – bigger than movies and television. Its customer base was decidedly narrow: mostly teenagers.

Without a presence in America, Nintendo Co., Ltd., had only a limited ability to cash in on the boom. The arcade games it made and sold in Japan were licensed through a trading company to American companies. Nintendo saw only a fraction of the take made by the companies that sold their games directly in the market.

Minoru and Yoko spent many evenings at video arcades. They looked over players' shoulders until it made the young kids nervous. 'What the fuck's your problem, mister?' one kid in a Kiss T-shirt barked at Minoru. Arakawa asked him, 'Would you like a job?'

He watched kids stand in front of the machines, transfixed, their hands melded to controllers, their bony arms like umbilical cords joining human and machine. He asked the kids questions about what made a game good. Arakawa realized that the most successful games had something the players couldn't articulate. The words used to describe them were those usually reserved to describe forms of intimacy between people. It was as if the players and the game itself somehow merged.

The other phenomena that made successful games were more obvious. They had to have immediate impact and exciting noise and graphics; a player had to be captivated within the first thirty seconds. There could be no letup in the intensity for two minutes, the time that one quarter lasted. If the players weren't engrossed by then, they left the machine for good. If the game snared them, the string of quarters to follow could have bought dinner for a family of four.

Arakawa hired kids he met at video arcades. They worked in a run-down warehouse he rented in New Jersey. There were enormous rats, a loading elevator that worked once in a while, and loading-dock doors that always got jammed. There was no heating or air conditioning. In winter the place was damp and frigid, in summer a muggy, relentless oven. Coin-operated arcade games were shipped by boat from Japan to the port of Elizabeth, New Jersey. From there they were transported to the warehouse.

Since there were so few employees – a warehouse manager and a few kids – everyone helped out. When Mr. A., as the Americans called him (Yoko hated the nickname because it reminded her of the TV character Mr. T), wasn't making calls on customers, he worked alongside the half-dozen young employees. He wore jeans just like the kids, and he put in as much effort as anyone.

One of Arakawa's first tasks was to hire a sales team; Nintendo of America needed an entrée to the large video-game operators and distributors around the country. He approached the pair who had been selling Nintendo's games in America for the past few years, Al Stone and Ron Judy.

Stone, who had attended Lowell High School in San Francisco and then the University of California at Berkeley, had once set his sights on a career in professional baseball, although he had more of a football-player's physique – the square head and wide shoulders of a linebacker. After playing some minor-league ball in Reno, he finished college at the University of Washington, graduating with a degree in finance and economics, and then tried selling sausages and representing a steamship line. Eventually he moved to Silicon Valley to work for Intel, the semiconductor giant.

Stone had met Ron Judy when they were both at the University of Washington. They lived in the same fraternity house and became business partners, running the *Business Week* franchise on campus. On one occasion they bought a huge shipment of cheap wine that a local company was going to dump and sold it to students.

Judy was a compact man with deep blue-gray eyes, eyebrows that seemed stenciled on, and a pencil-thin mustache. For fourteen summers, from grade school through college in Seattle, he had worked in his father's construction business. Most of his time was spent clearing land for interstate freeways. For a time he worked on the Alaska pipeline in fifty-degrees-below-zero weather, so that Chicago, where he headed later to finish his degree (at the University of Illinois), seemed mild by comparison.

After graduating in 1972, Judy moved to New York to consult for Chase Manhattan Bank on mergers and acquisitions. Then he moved to San Francisco to work for a small company that consulted with high-technology firms. He and Al Stone, then at Intel down the peninsula, got together sometimes after work to drink beer and mull over ideas. They agreed on two things: they were fed up with working for other people, and they wanted to make more money.

They formed their first business in Seattle, a trucking company they called Chase Express. They managed a fleet transporting containers from Seattle's piers when a friend of Judy's called from Hawaii with a proposition. He said it was a sure thing. Judy found himself at the air-freight dock of the airport, claiming a giant crate. He tried, unsuccessfully, to get it into the back of his station wagon. He finally gave up and tied it on the roof.

Judy unpacked the crate in his living room. Inside was something that looked like a cocktail table with a TV screen that faced upward, like a tabletop. It was, he had been promised, the latest thing in Japan, great for a lounge or pizza parlor, where customers stuffed in coins while they sucked down pizza and beer. A video game called 'Space Fever' was played on the machine, and it was made by a company called Nintendo.

Judy convinced a local hotel owner to let him put the game in the cocktail lounge, agreeing to a sixty-forty split of the take. It did fairly well, although one game wasn't worth the effort. His friend sent along two more tabletop games from Hawaii, explaining that all the big Japanese companies had representatives in the United States except for Nintendo. A trading company in Japan was buying games from NCL and sending them to him in Hawaii, and they needed someone to bring them into the mainland.

When the games arrived from Hawaii, Judy arranged to have them set up in another Seattle bar. The games made, in Judy's words, 'obscene profits.' It was enough to convince him and Stone to enter the video-game business. They formed a new company, Far East Video, and set out to sell Nintendo machines throughout the United States. They bought machines from the trading company and tried to sell them to local operators or small distributors. In the process, they became masters at convincing airline-ticket agents to ignore baggage weight and size limitations so they could get their game machines on commercial flights. From Peoria to Phoenix, they begged taxi drivers to let them load the game machines into the trunks of their cabs. Video games were so hot that even the bad games were selling. They bought the machines for less than $1,000 each, and customers were happily buying five or ten of them at roughly $1,500 each. Distributors sold them to operators for as much as $2,500. It made their backaches worthwhile.

Mino Arakawa contacted Judy and Stone in late 1980 and asked them to see him on their next trip to New York. The meeting coincided with Hiroshi Yamauchi's first visit to his new subsidiary. Yoko worried that her father couldn't avoid meddling; she feared a blowup.

Although he timed the visit so that he could accompany Arakawa to an arcade-game industry trade show, the other reason Hiroshi came to New York was to check up on Yoko and his grandchildren. His wife had pressed him to go; she felt that Yoko was drifting away from them. She seemed distant on the telephone; she was working too hard; America was too far away.

Soon after Yamauchi arrived in New York, he began to see that Michiko's perception was correct; something *had* changed. Yoko, however, was hardly unhappy. She seemed content and confident in a way that surprised him. In all the years she smoked, Yoko had never lit up in front of her father. Despite his lifelong habit, Hiroshi was part of the generation that held the double standard that smoking was unladylike. It never stopped Yoko from smoking, only from letting him know about it.

Sitting in a Manhattan restaurant after dinner one night, Yoko turned to her father and asked nonchalantly, 'Do you mind if I smoke?' He looked at her sharply, paused for one long moment, then pulled out his own pack and shook out a cigarette, offering it to her. She accepted it and leaned over to meet the match he held out for her.

Nothing was said, but that moment was the start of a change in their relationship. Yamauchi saw for the first time that his daughter was a strong, independent woman. He also realized that he liked her very much.

'Dad,' she said as they walked through midtown Manhattan, 'I know you're worried about how things are going here.' She took a drag of the cigarette and continued. 'But hold back a little longer; let Mino do it his way.'

Yamauchi said he would – for a while.

One afternoon, Al Stone and Ron Judy came in to meet with Arakawa and Yamauchi at the Manhattan office. Arakawa did the talking, although Stone and Judy noticed that he frequently looked to Yamauchi.

Arakawa said he intended to import Nintendo's arcade games directly to America and he hoped that Stone and Judy would work with his new company. From their perspective, it was a risk-free deal: they would remain independent and Arakawa would cover their expenses. Their per-game take would remain about the same, so they stood only to gain by the arrangement.

Stone and Judy told Arakawa and Yamauchi that they could sell every game Nintendo made if the games were better. Games such as 'Space Fever' and 'Sheriff' did fairly well, but what they all hoped for was a killer game from NCL – a 'Space Invaders' or a 'Pac-Man.'

Yamauchi said nothing. He left New York repressing his intense urge to take over. There hadn't been even one conflagration with Arakawa. Judy and Stone took their contract to an attorney, Howard Lincoln, of the Seattle law firm of Sax and MacIver. Lincoln had quite a reputation in Seattle. Someone said of him, 'To call Howard Lincoln forthcoming would be an oxymoron – like jumbo shrimp.' The thirty-eight-year-old attorney had the down-home affability of an old Kentucky colonel, but he was also capable of intimidating almost any adversary. And when he lost control, which was rarely, wise men and women got out of his path. He carried himself with effortless confidence and ease. When he spoke, he was jocular and warm; there was reassurance in his voice. He was dapper, almost preppy, and fox-sharp.

Lincoln had intense, circumspect brown eyes, small for his face, and the flushed cheeks of an outdoorsman (his fishing buddies had given him the nickname Cato, after the Green Hornet's sidekick, for his reckless pursuit of king salmon). Every chance he got, he headed into the mountains or, at least once a year, up to Alaska to fly-fish in high-country rivers. He relaxed then, but at other times his neck muscles were taut and he held his shoulders high, as if ready to protect his face in a fight. It was one of the few signs that betrayed the quick thinking beneath his composure.

Lincoln was born in Oakland, California, where his father was an executive with the Pullman Company, makers of Pullman railroad cars. The elder Lincoln was a reserved man, hard of hearing, who was well liked in his community and by his employees. His wife was an elegant woman, delicate and gracious.

Throughout World War II, the American government moved troops by the nation's railroads, which kept Lincoln's father particularly busy. Howard remembers being taken, at age four or five, to visit trains carrying wounded soldiers who had been shipped back to San Francisco.

Lincoln attended high school in the fifties. A skinny, short-haired boy, he dressed in short-sleeved shirts and cuffed pants. He was active in his local Baptist church and the Boy Scouts. In 1954 he was a model for a Norman Rockwell painting that appeared on the Boy Scout calendar for 1956. A scoutmaster stood over a well-tended campfire near a bunch of scouts in sleeping bags. Lincoln was the blond boy with the angelic smile.

With the rise of commercial air travel, the Pullman Company's fortunes inevitably declined. After forty-eight years with the company, Howard's father presided over its slide, but by then his son had entered college. At the University of California, Berkeley, he gravitated toward law.

When he arrived in September 1957, fraternities still controlled campus life. The situation soon changed: the budding Free Speech Movement rocked the campus. Lincoln watched it from the distance of a student determined to go to Boalt Hall, where he succeeded in gaining admission in 1962. He graduated high in the same class as Rose Bird, who would later become a chief justice of the California Supreme Court.

The draft for the Vietnam War was in effect, and three days before he took the bar exam, Lincoln was called to report for a physical. He headed downtown to Oakland's Naval Reserve center, where he signed up to be a seaman recruit. He was stationed at Sand Point Naval Air Station on Lake Washington, aching as a judge advocate for the navy. There he met a striking blond naval lieutenant, Grace Lincoln, and they married six months later.

When Lincoln and his new wife Grace entered civilian life in 1970, the couple had to decide where to settle down. He considered looking up Ed Meese, then in Sacramento with Governor Ronald Reagan, but in the end they chose to stay in Seattle. He sent his résumé to all the top Seattle firms and was hired by Sax and MacIver, where he built up a sizable practice, specializing in banking and corporation law.

Lincoln often worked with a CPA who did the books for Ron Judy and Al Stone. The CPA asked Lincoln to look at a contract between his clients and Nintendo of America. It confirmed that the pair would be the sole U.S. distributors for Nintendo in the coin-operated video-game business, in exchange for the payment of a set figure for each machine they sold.

The contract was, Lincoln told them, 'completely screwy.' When he asked who had put the document together, he was told it was NOA's president, Minoru Arakawa. He helped Stone and Judy fix the contract before they headed off to New York to set up Nintendo's distribution network.

Nintendo's new sales team, Judy and Stone, had good connections throughout the industry. The two had worked with numerous distributors and operators (who often owned machines in locations such as bowling alleys, bars, and restaurants). Occasionally they ran into some shady characters – one aggressive operator, wanting more liberal payment terms, hinted that he was well connected with the mob – but more often the business was straightforward. If buyers liked a game, they paid cash for consoles. That was it. There were none of the complications of the consumer business: almost no advertising, marketing, promotion, or royalties. The industry had slowed, however, and the new company's sales were weak. Ron Judy told Arakawa that they needed a big hit if he and Stone were going to stay with Nintendo. By 1980 they were barely keeping above water.

The game that was to turn things around was 'Radarscope,' an uncomplicated shooting game in which the player lined up an enemy fighter in a site and blasted away. Arakawa placed some samples in test locations around Seattle and the results were good. 'Radarscope,' he decided, was the game he would use to push his operation into the big time. He ordered three thousand units. By placing an order that large, Arakawa was committing almost all of NOA's resources.

It took almost four months for the ship, heavy with the game consoles, to travel from Japan to Elizabeth. Arakawa was already in a panic when it arrived, because the excitement for 'Radarscope' seemed to be evaporating. The games in the test locations sat idle, and he had no idea if he would be able to sell them. He was learning the hard way about the fickle tastes of video-game devotees. A hot game could become passé overnight. Tried-and-true games such as 'Pac-Man,' some of the classic shoot-outs, and sports and car-racing games always brought in decent returns, but it was impossible to count on new games. By the time 'Radarscope' arrived, it seemed old, and Arakawa's in-house gamers gave him feedback he didn't want to hear: the game was boring.

Ron Judy and Al Stone did their best to peddle 'Radarscope,' but operators who previously had indicated they might buy dozens took only two or three. Arakawa lowered the price, but he was still left with more than two thousand games. Stone and Judy were going broke. To keep going, Judy borrowed $50,000 from his aunt, her life savings. He thought, I've lost everything. I'll be in debt for the rest of my life. Arakawa was deeply worried. 'I was thinking it was a big mistake to take this job,' he says. He was loath to tell Yamauchi he was in trouble, but he had no choice. Nintendo of America would sink under the weight of all those 'Radarscopes.'

Yoko Arakawa's worst fears were being realized. She was smack in the middle of the clash she saw coming between her husband and father. Arakawa had postponed making the telephone call, but finally he called Yamauchi and told him that 'Radarscope' wasn't selling and NCL's fledgling subsidiary was in trouble. Yamauchi snarled, telling Arakawa that he knew he had overstepped himself with that huge order. What did Mino want him to do? He never would have made that many games if Arakawa hadn't ordered them . . .

All coin-operated video games looked essentially the same on the outside: a cabinet, joysticks, and a screen. What made the games unique was inside the cabinet, the PC board, or 'mother board' – the game's processor, chips, and circuitry. Arakawa could have the 'Radarscope' cabinets repainted, and he could have the 'Radarscope' program chips removed. The problem was that he had nothing with which to replace those chips. Arakawa weakly told Yamauchi that he needed a new game quickly.

On the phone to Yoko, Yamauchi screamed about her husband's ineptitude. He said he felt he had made a serious mistake of the kind he had never made before: judging character. Arakawa, irritated by Yamauchi's I-told-you-so arrogance, bellyached about his father-in-law. He felt he should have listened to his wife and stayed away from Nintendo. Yoko, meanwhile, felt torn apart. 'It was like I was on a ship that was going down in the middle of the ocean,' Yoko says. 'Two captains were shouting into my ears about what must be done, about how disastrous things were.' When she called to get sympathy from her mother, Michiko was anything but helpful. 'Be patient, be cheerful,' she said. The advice incensed Yoko. 'If all I needed was encouragement, I wouldn't be calling,' Yoko snapped. Reluctantly, when summer arrived a few months later, she followed through with her plans to take the children to Kyoto for a visit, even though the tension was hardly bearable.

In America, while they waited for the new game chip, Arakawa pushed Nintendo's other games, and also decided to move his base of operations. It was a mistake to be in New York. The 'Radarscope' disaster illustrated the repercussions of being so far from Japan. Shipping to North America's West Coast would cut out weeks, even months, of delay. The decision was personal, too. He and Yoko had loved living in Vancouver, and neither of them was comfortable in New York. The frenetic pace was exhausting, and all the driving between the midtown Manhattan office and the warehouse and service center in New Jersey was inefficient.

Arakawa had agents search for offices in California, Washington, and Oregon. The major urban center in the United States that was nearest to Vancouver was also the closest to Japan: Osaka harbor to Seattle took nine days by boat. Seattle was a thriving region of new industry, yet it was hardly exploited. Real estate was still affordable, and there were other pluses: as a lumber-producing area, there were companies that made fine-quality wood products, and they could make cabinets for arcade games. There was a high-quality labor pool because of Boeing and the many high-technology companies in the Seattle area. The city's population, of about 2 million, was enough to support good restaurants and arts and entertainment, yet not so big as to make it overwhelming, like New York.

To search for a place in Seattle, Arakawa contacted Phil Rogers, from his days with Marubeni. Rogers put him in touch with a broker who found a warehouse to lease in a suburb called Tukwila, not far from Seattle-Tacoma International Airport.

In the Segali Business Park Nintendo leased a 60,000-square-foot warehouse with three small offices built into a corner. Arakawa took one for his main office, and Judy and Stone moved into another. The main warehouse became the assembly and distribution site for the game machines. The service center was there too. All the games remaining in New Jersey, including the two thousand 'Radarscopes,' were shipped by rail to the Seattle warehouse.

Minoru called Yoko in Japan and asked her to come back to help with the move from New York. She flew to Seattle and they found a home to rent – an attractive four-bedroom place on a half-acre in Bellevue, across Lake Washington from Seattle. Then, in New York, she arranged movers to ship their furniture and clothes back west.

In Japan, Yamauchi made a quick check of his R&D groups and found that all the key engineers and programmers were too busy to be diverted to help with Arakawa's problems. The United States represented an infinitesimal portion of NCL's business, and he couldn't justify taking one of his top designers away from more important work. He told this to Arakawa, who was growing more and more desperate.

Arakawa pleaded with Yamauchi until his father-in-law finally agreed to put someone on the project. The chairman told Gunpei Yokoi to oversee the work of the young apprentice he had asked to come up with something. 'But he knows nothing about video games,' Yokoi said.

Yamauchi responded that there was no one else available.

The young man Yamauchi had chosen wasn't from any of the engineering groups; in fact, he wasn't even an engineer, but he had enthusiasm and some interesting ideas about the ways video games should be designed.

When Yamauchi so informed Arakawa, his son-in-law fumed. He needed a superior game to save the business and Yamauchi had put an inexperienced apprentice on the job! Why had Yamauchi seduced him into going to America if he was going to sabotage the operation? But there was nothing Mino could do, and he weakly asked his father-in-law, 'What is this apprentice's name?'

Yamauchi answered, 'Sigeru Miyamoto.'

6
FOR A FISTFUL OF QUARTERS

The Nintendo employees Arakawa took to Seattle with him from New York waited for the new game. The team included a service manager, a technician, and a secretary. To manage the warehouse Mino hired a friend of Ron Judy and Al Stone.

Don James, a stocky man with large arms and a thick mustache, grew up in Seattle and studied industrial design at the University of Washington. After graduating, he went to work for Far East Video. At Nintendo, his first job was to prepare the warehouse to receive the two thousand 'Radarscopes' from New Jersey. Arakawa gave him permission to hire an assistant. The help-wanted ad in the *Seattle Times* read: 'Have Fun and Play Games for a Living.'

Twenty-year-old Howard Phillips, who looked remarkably like Howdy Doody with a Charles Manson beard, applied. He had wavy orange hair, freckles, cobalt-blue eyes, and a goofy grin. Phillips, though originally from Pittsburgh, had grown up in

Seattle, where his father worked for Boeing. Howard had attended grammar school with Bill Gates, who went on to found Microsoft. They had been in the same carpool.

The shipment of 'Radarscopes' arrived by the truckload from the train station after their cross-country journey. Phillips excitedly uncrated a game, plugged it in, and stood before the console. 'It was like when a car dealer gets in a new car,' he says. 'I would test 'em out, drive 'em.'

Arakawa watched him. 'It was like he was sleepwalking,' he says. Phillips was disappointed with 'Radarscope.' 'It's hopeless,' he said. He joined the other Nintendo employees who were waiting for the new game to arrive from Japan.

One day a courier delivered a package that had arrived by air from Kyoto. Don James signed for it and delivered the small box to Arakawa. He opened it and saw the board that contained the new game's program. As the service technician installed it in a console, Arakawa called in Judy and Stone. They watched as the power was turned on. The opening screen announced the game: 'DONKEY KONG.'

They looked at one another. Stone swore. He and Judy tried the game and concluded that it was a disaster. Two thousand 'Donkey Kongs' were worse than two thousand 'Radarscopes.' Al Stone walked out. 'It's over,' he said.

Arakawa worriedly complained to Yamauchi, who was thoroughly unsympathetic. He implored Yamauchi at least to change the name, but Yamauchi refused. 'It is a good game,' he said.

Arakawa had no choice but to attempt to sell it. Judy reluctantly agreed to try, and he convinced Stone to cooperate. There was one promising sign: when the new flame-haired kid in the warehouse, Howard Phillips, test-drove 'Donkey Kong,' they had to pry him off it to get him back to work.

Before NCL could begin mass-producing the game boards, the American team had to provide an English text in place of the Japanese in the introductory storyline, which flashed on the screen at the start of a game.

The NOA staff gathered in a corner of the warehouse around a couple of card tables. They came up with a simple translation of Miyamoto's story and they had to name the characters. Arakawa christened the princess Pauline, after James's wife, Polly. They were trying to decide what to call the rotund, red-capped carpenter, when there was a knock on the door.

Arakawa answered it. Standing there was the owner of the warehouse. In front of everyone, he blasted Arakawa because the rent was late. Flustered, Arakawa promised that the money was forthcoming, and the man left.

The landlord's name was Mario Segali. 'Mario,' they decided. 'Super Mario!'

The Spot Tavern, near Nintendo's office, was a small, darkly lit hangout that served greasy hamburgers, excellent french fries, and draft beer in tall glasses. In a back corner was a pinball machine. Ron Judy convinced the tavern's owner to allow him to set up a 'Donkey Kong' game. The next morning he wheeled a console in on a dolly, set it down next to the pinball machine, and plugged it in.

He didn't expect much when he returned that night to check the cash box. But there were 120 quarters inside, $30, a phenomenal amount.

Judy assumed it was an aberration. He checked at around 10:00 P.M. the second day and found $35. The next day there was $36. The Spot's owner was happy to have more 'Donkey Kongs' delivered. His bar was packed with people lined up to play Sigeru Miyamoto's first game.

The NOA team, especially Stone, hated to admit that Yamauchi had been right, but Arakawa was greatly relieved.

The components – the mother board, power supply, and unassembled cabinets – arrived from Japan. Arakawa, James, Phillips, Judy, Stone, Yoko Arakawa, and virtually all the other employees assembled consoles throughout long days and nights. Completed games were crated and loaded onto trucks, which headed out to cities throughout America. Nintendo had a hit on its hands.

Nintendo of America had its first company Christmas party at a restaurant near the warehouse. All of the dozen founding employees attended. The centerpiece of the party was a sculpture of

Donkey Kong made out of fifty pounds of butter covered with shredded coconut. Afterward, the sculpture was dried out, shellacked, and hung from a rafter in the warehouse, from which it watched over the Nintendo crew until it turned green with mold.

'Donkey Kong's' popularity grew, and Taito, the Japanese company behind 'Space Invaders,' offered to buy all rights to the game for an exorbitant sum. Almost everyone associated with Arakawa counseled him to take the money.

Arakawa pondered the offer for days and called Yamauchi to discuss it with him. Yamauchi felt that a large advance in hand was better than profits they might never see, but he said he would back Arakawa in any decision.

Arakawa told Taito the rights weren't for sale. In Kyoto, Yamauchi told Hiroshi Imanishi, 'Arakawa insists, so okay. We will see if it is a mistake.'

All two thousand 'Donkey Kongs' sold. The NOA staff was astonished. Arakawa called Yamauchi and placed orders for thousands more.

Arakawa enlarged his staff, hiring salesmen and service technicians. Don James hired twenty-five people to assemble and test games. When they were ready, serial numbers were affixed and they were packaged and shipped. Fifty games went out each day. To increase production James began to purchase control panels, cabinets, graphics controllers, and monitors from local sources. His staff, which grew to include most of Nintendo's 125 employees, were building up to 250 game machines a day.

Sixty thousand more 'Donkey Kongs' were sold, and Nintendo of America's second year ended with more than $100 million in sales. The Arakawas realized they might be in Seattle for some time, so they bought the house they had been renting in quiet, peaceful Bellevue. Yoko took up tennis, and she dragged Mino onto the golf course.

Judy and Stone were having a good 1981 too. Their accountant called Howard Lincoln to tell him they had to form corporations for their clients. Lincoln thought it was a joke. 'They're half bankrupt, what are you talking about?' he asked. The accountant explained that a Nintendo video game was selling like mad. Stone and Judy were making a fortune.

Lincoln formed Ron Judy Inc. and Al Stone Inc. and, with the accountant, closed the companies' first fiscal year. Stone says they each made in excess of $1 million.

That same year, Atari and Mattel were battling for the home video-game market in America. Coleco, which began in 1932 making swimming pools, went up against them with a system called ColecoVision. All three companies wanted the exclusive rights to create a version of 'Donkey Kong' that would play on their system. Atari and Mattel contacted Arakawa, but Coleco went directly to Yamauchi in Japan, who decided that Nintendo should work with the company with the most at stake. He told Arakawa a deal should be made with Coleco. 'It is the hungriest company,' he said.

Before he could sell the rights, Arakawa needed a lawyer to trademark the 'Donkey Kong' name and copyright the game, so Ron Judy introduced him to Howard Lincoln. Lincoln had never done this kind of work and had no idea where to begin. He told Arakawa, 'No problem.' It was, he says, 'a typical lawyer response. You never tell a client that you don't know what you're doing.'

Once 'Donkey Kong' was legally protected, Lincoln helped put together the deal with Coleco in 1981. He used a legal form book and prepared an agreement. When Arakawa went over it, he asked why Nintendo had to warrant that they owned any of the rights to the game. Lincoln explained that it was just the way it was done. Arakawa asked again. 'But why do *I* have to do it?'

Lincoln shrugged. 'I guess you don't *have* to.'

Lincoln had Nintendo disclaim any warrant about ownership, and he noted in the contract that Coleco assumed the entire risk. There was no practical reason for Arakawa to change this provision other than his instinctive way of doing business: Never give anything away that you don't have to. 'I knew Nintendo owned the game, but I figured, What the hell, might as well be bold,' Lincoln says. Taking his cue from his client, Lincoln skewed the rest of the contract to favor Nintendo, 'mostly because we didn't know how things were normally done,' he says.

The agreement between Nintendo and Coleco was to be signed before the end of the year, and Lincoln spent most of the night of

Christmas Eve 1981 completing it. On Christmas Day he sent it to Arakawa for his signature. Arakawa hurried it to Japan for Yamauchi to sign with a representative of Coleco, who had been sent to Kyoto to nail down the deal. When they met at NCL, the Coleco executive told Yamauchi that he would take the contract back to America to have the company's attorney check it over and return it signed. Yamauchi refused, saying, 'You must sign it now, or we are going to go with someone else.' The man froze. He had no choice. Nervously, he signed the agreement.

Meanwhile, Nintendo had outgrown the warehouse at Segali Business Park, and Arakawa wanted to move to a larger and better location. Another manager would have been more cautious. One successful video game in that volatile business did not necessarily mean there would be more. Arakawa, however, viewed 'Donkey Kong' as the break he needed, and invested in twenty-seven (and later, an additional thirty-three) acres of cleared and plowed Redmond land. He paid cash and the deal was closed in July 1982. By then he talked Phil Rogers into joining Nintendo full time. Rogers said he wanted to be a vice-president. When Arakawa balked, Rogers said, 'Don't worry about the title; everybody is a vice-president in the United States.'

Arakawa said he would talk to Howard Lincoln, who advised against it, and Rogers was persuaded to accept the title of director of real estate. His first job was to oversee the construction of the first of several Nintendo corporate buildings – three-layer rectangles, like high-tech sheet cakes. Eventually he also bought 125 acres in nearby North Bend for a larger new warehouse, as well as several small parcels in Seattle. The first building was ready in November 1982. By the time the additional warehouse and production buildings were completed and the warehouse at Mario Segali's industrial park was vacated, Rogers was Nintendo's director of product development and manufacturing. Six months later he became vice-president of operations.

Rogers worked with Don James to design a production system to build video games more efficiently. After 'Donkey Kong' there were 'Donkey Kong Jr.,' 'Popeye,' 'Punch-Out' (later introduced as 'Mike Tyson's Punch-Out!' as a home video game when an endorsement deal with the heavyweight champ was negotiated), and then a new kind of arcade game designed by Nintendo Japan. Called the VS System ('VS' for *versus*), it was a console video-game system that had two monitors, side by side, with two play options: you versus the machine or you versus another player. The first VS game was a baseball game. Four kids held on to joysticks and controlled pitching, batting, and fielding.

By 1982, Howard Lincoln found himself occupied almost exclusively with Nintendo-related matters. He was asked to draw up a new contract between Nintendo and Al Stone and Ron Judy and terminate their past agreement. Judy was becoming Nintendo's vice-president of marketing and Stone its vice-president of sales.

Next Lincoln was asked to work with Nintendo to do something about the extraordinary number of counterfeit 'Donkey Kong' games on the market – as many as half the games sold were counterfeit.

Lincoln and his staff went after the counterfeiters and their customers, employing detectives and cooperating with police and customs officers throughout the country. One distributor in Texas who dealt in phony Nintendo games disappeared, but many others were brought to court. Organized-crime connections were never concretely proved in any of the cases, but one prosecutor insisted that the distribution of the illegal games never could have become such a large business without the mob.

When Lincoln's team of lawyers tracked down a source of bootleg games, they would get U.S. marshals to raid the offenders, court orders in hand. Many thousands of mother boards and cabinets were confiscated.

Nintendo litigated thirty-five copyright infringement suits against individuals and companies selling counterfeit 'Donkey Kong' games, but in spite of all the efforts, the company lost at least $100 million in potential sales because of counterfeiters.

While planning legal strategies, Lincoln and Arakawa spent a great deal of time together, consulting at each other's offices or, on occasion, on airplanes, flying between Seattle and Japan and throughout America. In Seattle, Mino and Yoko frequently dined with Howard and Grace Lincoln. These evenings, though ostensibly social, inevitably turned to Nintendo business.

One late night in April 1982, Arakawa called Lincoln at home. There was an unusual urgency in his voice. Arakawa explained that his father-in-law had just called from Kyoto, where it was early morning. A telex had arrived at NCL from Sidney Sheinberg of MCA Universal, the huge entertainment conglomerate. The telex was short and direct. It said that Yamauchi had forty-eight hours to turn over all of Nintendo's profits from 'Donkey Kong' and to destroy any unsold games. The game, MCA claimed, was an infringement on a Universal Studios copyright – for the movie *King Kong*.

The telex was ominous. Just as Nintendo of America was finally succeeding, here was a threat from one of the most litigious, hostile men in the entertainment business. Sheinberg, MCA's indomitable president, second in that organization only to chairman and CEO Lew Wasserman, was an attorney who was known to work, as one colleague put it, 'like a python, strangling his prey before devouring it.'

After a sleepless night, Arakawa and Lincoln headed to their respective offices and consulted on the telephone. There was every reason to believe that MCA, with its enormous clout and bank account, could crush a relatively small, foreign-owned company like NOA. Why, Arakawa wondered, hadn't anyone considered that 'Donkey Kong' might infringe on the *King Kong* copyright?

Lincoln tried to reassure him. He explained that the threat from MCA wasn't unusual in business, and it certainly didn't mean that Nintendo was in the wrong. If nothing else, it was undeniable proof that Nintendo had made it into the big time.

After a week or so of frantic research, Arakawa and Lincoln prepared to leave for Los Angeles for a meeting with the MCA brass. The pair arrived in L.A. and headed for Universal's main office building, known as the 'black tower' (appropriately forbidding, the two felt), in Universal City. Bob Hadl, an MCA attorney, escorted the men into an elaborate office crowded with antiques and expensive artwork. There was a sweeping view of the smog.

Also present were two attorneys from Coleco, MCA's in-house attorney, and an outside counsel. Coleco, which had invested a fortune in its impending launch of the ColecoVision system, which would include a home version of 'Donkey Kong,' had apparently received the same threatening letter.

Hadl and another MCA attorney explained their boss's position: Sheinberg planned to sue and immediately seek a preliminary injunction that would stop both Nintendo and Coleco from selling any games while the litigation continued. There was only one alternative: Nintendo and Coleco had to settle.

It was expected, but chilling nonetheless. Coleco had virtually bet the store on 'Donkey Kong.' For Nintendo, 'Donkey Kong' *was* the store.

MCA's lawyer waited for a response. Lincoln spoke first. 'If you own *King Kong* and it is infringed by "Donkey Kong," then we'll settle,' he said. 'But I'm not going to buy the goddamn Brooklyn Bridge. First you'll have to prove to me that you own *King Kong*.'

There was silence. The MCA team looked at him and Arakawa as if they were Martians, Lincoln recalls – 'Like, come on, what are you smoking?'

There was lawyerly huffing and puffing and large bodies fidgeting in uncomfortable chairs until the MCA outside counsel spoke. 'Of course we own it,' the lawyer said.

He was back on the offensive, listing everything that MCA was going to go after: royalties, inventory, damages . . . He suggested that the Nintendo and Coleco representatives discuss their course of action in privacy. Before the others adjourned to a private conference room, MCA's attorney told Lincoln that the only way to avoid a lawsuit was a settlement. 'You don't have a chance in court,' he said.

When the lawyers and Arakawa were alone, the Coleco team said they agreed; there was no alternative but to acquiesce. 'What else can we do?' they said. 'The gorillas look the same, the name is almost the same . . .' They attempted to convince Arakawa and Lincoln to settle, never letting on that they already had. Coleco, terrified of MCA and looking to appease Sid Sheinberg, who had dangled the possibility of investing in their company, had promised to try to convince Nintendo to settle too.

'Sid Sheinberg had put the screws to Coleco's CEO, Arnold Greenberg,' said Howard Lincoln. 'He told him to get Nintendo to settle up.'

MCA also went after other companies to which Nintendo had licensed 'Donkey Kong.' By then Atari was selling a 'Donkey Kong' computer game, and MCA was also pressuring Atari's parent company, Warner Communications. Sheinberg personally threatened Warner CEO Steve Ross. 'I told him . . . I didn't want to be in the position of suing him,' Sheinberg says. Ralston Purina, which had licensed the 'Donkey Kong' character for a breakfast cereal, responded to Sheinberg's threat by offering a $5,000 settlement. This incensed Sheinberg. 'It's the most stupid thing I ever heard of,' he said. 'Throw them out of the building.' Thereafter Ralston Purina refused to settle, as did Milton Bradley, which had a 'Donkey Kong' board game.

In the meeting in the black tower, Coleco's lawyers never so much as intimated that they had cut a deal with MCA. All they said was, 'There is no alternative to settling.' Lincoln listened intently and never let on that he felt they were probably right, that Nintendo would have to settle (he calculated that it would take a minimum of $5–$7 million). Still, he refused to agree to anything. 'We need more time,' is all he told the Coleco team.

They pressed him, seemingly in panic. Lincoln told them, 'You can do whatever you want, since there was no warrant about the rights you bought from us.'

The Coleco lawyers glared at him. 'We know that,' one of them said. Arakawa glanced over at Lincoln. They shared a fleeting moment of schoolboy glee. The no-warrant clause in the contract Yamauchi had intimidated Coleco into signing was paying off. Even if they did have to settle, Nintendo was not responsible for Coleco's losses. As the men left the room, Lincoln tugged Arakawa's arm. They slowed up and Lincoln whispered, 'Something's going on.' The reaction to his crack about the Brooklyn Bridge made him wonder if MCA actually *did* own *King Kong*. 'Don't agree to anything,' he said.

Back in Hadl's office, the Coleco attorneys excused themselves, saying they would meet alone with Hadl at another time. It made Lincoln suspicious. 'Something was wrong. Something was going on between Universal and Coleco,' he says. He decided he had better buy some time. 'We have to sort things out,' Lincoln told

Hadl when he and Arakawa prepared to leave. Hadl told him he had better not take too long.

Lincoln and Hadl spoke by telephone throughout the next month. In June, the MCA attorney said, 'You've had all the time you need. It's time to meet and sew things up.' Lincoln said he was ready and he and Arakawa planned to return to Universal City.

The morning the pair left for the Seattle airport, Arakawa was running a fever, fighting off the flu. He asked Lincoln if he was really needed. Lincoln insisted. Under no conditions would he do this alone.

They flew back to Southern California and taxied to the black tower. Soon after they met with Hadl, they were told that if they were ready to 'resolve things' they should head down 'to meet with Mr. Sheinberg.' Arakawa looked at Lincoln, who said nothing.

They accompanied the MCA lawyer through the corridors to the elevator.

Sheinberg had risen in the ranks of MCA to become one of the most powerful movie moguls in Hollywood. MCA was comprised of a record company, a television production company, a book publishing house (G.P. Putnam's Sons), a retailing division, theme parks, and massive real estate holdings. Sheinberg was savvy about future technologies, and he did his best to place MCA in a strategic spot by investing in them.

Before Nintendo had been threatened, a meeting was arranged between him, MCA chairman Wasserman, and Coleco's president. Arnold Greenberg had big plans for Coleco, but he needed volumes of cash. The three men were talking about the possible acquisition of – or at least an investment in – Coleco by MCA when Sheinberg casually mentioned that Coleco's association with Nintendo was a stumbling block to any arrangement they might make. 'We believe some rights of ours are being violated,' he said.

Greenberg smiled wryly and asked, 'What took you so long?'

Later Sheinberg said he remembered the moment. The line, he said, was 'that . . . famous movie line where the hero rides off into the sunset and then somebody always comes running after him, and the hero turns around and looks at the guy or the woman, always John Wayne or Gary Cooper or somebody, and says, "What took you so long?" and you do a fadeout.' The message was clear: Greenberg had come prepared to negotiate.

A deal was made. As leverage to convince Greenberg to settle with MCA, Sheinberg dangled the prospect of a partnership or some agreement that would bring a cash infusion into Coleco. Coleco could continue to sell 'Donkey Kong' in exchange for a modest royalty. 'We entered a covenant not to sue,' Sheinberg said. 'And we received from Coleco an agreement that they would pay us 3 percent of the net sales price [of all the "Donkey Kong" cartridges Coleco sold].' It turned out to be an impressive number of cartridges, 6 million, which translated into $4.6 million. (In subsequent negotiations, Sheinberg's interest in Coleco evaporated.)

The Coleco negotiation wasn't Sheinberg's first attempt to bring MCA into the video-game business. 'There was a point in time when the video-game business looked like it was going to be the biggest business around,' he said. He wanted MCA to be, as he put it, 'a principal' in video games, as it was in records, movies, and videocassettes. He formed MCA Video Games and later bought a company called LJN, makers of toys and Nintendo games.

On that June day when Arakawa and Lincoln followed Hadl out of the black tower, they walked through the Universal lot, past actors in costumes and palm trees traveling by on a trailer. When they reached a long warehouse-like building, Hadl announced, 'The executive dining room,' as he grandly opened a side door.

Inside was one massive table, that could have seated dozens, set for four. They sat down and waited. Arakawa's fever worsened.

Sidney Sheinberg, tall and lanky, wearing large horn-rimmed glasses, arrived and settled into his chair. Arakawa was feeling so ill that he felt he might pass out when, after a round of introductions, an elaborate lunch was served. There was interminable small talk, and by the time Sheinberg announced how pleased he was that Nintendo had agreed to settle the case, Arakawa was ready to keel over.

He looked at Howard Lincoln, who had been charming Sheinberg and Hadl with stories of video games and fishing, and watched the attorney transform. 'It's real simple,' he said, eyeballing the

MCA chief. 'We have done a lot of research on this thing, looked at it from top to bottom, and we feel that there is no infringement.' Firmly, coldly, he said, 'We have no intention of settling.'

Arakawa had never seen Lincoln this icy, and he was shaken. He had no idea how Sheinberg would react.

His face reddening, Sheinberg pushed back his chair, placed his hands on the edge of the table, and boomed, 'What is going on here?' He took a deep breath. 'I understood that you were coming down here to talk about a settlement! For Christ's sake, you're wasting my time. What the hell is going on?'

He looked toward Hadl, who went white. Hadl threw a pleading glance at Lincoln, who continued. 'It's simple,' he said. 'I wanted to tell you we aren't going to settle and I wanted to do it by looking you right in the eyes. That, Mr. Sheinberg, is what I'm doing.'

Rising from his chair, Sheinberg said, 'I've heard enough. You'll hear from our legal department.' He glared at Lincoln. 'You are making a major mistake,' he fumed. 'I view litigation as a profit center.'

The three men rose, too, and walked behind him to the elevator. Hadl followed Sheinberg in as Arakawa and Lincoln hung back, watching. Before the doors closed, Lincoln called out – 'Mr. Sheinberg?'

Sheinberg looked at him and grunted.

'Have a nice day,' Lincoln said.

Sheinberg kept his promise and filed the lawsuit in New York State, so Lincoln flew East to meet with John Kirby of Mudge, Rose, Guthrie, Alexander and Ferdon, the well-known New York law firm. Kirby was one of the top litigators in the country, and had handled antitrust cases for PepsiCo and Warner-Lambert and franchise cases for General Foods. 'When I initially met him, I wasn't all that impressed,' Lincoln says. 'He was kind of disheveled looking and out of sorts. But it didn't take long to figure out that this guy was one hell of a lawyer.' Kirby had a reputation for vigorously defending his clients. Importantly for Nintendo, nothing intimidated him.

Lincoln and Kirby headed to Kyoto to meet Yamauchi and discuss the case with him and other NCL executives. It was Lincoln's first meeting with Yamauchi, and he had heard enough about the Nintendo chairman to be on guard. Inside the Mother Brain they inspected each other. 'I have no liking for lawyers,' Yamauchi said.

Lincoln restrained a smile. 'We have more lawyers in Seattle, Washington, than you have in all of Japan,' he said. 'Few lawyers is the greatest business advantage Japan has over the United States.'

'I could tell that he was a very strong person who was used to getting his way,' Lincoln says. 'There was no small talk. He didn't waste time.'

Yamauchi wanted to know one thing from the attorneys: What must be done to guarantee that Nintendo would win the lawsuit? 'We *must* win,' he said.

After interviewing Nintendo employees, including Gunpei Yokoi and Sigeru Miyamoto, Lincoln and Kirby returned to the United States and worked with their respective staffs over the next ten months to prepare their case. Arakawa was elated when he heard that Lincoln's instincts had proved correct: there was serious doubt that Universal owned the rights to *King Kong*. The company had never protected the *King Kong* trademark, and past litigation seemed to confirm that *King Kong* was in the public domain. The best news was that Universal had once prevailed in litigation by asserting just that: that the name King Kong was in the public domain and could not be trademarked.

There was more. Nintendo discovered that Coleco had settled with MCA, and that Sheinberg was negotiating an investment in Coleco with Arnold Greenberg. This brought to light other motivations for the lawsuit. Sheinberg wanted a place in the videogame business, and was suing the companies that would be his major competitors.

As the materials for the trial were being assembled, Arakawa asked Yoko one night if she thought Howard Lincoln would leave his law firm and come to work exclusively for Nintendo. Arakawa had come to rely on Lincoln's legal skills, but there was more to it than that. He had never found anyone, outside of his family, with whom he felt as close. He respected Lincoln, professionally and also as a friend, but he wondered if he was being presumptuous, too pushy, or too eager. Yoko replied that there was only one way to find out.

On one of their many flights together, Arakawa finally approached Lincoln. He said he knew that Lincoln was bored with his legal practice and he asked him to come work with him at Nintendo.

Betraying no emotion, Lincoln told Arakawa he would think about it. After a brief deliberative pause, he said that if he decided to gamble on Nintendo, he wouldn't come aboard as corporate counsel. He wanted to help run the company, to be involved in every aspect of the business.

Arakawa immediately responded that this was exactly what he had in mind. In a subsequent meeting that lasted no more than fifteen minutes, Lincoln and Arakawa came to an agreement. Lincoln would come aboard as Nintendo's senior vice-president, and would work alongside Arakawa in the number-two position. At the conclusion of the meeting, the Nintendo president shook Lincoln's hand. 'I got you,' he said.

Lincoln scheduled a meeting with his partners at the law firm on December 7, at which he gave them thirty days' notice.

In fighting the 'Donkey Kong' case, MCA and Nintendo presented evidence and testimony in the New York courtroom of U.S. District Court Judge Robert W. Sweet. Howard Phillips was called to court one day to play 'Donkey Kong' because John Kirby wanted to demonstrate that the game had nothing to do with *King Kong*. Sigeru Miyamoto was deposed in Kyoto. He recounted how he came up with 'Donkey Kong,' explaining that he had called the character King Kong before naming him Donkey Kong because 'King Kong' in Japanese was a generic term for any menacing ape.

Kirby also presented testimony and judgments from the past trials that brought into question MCA Universal's ownership of *King Kong*. He sought to prove that after its previous trials, MCA knew it didn't have those rights, and that they had filed suit against Nintendo in full knowledge of this fact.

A strong case developed so quickly that Nintendo's lawyers moved for summary dismissal of the suit, and Sweet granted it. In his written opinion, the judge described what appeared to be his favorite day of the trial. ' "Donkey Kong," ' the judge wrote, 'was demonstrated by a game master and pertinent parts of the 1933 movie and the 1976 remake were reviewed, an altogether satisfying court day enhanced by the argument of highly skilled and forceful counsel and marred only by the submission of affidavits, depositions, and briefs.'

There was nothing lighthearted about the judgment itself. Sweet concluded that Nintendo had not infringed on MCA Universal's rights because the company didn't own them. He also ruled that there was no infringement even if MCA had owned *King Kong*, since the game was completely different from the movie. The judge criticized MCA for bringing the lawsuit in spite of full recognition that it didn't own the rights, and this paved the way for Nintendo to be awarded damages.

MCA appealed the case all the way to the U.S. Supreme Court, and lost in each round. At one stage of the appeals, Howard Lincoln was called to testify. He pulled out the notes he had taken after his first meeting at MCA, when he said that Nintendo would not agree to buy the Brooklyn Bridge. He detailed the lunch meeting, during which Sid Sheinberg said that he viewed litigation 'as a profit center.'

When Sheinberg testified, he was asked to recall his lunch meeting with Arakawa and Lincoln. 'I believe that one of them was a relative or somehow related to the Japanese person who I understood owned or controlled Nintendo,' he said, dismissing Arakawa. Of Lincoln, Sheinberg said, 'I believe he was a kind of a general counsel to Nintendo, but not one of great authority, as it appeared to me.'

In his cross-examination of Sheinberg, John Kirby earned all the money Nintendo was paying him by reminding the judge why MCA sued in the first place. 'I gather it's a pretty big company you are running out there, Mr. Sheinberg?' he asked.

Sheinberg nodded. 'It's a big company with lots of legal involvements.'

Kirby asked about MCA's revenues for the past year. When Sheinberg said they were in excess of $1 billion, Kirby asked how much of this was profit.

'I think our profits were around $135 million . . .' Sheinberg responded. Total sales, Sheinberg said, were $1.6 billion.

Kirby continued. 'What portion of your total operating income was contributed by your *litigation profit center*?' he asked.

Sheinberg eyed him. 'By our litigation profit center?'

The point was not lost on the judge. Kirby continued, asking Sheinberg to confirm a report in *Business Week* that put his salary at $4,638,000.

Sheinberg's attorney jumped in. 'This is amusing and all,' he said, 'but what real relevance is there to it? We'll stipulate that he's a well-paid executive. Where do you go with this line?'

Kirby said that the line of questioning was concluded. He added, 'And I don't even think I need to make the argument about relevance in terms of an exemplary damages claim.'

Sheinberg's arrogance had, in the opinion of several spectators, infuriated the judge. But what sank MCA was the evidence that Sheinberg had already instigated and won a lawsuit proving that *King Kong* was in the public domain. MCA's suits (and the threats of other suits) were seen as MCA's 'litigation profit center' at work.

Nintendo was awarded $1.8 million. Months later, the arrival of a big, fat check from Universal was followed by a celebration at Arakawa's home. Yoko brought out caviar and champagne. Arakawa and Lincoln toasted each other and John Kirby, whom they would reward lavishly. Soon after in New York, they took the attorney, his wife, and some associates to dinner in the private dining room of an elegant Manhattan restaurant. After dinner they presented Kirby with a framed photograph of a thirty-thousand-dollar, twenty-seven-foot sailboat. The boat, Nintendo's way of saying thank you, had been christened *Donkey Kong* and included, they explained, 'exclusive worldwide rights to use the name for sailboats.'

Coleco, which had sold Nintendo out in its settlement with MCA, filed against MCA Universal to get back the royalties they had paid. Universal settled. Atari and the other companies MCA had shaken down were also paid back.

The experience did more than bolster Nintendo's bank accounts. 'We learned,' says Lincoln, 'that we could handle ourselves in the big leagues. And we learned that the kind of arrogance we saw at MCA is lethal.'

NOA, strong from 'Donkey Kong's' enormous success, headed cautiously into the consumer market. NCL sent over Game & Watches, which had sold like 40 million hotcakes in Japan and

Asia, where demand was never a problem. In fact, the demand was so great that all manner of counterfeiters started making them; the cheap imitations being made all over Asia were the problem. Perhaps as many illegal Game & Watches were sold as ones made by Nintendo.

To launch the business in America, Bruce Lowry, a vice-president at Pioneer, was hired to run Nintendo's new consumer division. Just the idea that they *had* a consumer division delighted Arakawa and Lincoln.

Entering the consumer and toy businesses meant learning a new industry. At the Redmond headquarters, in a conference room they had named 'Donkey Kong,' Lowry tried to educate his new colleagues about the rules of the toy business. There was much to do to prepare them for their first trade shows in January and February 1983. Don James worked on display booths while Lowry outlined the steps Nintendo ought to take.

There was no dissent when Lowry said that Nintendo needed an office in New York (they would rent space in the Toy Center building, at 200 Fifth Avenue). But when he explained the way billing was done in the toy business, the Nintendo executives balked.

Lowry said that toy companies expected all invoices to be dated December 10. But Nintendo sold coin-operated video games on net-thirty terms – all bills were due in thirty days. Simple.

Lowry explained that in the toy business, orders came in in, say, January or February for a product that was to be shipped in the summer. The toy stores had the winter season to sell it. Then, finally, they began to pay their bills on December 10, once much of the Christmas business was over.

Howard Lincoln jumped in. 'Wait a second! Why the hell would anyone agree to that? We build the product and take all the risk and we have to finance this whole thing and then sometime in December we're going to get paid – maybe?'

Lowry said this was correct. That was how the toy business worked.

In 1983, Arakawa attended his first Consumer Electronics Show to drum up business for Game & Watch. At this crucial trade show for businesses from Walkmen to VCRs, a company's placement in the CES's convention-center display rooms says volumes about its stature in the industry. Nintendo was hidden in a tiny booth on a high floor in an out-of-the-way building. Buyers couldn't have found the company's modest display of Game & Watches even if they had been looking for it.

Things weren't much more promising at the Toy Fair the following month. The shows were barometers of what was to come; NOA lost millions on Game & Watch in the United States. The lessons, however, were valuable. The next time NOA entered the consumer business, the Nintendo team was prepared. They knew never to call their product a toy, whether or not it was. That way they didn't have to offer December 10 invoicing. They also didn't have to give mark-down money, which was another unsettling new concept for Howard Lincoln.

When it finally came time for a major chain to pay its Game & Watch bills to Nintendo – after December 10, 1983 – Lincoln received a call from the chain's controller. The gentleman asked for mark-down money, and Lincoln didn't know what he was talking about. 'You know, mark-down money,' the man said. 'We still have a lot of those Game & Watches, you know. We have to mark them down to sell them.'

'We sold them to you and sent the invoice,' Lincoln said. 'We shipped them to you, so you owe us the money. If the product doesn't sell, that's not my fault. You took the risk. You owe us the money.'

The man said, 'You may have learned a lot of things in law school, but we're in the toy business. If the product doesn't sell, you have to give us mark-down money; you have to reduce the price so that we maintain our margin.'

'You gotta be nuts,' Lincoln said, but the man explained that the practice was standard. 'We're long-term partners,' he told the Nintendo manager. 'If you don't want to give us mark-down money, fine, but don't have your salesmen call anymore.' Nintendo gave the mark-down money.

Another lesson Nintendo learned from the Game & Watch disaster was how *not* to make television commercials. An agency Nintendo had hired came up with a creative television campaign it dubbed 'the bored campaign.' In one thirty-second spot a boy was sick in bed. The second after his mother tucked him in, he pulled a Game & Watch out from under his pillow. In another 'bored' commercial, a young boy was bored to tears at a wedding. He said, 'My parents brought me to this stupid wedding and I'm bored . . .' until he pulled out his Game & Watch.

Rather than allow the agency to produce the commercial with professional actors, Ron Judy and the marketing group decided to cast it. They thought they could make the commercials more believable by using nonactors. It was an expensive, though hysterically funny, mistake. They used Nintendo employees. The company's new credit manager, for instance, a kindly older woman who froze in front of the camera, played the mom. The resulting ads were so bad that television stations refused to air them.

Nintendo's Game & Watch business was dissolved in the summer of 1985. By then, although NCL was making an enormous amount of money on the Famicom in Japan, almost all of the revenues of its American subsidiary were still from coin-operated games. Hiroshi Yamauchi wanted to change this and he told Arakawa it was time to launch the Famicom in America. To determine if it was feasible, Arakawa undertook an investigation of the American home video-game business.

It was like surveying a car wreck. In the early 1980s, companies such as Atari, Mattel, and Coleco had been sharing a multibillion-dollar business. By the end of 1983, all that was left was the wreckage of a devastating crash. The industry had shrunk to an insignificant size, amounting to only a few hundred million dollars. Companies that had been raking in the cash were bankrupt. It seemed clear that the American market just wasn't interested in home-video games.

Arakawa talked to people who had worked in the home video-game industry. He met with manufacturers, wholesalers, and distributors, with buyers for department stores, discount stores, toy stores, electronics stores, and software companies, and with parents. From everyone he heard the same message: the last thing anybody wanted to hear about was a new video-game system. Everywhere he went, he heard one name over and over again: Atari.

REVERSAL
OF FORTUNE

7

In the early 1980s, Nolan Bushnell had had two fully decked-out Learjets to shuttle him between his Woodside, California, estate and his homes in Aspen, Georgetown, and Paris (where his palace's back-yard opened onto a view of the Eiffel Tower). When he wasn't sipping Dom Perignon above the clouds, he was often racing his sailboat, in training for the Transpac, one of the oldest yacht races in the world, which he won in 1983. When he took to the roads, he chose from among a Rolls, two Mercedeses, and a Porsche.

At the time, there were few models for the kind of wealth and notoriety Bushnell had acquired so quickly and so young; he was the first of that generation of much-hyped super-successful high-tech entrepreneurs, the founder of one of the fastest-growing companies in history.

Bushnell, the son of a cement contractor, grew up in a bleak outpost near the Great Salt Lake. When he was a child, he was already obsessed with innovation. 'I read science fiction,' he says, 'and I really wanted to live there, without all the limitations we have in our world.' He spent much of his youth in the family's garage, trying to create the things he read about. He was only six years old when he built a control panel for a spaceship out of an orange crate. He was the youngest ham radio operator in Utah – but not the shortest; he was six-foot-four by the time he was in seventh grade. When he launched a 'UFO' he had made – a hundred-watt light attached to an enormous kite – he convinced a fair percentage of the local population that the planet was under attack.

Another time he took a few shotgun shells, removed the shot, and, wearing a ski mask, drove a borrowed car up to a buddy of his, who was standing in the schoolyard among a group of their friends. Bushnell aimed and fired both barrels into his friend's chest. The boy smacked two handfuls of catsup against his shirt and fell to the ground.

In college, at Utah State and later the University of Utah, Bushnell studied engineering, economics, business, and philosophy. Once, when he had lost his tuition money in a poker game, he had to take work guessing people's weights and ages at an amusement park. Eventually he ran the arcade there. At college he often hung out in the school's computer lab playing a game called 'Spacewar', one of the first computer games ever made.

Bushnell graduated with an engineering degree in 1968 and moved to California, where he worked briefly as an engineer in the computer-graphics division at Ampex. At home, meanwhile, in a laboratory he made in his daughter's bedroom (the little girl was exiled to the living-room couch), he created a simpler version of 'Spacewar,' which by then could be found on computers at most universities around the country.

The game had been invented in 1962 by an MIT graduate student named Steve Russell (who based it on a series of science fiction space operas called *Lensman*, written by 'Doc' Smith). Bushnell's version, 'Computer Space,' was made of integrated circuits connected to a nineteen-inch black-and-white television. Unlike a computer, it could do nothing but play the game, a primitive simulation of air combat between a spaceship and flying saucers. The key to Bushnell's invention was that since it didn't require a full-fledged computer, it could be produced relatively cheaply. He envisioned video games like his standing alongside pinball machines in arcades, pool halls, and bowling alleys.

With hopes of having his machine put into production, Bushnell left Ampex for a small pinball-machine company, which manufactured 1,500 of them. They never sold, and Bushnell, then twenty-seven, left the company. He had determined that 'Computer Space,' which required players to read a full page of directions before they could play, was too complex.

He set out to make a simpler game, and this time he would sell it himself. Kicking in $250 each, he and a friend formed a company they called Syzygy (from a word meaning the nearly straight-line configuration of three celestial bodies in a gravitational system – for example, the sun, the moon, and the earth). The name was already taken by another company, so Bushnell chose the Japanese word that was the equivalent of *check* in the game *go: atari*.

In his home laboratory, Bushnell built a new game, 'the easiest one I could think of. People knew the rules immediately, and it could be played with one hand, so people could hold a beer in the other.' A 'ball' – really a squarish dot of light – was batted back and forth by two inch-long paddles that were projected on a screen. The paddles, on the far sides of the 'court,' could be moved up and down when players twisted knobs on the front of a crudely built cabinet. 'I made it with my own two hands and a soldering iron,' Bushnell says. He named it 'Pong,' after the sonar-like 'pongs' that sounded each time the ball made contact with the paddle.

In the fall of 1972, Bushnell placed 'Pong,' the first commercial video-arcade game, with a coin box bolted to the outside, in Andy Capp's tavern, a popular Sunnyvale pool bar that holds a place in Silicon Valley lore rivaled only by the garage in which Steve Jobs and Steve Wozniak invented the Apple computer.

Set beside a pinball machine, 'Pong' was an oddity, a dark wood cabinet that held a black-and-white TV screen on which cavorted a white blip like a shooting star in a black sky. One of the bar's patrons stood over the machine, examining it. 'Avoid missing ball for high score,' read the only line of instructions.

The young man reached into his pocket, extracted a quarter, and slipped it into a slot on the console as he called a friend over. The machine, announcing its name with its trademark bleat, 'served' a ball automatically from one side of the screen. The players missed the first few serves until they got the hang of the controls, but two bucks' worth of quarters later, they were having lengthy volleys. A crowd had gathered around to watch. There was a long line in front of the machine for the entire day, and the next day too.

The 'Pong' machine stopped working toward the end of the second day; the coin box was stuffed with so many quarters that the game had short-circuited. A new coin box (actually a casserole dish) was installed inside the machine. It took about a week to be filled to its capacity of about 1,200 quarters. Bushnell was ecstatic. His simple, monotonous game was bringing in $300 a week. The pinball machine that stood next to it was earning only about $30 or $40.

Lacking the money to do a major 'Pong' production run himself, Bushnell approached the established amusement-game makers, companies like Bally's Midway. The pinball companies unceremoniously showed Bushnell the door. He was left with two alternatives: he could either finance the venture himself or forget it.

To get some quick cash, Bushnell accepted jobs consulting for electronics companies, and he talked his way into a $50,000 line of credit with a local bank. Employing a band of long-haired techies whom he paid next to nothing, he started an assembly line in an abandoned roller-skating rink. The rowdy gang assembled machines for twelve to sixteen hours a day as the Rolling Stones and Led Zeppelin blared from a staticky stereo system. Dan Van Elderen, a young engineering graduate who came on to assemble games, recalls that 'there wasn't even a monitor business in those days. All the original "Pong" games were built with Motorola TVs. We threw away the plastic case and the tuner and RF circuitry and used the raw tube and video drivers.'

Bushnell met potential customers, mostly distributors who handled pinball machines and jukeboxes, and was able to sell all the machines his small staff could make, about ten a day. If he was going to make any real money, however, he had to expand; he needed more cash. Banks and investment bankers declined to put up money because of rumors that Atari was connected to the Mafia. Also, they were worried about an inherent flaw in the whole idea of video games: people would steal the TVs from the consoles.

Investors whom Bushnell fast-talked past these concerns were turned off when they visited the company's site. Employees in ripped jeans and worn sneakers (if they wore shoes at all) worked whenever they wanted to. Staff meetings were a rarity. The founder wore T-shirts or flower-print shirts with polka-dot ties. As Steve Jobs, one of Atari's early employees, remembers, 'The smell of marijuana ran freely through the air-conditioning system. A few of the people there had beards so large that I never once saw their faces.'

Bushnell was a consummate salesman, obnoxiously persistent. This and his immodest, even grandiose, vision – he projected sales of hundreds of millions of dollars – finally convinced one of the Valley's most astute and credible venture capitalists, Don Valentine, to back the company. The cash infusion allowed Atari to grow. Bushnell hired more staff and rallied his team with cheerleading, charm, and anything else that worked – including lying; he persuaded one employee to work double-time on some revised circuitry for 'Pong' by telling him that General Electric was waiting anxiously for units, even though GE had refused to return his calls.

'We were all so young,' he says. 'I was in my twenties. My vice-presidents were in their twenties. Many of the people were teenagers.' Atari had a fund for 'unwanted pregnancies' and another to bail staffers out of jail. The average age of the staff was so low that when Bushnell decided to get group health insurance, the rates for extraordinary benefits were dirt-cheap – 'until everyone started getting braces,' he remembers. 'Not for their kids, for *themselves*!'

A typical early staffer was Steve Jobs, who came on board when he was only seventeen. At the beginning of 1974, he had dropped out of Reed College and returned to his parents' Los Altos home. When he began looking for work, in a local newspaper he saw a help-wanted ad that read 'Have Fun and Make Money.' He visited Atari. 'We've got this kid in the lobby,' Bushnell's partners' secretary announced one day. 'He's either a crackpot or he's got something.'

Jobs, skinny, long-haired, with a Ho Chi Minh beard, filled out an application and listed all the things he had done – nothing relevant, as it turned out, except for some courses in engineering at Reed. 'Don't call us, we'll call you,' he was told.

The phone rang the next day. Jobs became Atari's fortieth employee. He was hired as a technician, earning $5 an hour. His first assignment was to help an engineer on a new game, 'Video Basketball.' Atari was trying to model its games after field sports, for 'Pong' circuitry was easily adapted to such simulations.

Although Atari games were selling, Bushnell was in over his head and Atari's survival was continually precarious. 'A lot of people don't understand that you can be successful and profitable and still not have enough cash; a growing company consumes *tremendous* amounts of cash,' he says.

The company literally couldn't afford the payroll twice one month. Don Valentine's money had helped build up production, but the returns lagged. A big success that followed 'Pong' bailed them out. It was the first video car-racing game that was controlled by a steering wheel attached to the cabinet. The game, 'Gran Trak,' gobbled up quarters even faster than 'Pong.'

A friend of Steve Jobs, Steve Wozniak, an engineer at Hewlett Packard, was a 'Gran Trak' addict. Most evenings after work he headed to a pub, where he put great quantities of quarters, money he could not afford, into 'Gran Trak.' Jobs began to sneak him into Atari's production facility at night, where he could play the game for free. In exchange for the free-game time, Woz, a whiz with computers, helped out whenever Jobs hit a stumbling block with some particularly tricky circuitry.

Bushnell found Jobs tactless on occasion, but he liked the head-strong young man and took him under his wing. Jobs was working in order to earn enough money to travel to India. Bushnell helped him by paying Jobs's expenses to Europe in exchange for a service call in West Germany. Some games Atari had shipped there were causing local TV interference.

Jobs flew to Europe, adjusted the 'Pong' games, and continued on to New Delhi, where he met a guru who shaved his head. He stayed in India for six months before returning to Palo Alto and his old job, and then was assigned to work on one of Atari's oddest games. 'Gotcha' had been dreamed up in a brainstorming session during which a young technician joked that the joystick used to control most arcade games was a phallic symbol. The boy suggested that Atari try out a 'female' game; 'Gotcha' was the result. On the game's console were two rounded mounds made of rubber that were squeezed to control game play. Insiders called it 'the boob game.'

Steve Wozniak came over to Atari to help Jobs build another 'Pong'-based game for Bushnell called 'Breakout.' A paddle hit a ball against a wall of bricks that disappeared, one by one, when hit, until there were none left. Bushnell liked the game, but the circuitry required too many expensive computer chips. He offered Jobs a bonus of $100 for every chip he was able to eliminate. Jobs made himself $5,000.

When they weren't working their day jobs, Jobs and Wozniak were busy on their own, in the Jobs family garage. They built a makeshift computer – a circuit board, really – which they called the Apple I. Some of the parts had been lifted from Atari. The Apple I didn't do much, but when Wozniak showed it off at a computer club meeting and the result was orders for fifty of the contraptions, it dawned on Jobs that there might actually be a market for personal computers, and he left Atari to found Apple.

Wozniak's interest was primarily technical; Jobs set about making the computer accessible to people. Together they added a keyboard and memory, and Wozniak developed the disk drive and added a video terminal. Jobs hired experts to design an efficient power supply and a fancy casing, and thus was born the Apple II – and with it an entire industry. Needing investors, Jobs went to Nolan Bushnell and asked him to become a partner in Apple Computer. Bushnell unwisely declined.

Jobs and Wozniak were only two of the computer and video-game industry executives who cut their teeth at Atari. A decade after Bushnell founded the company, there were Atari alums in high-level spots at Electronic Arts, Lucasfilm and LucasArts, Apple, Microsoft, and a number of other companies. 'It's because we provided a place for creative people to be part of something completely new,' Bushnell says. 'These were people who wanted to create something intellectually stimulating and fun. They wanted to put their talent into making games, not bombs.'

* * *

Atari, meanwhile, continued to grow. In 1973, after six thousand 'Pong' games were sold for more than $1,000 each, Bally's Midway approached Bushnell with a huge offer to buy the rights to the game. Bushnell agreed, and Bally's sold about nine thousand more 'Pongs.' Atari now had eighty employees, 'long-haired freaks, bikers and dropouts, hired not for their skills but on the basis of their good vibes,' according to Scott Cohen in his book *Zap! The Rise and Fall of Atari*. *Fortune* reported that 100,000 'Pong'-type games were produced in 1974 alone. Although only a tenth of those were made by Atari ('Pong' was copied with abandon), the company earned $3.2 million that fiscal year. In the three years that followed, Atari sold $13 million worth of video games, including 'Quadrapong,' for four players, and 'Puppy Pong,' in a Formica doghouse.

In 1974, after Atari's success with 'Gran Trak,' Bushnell decided to make a 'Pong' system for the home. The trick would be to compress a coin-operated game down to a few inexpensive components. Magnavox had been selling a home video-game system for the past two years that had been created back in 1966 by Ralph Baer, a supervising engineer at a company called Sanders Associates. Baer had come up with a game almost identical to 'Pong' that played on a seventeen-inch RCA color set, but Sanders did nothing with the technology until Magnavox licensed it. Magnavox's Odyssey used Mylar overlays taped to the TV screen that depicted different game boards or playing fields. One hundred thousand Odysseys sold in 1972, its first year on the market.

Atari's home 'Pong' had a sharper picture and more sensitive controllers than the Magnavox system, and it also cost less. Still, when Bushnell showed 'Pong' off at toy shows, none of the major chains showed interest. Dejected, he returned to Atari with no idea where to turn next. Then the buyer for the sporting goods department of Sears Roebuck came to see him, and before he left, he had offered to buy every home 'Pong' game Atari could make.

With the backing of Sears, Bushnell had the ability to boost Atari's production capacity. The retailer mounted a major television ad campaign, and Atari's 1975 sales shot up to almost $40 million. Bushnell spent as much of it as he could– on parties, expensive suits, and sports cars. 'We were absolutely no more or less irresponsible or crazy than Ross Johnson and those guys at

RJR Nabisco,' Bushnell says. 'The only difference is they were running corporate America.'

Arcade games became more sophisticated when microprocessors dropped in price by the mid-1970s. Dan Van Elderen was part of the team that built Atari's first microprocessor-based game, 'Sprint,' a driving game with oncoming traffic that required realistic, quick reactions. Up until this point, Atari had basically been a hardware business. With microprocessors – which used stored information from programs as needed – software became integral to video games, and rooms full of programmers were hired.

With income from the arcade games, the deal with Sears, and more venture-capital money, Atari was poised to expand and take on the competition. By the end of 1976, twenty different companies, from RCA and National Semiconductor to Coleco, were making home video-game systems, each trying to outdo the next with marketing dollars and technology. When Fairchild Camera introduced the first full-color system with changeable cartridges (created by Alpex), Atari's entry had to be that much better. It was. Atari's engineers assigned their new products code names. Their programmable video-game system was Stella, named after a woman in the personnel department. Officially named the Atari 2600, it was a powerful and inexpensive machine, but the outlay required to manufacture and market it on a big-league scale was beyond Bushnell. He considered going public but decided to try to find a corporate investor first.

MCA and Disney declined. It would be a year or two before the likes of Sid Sheinberg fathomed the significance of the new video-game industry. Warner Communications, on the other hand, approached Bushnell.

Steve Ross, the company's silver-haired chairman, who later drove the Time Inc.-Warner Communications merger, heard from one of his executives that Atari was looking for investors. Ross knew about Atari. Once, at Disneyland, he had briefly lost track of his kids. When he found them they were gathered around an Atari video game called 'Indy 8,' an eight-player road-race game. 'His family was hypnotized and he sat there and watched the machine suck up quarters,' according to Manny Gerard, the executive who told Ross that Atari was looking for an investor in 1976.

Gerard saw the video-game business for what it was: the computer, entertainment, and consumer-electronics business rolled into one. 'I saw the 2600 in an Atari lab and said, "Holy shit! This is going to take over the world." ' He convinced Ross that Warner should not make an offer to invest in Atari but rather buy it outright. When Ross gave him the okay, Gerard negotiated with Bushnell and his highest-ranking cohorts.

At first, the Atari team said they weren't interested in an acquisition, but it was more a pose than anything. 'We were exhausted,' Bushnell says. 'The offer from Warner was a relief.' The size of the offer encouraged them too, and a deal was struck. Warner paid $28 million, a pretty good return on Bushnell's $250 investment. Bushnell and his friends made a fortune, and anyway, the deal had him stay on as chairman. Bushnell reportedly said, 'I've always been telling people I was a millionaire. Now I am.'

The relationship, however, was ill-fated. 'I should have known it wouldn't last,' Bushnell says. 'It just wasn't fun anymore when it wasn't mine.' He worked under Gerard for two years, but he had lost his focus. Gerard claims that Bushnell spent more time managing his personal investments than running Atari. 'He wanted the business, wanted to run it, but didn't want to come to work,' Gerard says.

When Bushnell did, he clashed with the Warner management on most issues. He says he wanted Atari's new computer, the 800, to blow the inferior Apple II out of the water (partly as revenge, after he passed up on the opportunity to be a founding partner in Apple).

However, while Steve Jobs was encouraging developers to write programs for the Apple II, Atari threatened to sue anyone who tried to make software for the 800. If customers wanted a spreadsheet or word processor for the 800, they had to buy Atari's. Meanwhile, outside developers came out with software for the Apple II – VisiCalc spreadsheet, for one – that sold millions of the machines.

Bushnell also disagreed with Warner's handling of the video-game business. He felt their huge stock of 2600s should be dumped for cost because Atari would make its profits on software, but Warner management vetoed the idea.

Atari was poised for a big year in 1978, but so were National Semiconductor, Fairchild, General Instrument, Coleco, Magnavox (which had released Odyssey 2), and a dozen other companies. The Christmas season came and went, and few consumers, perhaps because they were confused by all the choices, brought video games home that year. Of all the entrants, only Atari and Coleco survived, and Atari was in shambles.

Manny Gerard, who had to answer to Steve Ross, put the screws to Bushnell, who was never known to respond well to anyone else's ideas, never mind anyone else's ideas about *his* company. 'You can't rule by the divine right of kings,' Gerard told him, whereupon Bushnell stopped returning Gerard's calls.

Gerard decided to bring in someone new to run Atari. He chose Ray Kassar, a former marketing vice-president from Burlington Industries. Kassar was as buttoned-down as Bushnell was northern-California-casual, and a clash was inevitable.

Bushnell, his necktie flying over his shoulder, arrived late to the November 1978 annual budget meeting at Warner's headquarters at 75 Rockefeller Center in New York. Winded and pink-cheeked, he threw his jacket onto a coffee table and plopped into the only empty chair, at the far end of the marble conference table. He looked carefully around the table at the Warner brass, who began 'the inquisition,' as he remembers it. They wanted to know what Bushnell planned to do in the coming year with their subsidiary (which was generating $250 million in sales but no profits).

Bushnell let loose, attacking virtually everything Manny Gerard and Ray Kassar wanted to do. First, Atari should fold its sinking pinball-machine business. Second, Atari shouldn't even think about launching the 800 computer unless it changed its policy and encouraged software companies to create programs for the platform. Third, the 2600's price should be slashed. Warner, he said, should invest whatever it took in the short term for the profitable long-term business. Greed would destroy the company.

Manny Gerard was outraged that Bushnell had aired his dissatisfaction in front of the Warner bosses. 'Man, was he pissed off,' Bushnell says. Gerard says he was countering Bushnell's 'bullshit and lies.' Gerard contradicted everything Bushnell said. He said that Bushnell was the one who was going to sink Atari. The two shouted each other down. In the end, as Scott Cohen writes, 'Gerard yelled louder.'

After the meeting, the two men met. Gerard said, 'You don't believe in the program. Maybe you should leave.'

Bushnell did: with $1 million cash, about $12 million in debentures (which Warner eventually bought back), a $100,000-a-year salary, and bonuses and options. The only condition was that he couldn't compete with Atari for the next seven years. 'They saw me as an extremely creative gamer as well as a strategist,' Bushnell says. 'They knew that I at least *might* be right, and they didn't want me to be able to shove it in their faces. They were also afraid because I had tremendous relationships with all the engineers. They thought the engineers would leave Atari and we'd go up against them and blow them away.'

By 1978, Americans were spending more than $200 million a year on home video games. By 1981, the amount had increased to $1 billion. Mattel had entered the fray with Intellivision. In 1982, video-game sales skyrocketed. Atari accounted for half of the revenue for Warner Communications and more than 60 percent of its operating net.

It seemed as if Atari could do no wrong. The 2600 was everywhere; 20 million units were sold, and there were 1,500 games available for it. Activision, Epyx, and many other independent companies began making millions manufacturing game cartridges for the 2600. Coleco came up with its strong competitor, ColecoVision, which promised, for the first time, arcade-quality video games on a home screen. With an expansion module, ColecoVision was able to play all the Atari 2600 cartridges. ColecoVision sold well, partly because it played a home version of one incredibly popular arcade game it licensed from Nintendo: 'Donkey Kong.'

Soon Mattel and Atari were making ColecoVision games for their own systems. Milton Bradley tried to keep pace with Voice Command video-game cartridges tied to the Texas Instruments 99/4A home computer, but the attempt fizzled. It was the exception in a rapidly expanding market: the home video-game business was bringing in over $3 billion a year.

Arcades, meanwhile, were bringing in even *more:* $5 or 6 *billion*, in spite of a backlash against them. Communities as far apart as

Babylon, Long Island, Oakland, California, and Pembroke Pines, Florida, passed ordinances restricting play by teenagers of various ages. The United States' surgeon general, C. Everett Koop, issued a statement indicting video games for producing 'aberrations in childhood behavior' and causing users to become addicted 'body and soul.'

But video games were sweeping the world. 'Fascination with the games, often accompanied by cosmic brooding about their presumed bad effect on faith, morals and school attendance, seems to be universal,' wrote John Skow in *Time* in 1982. The article reported that games such as 'Asteroids,' 'Defender,' 'Missile Command,' 'Pac-Man,' and 'Donkey Kong' were consuming, in addition to all those quarters, 75,000 man-years in the United States alone.

Yet Nolan Bushnell's timing in leaving Atari was fortuitous. The company fell further and further behind Apple in computers, and then its bread and butter, the video-game business, crashed.

Bushnell winces when he remembers some of the mistakes Atari made under Warner. 'The number of horrendous management decisions that went on in that place is amazing,' Bushnell says. 'A lot of people got involved with the company who really were underqualified, and there was a tremendous revolving door of vice-presidents. The company had been very successful, but nobody really knew why. All they were doing was pumping out cartridges and selling millions of units, but there was no strategic thinking going on.'

By 1983, the $3 billion video-game industry had turned into a trickle – $100 million in sales for the entire industry – yet Atari and dozens of other companies were still churning out games by the millions. Bushnell says it was 'an absolutely unconscionable screwup' on the part of Atari that destroyed the video-game industry. 'They expected the market to double when all rational thought said that it couldn't. The red ink poured forth.' This devastated Warner Communications. Its stock went into a tailspin, plunging the company into a takeover battle with Rupert Murdoch. Steve Ross announced that Atari's troubles were responsible for Warner's announcement of a $283.4 million loss for the second quarter of 1983, 'the worst in the company's history and triple even the most pessimistic Wall Street forecasts,' according to *The Wall Street Journal*.

Inventory levels were mammoth. Atari built and then bulldozed almost 6 million 'ET: The Extraterrestrial' games. Even more astounding, after licensing the game from Namco, Atari built more 'Pac-Man' cartridges than there were players.

With the ludicrous number of games in inventory, prices were slashed. During the years of the decline, total unit sales actually increased, but the dollar sales went to a tenth of what they had been. 'Atari hit two billion in sales, and that third year they were going for three,' Bushnell says. 'And that was why they hit the wall running as fast as they could.' Bushnell made a substantial amount of money *shorting* Warner stock.

'Very seldom do you have an industry in which the dominant player not only abandons leadership but abandons the *industry*,' Bushnell says. 'There was nothing left. Basically they retrenched, retrenched, retrenched, and didn't really try anything innovative. Nobody had enough cash to do anything for a long time. There was not a single innovation in product line at Atari after the day I left. Everything they did was just variation on the chip sets and the business I created. Atari abandoned the game market to Nintendo, pure and simple, and it abandoned the computer market to Apple and then IBM.'

The dumping and discounting of cartridges eroded the market, and Atari and Mattel nearly went bankrupt. Coleco did better, but not because of video games. It released Cabbage Patch Kids and sold, in all, more than half a billion of them.

The year Atari recorded losses of $200–$300 million, Ray Kassar, who, as Atari's chairman, was running everything for Warner, needed to find a way to keep things going in a video-game market that had suddenly vanished, as well as in the rough-and-tumble computer business. He tried a number of things, several of them having to do with a certain company that had been doing phenomenal business in Japan.

Nintendo's dealings with Atari began when Atari licensed 'Donkey Kong' for its home computer. Kassar and Skip Paul, Atari's senior vice-president, invited Minoru Arakawa and Howard Lincoln to their Silicon Valley offices for a meeting. Arakawa and

Lincoln met with a dozen vice-presidents ('of everything imaginable,' Lincoln says), twenty executives in all, in the corporate dining room. Kassar boasted that his chef was from one of the best restaurants in the world, and the meal was exquisite.

The meeting paid off; Atari licensed 'Donkey Kong' for the 800. And because Hiroshi Yamauchi was pleased with the way the negotiations had gone, one day he called Arakawa and suggested that Nintendo approach Kassar to see if he was interested in buying the worldwide rights to the Famicom. Yamauchi's idea was that Nintendo would sell the machine in Japan, but Atari, which already had a worldwide distribution network, would sell it in the United States, Europe, and elsewhere. The benefit would be more than a per-unit royalty. Nintendo, which on its own might never be a contender outside Japan, would, as a partner of Atari, be able to sell software all over the world.

Atari's 2600 was outdated and the 5200 was going nowhere. There was a rumor that Atari was working on another, more powerful system, the Atari 7800, but Yamauchi was confident that his success in Japan carried far more weight than anything in Atari's R&D labs.

Arakawa made the pitch to Kassar, who decided that his proposition made sense. He either could release Nintendo's Famicom under Atari's name or sit on the Famicom and do away with a potential competitor.

A meeting was set up and Kassar told Arakawa he would send the Warner Communications corporate jet, a Gulf Stream, to collect him and Howard Lincoln. En route to the airport, Arakawa asked Lincoln if he expected lunch to be served on the plane. Lincoln said there would probably be no food on the short hop between Seattle and Sunnyvale. Arakawa was starved, so the two headed to a restaurant before meeting the jet at a private airport.

The jet, fitted with leather couches and gold-plated ashtrays, was empty except for Arakawa, Lincoln, and the crew. Once it was airborne, the pretty attendant set up dining tables with linen tablecloths and asked if the two were ready for lunch. Arakawa threw Lincoln a dirty look when she served pâté, fresh poached salmon, and Dom Perignon.

'Just eat the goddamn food,' Lincoln muttered.

When the jet landed in San Jose, two chauffeurs escorted the Nintendo executives down a stairway into a waiting limousine. They drove to Atari's headquarters, where they were led to a conference room. The entire upper-management staff was assembled, from Warner's Manny Gerard and Kassar to Atari's Skip Paul and numerous lawyers and vice-presidents familiar from the 'Donkey Kong' negotiations. In the middle of the meeting, Steve Ross poked his head in to say hello. He wanted to apologize for the fact that he had to use the company's jet to go back to New York; he had, he said, rented another jet to take Arakawa and Lincoln back to Seattle.

The meeting began with Arakawa's description of the Famicom. Questions came from Gerard and Kassar, at the far end of the conference table, but also from each of the dozen lawyers and executives. Scribbling notes and fielding most of the questions, Lincoln watched Arakawa. 'I can always tell when he understands something or doesn't, when he's pissed off or when he's happy,' Lincoln says. 'This time Arakawa was just amazed by all those people, all that bureaucracy.'

Arakawa and Lincoln left the meeting exhausted and uncertain of how much progress they had made. Back at the airport, where they boarded the smaller jet Ross had arranged for them, they were trying to relax and sort out the meeting when the copilot came back to tell them, 'Mr. Ross left you some wine.' An attendant served them bottles of a rare Bordeaux. 'I don't know how we got home,' Lincoln recalls. 'We still had a buzz the next day.'

The next step was for Atari to see the Famicom. Skip Paul, along with half a dozen Atari managers, joined Yamauchi, Arakawa, and Lincoln in a conference room at NCL in Kyoto. The system was demonstrated by Masayuki Uemura, who explained, through an interpreter, why it was better than any that preceded it.

Yamauchi came and went several times during the meeting. He used this disappearing act as a diversionary tactic: he wanted everyone to believe that he had far more important business going on elsewhere.

At the end of the first day of meetings, Yamauchi had so successfully confused the Atari delegation that Paul called Lincoln at his hotel to clarify some issues. Yamauchi had Atari manufacturing the machines at very low cost. They would have the worldwide rights outside Japan, and they would have software support from NCL. Nintendo would receive a relatively large royalty on each machine.

Throughout the week there was persistent haggling over percentage points of royalties, but Yamauchi was getting everything he wanted. Finally Lincoln used one of Yamauchi's dramatic disappearances to full effect: he said that Yamauchi was growing impatient. The deal had better be sewn up immediately or Yamauchi might decide to forget the whole thing. 'You don't want Mr. Yamauchi to become annoyed,' Lincoln said.

At the eleventh hour, the Atari negotiators retreated to a private office to telephone Ray Kassar in California, who was in touch with Manny Gerard in New York. Yamauchi came back into the room with Arakawa and Lincoln. Lincoln said, 'Mr. Yamauchi, you shouldn't be in here. If the Atari people come back in and you're here, they'll take it as a sign that you are overanxious.'

The chairman gave Lincoln a look that instantly humbled the cocky attorney. Yamauchi had his own negotiating tactics; he didn't need an arrogant young lawyer from America to tell him what to do. He remained in the room as the Atari team returned. Paul said that the deal was as good as done and asked Lincoln to write up the contracts. They would all meet again in a month at the June Consumer Electronics Show in Chicago to sign the papers. Yamauchi rose and left the meeting. Handshakes and backslapping signaled that the negotiations had been a success.

Yamauchi flew to Chicago for the CES, which he attended with Arakawa and Lincoln. In the convention center, they walked past Coleco's booth, where the company was showing off its new home computer, Adam, set in an artfully lit glass case. There, playing on the sharp color screen, was 'Donkey Kong.'

Coleco's stock shot up almost twenty points that day, and Atari was not amused when it saw the Nintendo game playing on its competitor's machine.

Ray Kassar's office sent a tersely worded letter to Arakawa threatening not only to cancel the deal Skip Paul had made, but also legal action. Atari, which owned the floppy-disk computer-game rights to 'Donkey Kong,' thought that Nintendo had double-crossed them and sold the game to Coleco.

Howard Lincoln arranged an emergency meeting with Coleco's president, Arnold Greenberg, that night in Nintendo's hotel suite. Present when the meeting began were Minoru and Yoko Arakawa, Ron Judy, Howard Lincoln, and, representing Coleco, Greenberg and several of his colleagues. There was also a translator.

Everyone sat around a table. Arakawa whispered to Lincoln, 'Don't say anything. Mr. Yamauchi will do this.'

Arnold Greenberg, a distinguished-looking man, gray at the temples, ready to celebrate because of the computer Adam's apparent success, asked where Yamauchi was. Yoko assured him that her father would be there in a moment.

Yamauchi entered the room abruptly and, without addressing anyone, stood at the end of the table. He became, as one of those present put it, 'unglued.'

He began with a breathy, high-pitched tirade in a Marlon Brando monotone and quickly became loud and abusive. With a piercing cry, he swung his arm in an arc in front of him, shooting his outstretched index finger toward Greenberg.

Yamauchi's diatribe, all in Japanese, completely stunned everyone in the room, with the possible exception of the Arakawas. Howard Lincoln says, 'it scared the hell out of me.'

The Coleco people weren't aware that they had messed up Nintendo's lucrative Atari deal – millions of dollars were in the balance – but they could see that they had somehow incurred Yamauchi's unfathomable wrath. When Greenberg turned to Arakawa for help, he was met with a cold stare. By the time Yamauchi wound down, no one in the room said a word.

The translator finally began to speak. 'Mr. Yamauchi is very upset,' the man said.

This understatement underscored the fact that the Coleco team could have no recourse but to roll over. The translator continued, calmly reciting the gist of the outburst, but Yamauchi had already won. Greenberg's excuses – he said that Coleco considered the Adam a computer with a video-game machine inside – were feeble. He then tried to turn it on Lincoln, blaming him for 'the misunderstanding.' This made Lincoln furious; he was about to jump up to respond when he felt Arakawa firmly grasp his forearm, holding him still.

Yamauchi spoke again, never wavering. He made it clear that there was nothing else to be said. No excuses would be listened to. Coleco had to refrain from selling 'Donkey Kong' on Adam and announce the mistake, or there would be a lawsuit that would leave nothing of the company. There was no doubt that he meant it.

Greenberg and his colleagues retreated from the suite, shaken. Afterward, at dinner in the hotel's Japanese restaurant, Yamauchi, his tie loosened, turned to Howard Lincoln, who was still in a state of shock, and said, 'Sometimes this is the way you have to handle people, Mr. Lincoln. What did you think about that performance?'

The Coleco imbroglio ended up being irrelevant to Nintendo's deal with Atari, which fizzled out of its own accord – mostly because Atari was itself unraveling. A month after the CES, in July 1983, Ray Kassar was axed from Atari.

In September, Manny Gerard hosted a meeting between Atari, Nintendo, and Coleco in his office at Warner in New York. Skip Paul and his staff came in from California. Arnold Greenberg and the Coleco bigwigs were there, as were Minoru Arakawa and Howard Lincoln.

Gerard's office, with inlaid wood paneling, had a ticker-tape machine spewing out the latest market numbers and a bank of telephones with some sixty lines. Gerard explained that he was changing the office's decor – some new artwork was expected any day. As Arakawa took all this in, he knew that Warner was also laying off hundreds of employees and losing a fortune each quarter.

At the meeting a tentative compromise was agreed upon – 'Donkey Kong' was divvied up so that Atari's deal with Nintendo could proceed – but the issues soon became academic. Coleco's Adam was a disaster and soon disappeared, and Nintendo learned (from an attorney who left Warner) that Atari never had the money to buy the Famicom; the negotiation was a charade orchestrated to tie Nintendo up and remove a potential competitor and perhaps to learn something new about video-game hardware and software. When the message reached Minoru Arakawa that the Atari deal was dead, he thought it was a disaster. He called Yamauchi with the bad news. Potential millions had slipped through their fingers, he felt.

The event, however, was seminal. Years later Arakawa said, 'Can you believe that we almost sold the whole thing? If we had, no one outside of Japan would know about Nintendo.'

Any remnants of the home video-game business in America all but disappeared. In 1984 Mattel sold off its electronics division. Arnold Greenberg folded Coleco. At Atari, to replace Ray Kassar, Manny Gerard brought in Jim Morgan from Philip Morris, where his background in marketing cigarettes hardly prepared him for the video-game business. Morgan bragged to employees that his seven-year, multimillion-dollar contract gave him the freedom to run the company any way he saw fit.

However, as a former Atari executive told *Business Week*, 'Rome was burning and he was fiddling around.' Atari reported a $536 million loss in the first nine months of 1983. Games that were meant to be priced at $40 were selling for $4. Morgan consolidated Atari's forty offices around Silicon Valley to about twenty-eight and killed all but nine of Atari's new development projects. He let go a quarter of the company's employees. But the cuts were too little too late.

Steve Ross, whom Morgan once called 'the best man with numbers I have ever seen,' had had enough. Atari was taken away from Morgan on July 6, 1984. He was never told that Steve Ross had decided to break up Atari and sell its pieces.

Atari's hardware divisions – the video-game systems and computers – were sold to Jack Tramiel, founder of Commodore Business Machines, for $240 million in notes (Warner retained 25 percent of the company). Tramiel believed that his new company, called Atari Corporation, could go up against Apple and Commodore. He had been virtually kicked out of Commodore, and he imagined a sweet revenge. Since Tramiel, who planned to run Atari with his three sons, had no interest in the coin-op business, Warner sold it to Masaya Nakamura, and Atari Games became a subsidiary of Namco. Under the agreement Atari Games could do anything except make hardware or software that competed with Tramiel's Atari Corporation under the Atari name.

'I look at it sadly,' Nolan Bushnell says, surveying the devastation of the company he founded. 'You can't help but have a certain feeling for a name that you chose out of the universe.' He adds, 'See, Atari could have been Nintendo and Apple under one roof.'

The home video-game business was dead. The consensus was clear: no one in America wanted anything to do with video games.

But Minoru Arakawa, picking through the rubble, noticed that there was one group of people who were oblivious to all the death notices and eulogies. Video arcades were still packed, bringing in more money than first-run movies: billions of dollars. Perhaps, Arakawa wondered, it was not a lack of interest in home video games that had killed off the American industry. Perhaps it was the kind of sloppy business he had witnessed during his glimpses inside Atari and Warner that was to blame.

He decided to find out.

ENTER THE DRAGON

8

'The reason I have this terrific job,' a buyer for a toy company began, 'is that the guy before me was fired after he lost so much in video games. Do you think there is any way *I'm* going to make that mistake?'

Throughout 1984, Arakawa heard variations on that theme over and over when he met with toy- and department-store representatives to tell them he was considering entering the home video-game business. They thought he was nuts.

Arakawa marveled at the intensity of the hostility toward video games – even the phrase was taboo. In the horror stories about the industry, hyperbole was unnecessary. One of the legions of former Atari vice-presidents (who retreated into his father's pharmaceutical business after the crash) said he watched millions of unsold game cartridges being bulldozed into a landfill. Destroyed careers, divorces, and a suicide were blamed on the Atari crash. 'It would be easier,' one former toy-industry executive told Arakawa, 'to sell Popsicles in the Arctic.'

On the other hand, there was no letup in the sales of the Famicom in Japan. Were Tokyo and Darien that different?

Arakawa, Howard Lincoln, Ron Judy, and Bruce Lowry visited arcades, toy retailers, merchandisers, discounters, specialty stores, software developers, former Atari and Coleco managers and executives, and anyone else with experience or opinions about video games. 'We kept trying to zero in on what we shouldn't do,' Lincoln says. What they most often heard was that they shouldn't do anything at all. But there was a consensus that the 'suck factor' was one of the biggest reasons for the industry's crash. The market had been glutted with terrible games. 'Pac-Man' was a blast in arcades, but the home version 'sucked.' 'ET,' ridiculously hyped, 'sucked.' 'Zombies from Pluto Stole My Girlfriend' *really* sucked.'

Bad games such as these would never have survived in the arcades; kids would have tried them and deserted them. But there had been no easy way to test home games. Fancy boxes and expensive advertising campaigns made promises, and when the promises were unfulfilled, the customers stopped believing them. Systems and games went into the garbage.

Arakawa came to realize that it didn't matter how much money was spent on marketing, advertising, and promotion if the games weren't good enough. As a Nintendo slogan later acknowledged, 'The name of the game is the games.' Arakawa also knew that he had, if nothing else, great games. Sigeru Miyamoto's 'Super Mario Bros.' and 'The Legend of Zelda' would blow these kids away. The question, then, was how he could get them to understand that Nintendo's new system was like nothing they had ever seen.

There was much to be done.

Arakawa felt it was vital that the Nintendo system be distinguishable from its predecessors. He decided it should be clear from the outset that the Nintendo system wasn't a toy. If it was marketed as a more sophisticated electronics product, the company could disassociate from the Atari, Coleco, and Mattel systems. There were other reasons to stay far away from the toy business. December 10 dating, which had helped devastate Nintendo when it was selling Game & Watches, was one. As a consumer-electronics company, Nintendo could take orders, deliver systems, and send bills that were due in thirty or sixty days. The marketing perspective would therefore be broadened: to include mass merchandisers, electronics stores, and discounters as well as the toy chains.

To interest an extended base of retailers, Arakawa wanted the system to be more than a game machine; it should have the capabilities of a small computer. NCL engineers were given the task of developing peripherals, including a keyboard, a music keyboard, and a tape-storage device. They came up with new, high-tech, infrared remote controllers and a cool Zapper gun to play shooting games. All these options indicated that the Nintendo machine was both a giant step forward from the old-wave systems and a new kind of system altogether. Parents would be more likely to buy it because it could do more for their kids (the keyboards, for example, promised educational and cultural value).

The R&D teams in Kyoto modified the system while Arakawa had some of his people in Seattle design the housing and packaging. A young designer named Lance Barr was assigned to make a system that looked high-tech sleek yet accessible. The main computer board and circuitry were nearly identical to the Famicom, but Barr fit them inside a slimmer and handsomer box. Gray and squarish, it looked more like a stereo component than the red-and-white plastic Famicom. The remote-control unit was understated; it could have been featured in a Sharper Image catalogue. The Zapper gun might have belonged to Luke Skywalker, the keyboards were slender and svelte, and the joystick looked like it belonged in a jet fighter. The system was given a name to reflect its maturity: the Advanced Video System, or AVS.

The major headache of counterfeiting also had to be addressed. The problem was the apparent impossibility of making an uncounterfeitable machine or uncopiable software. There was also a related problem. Ron Judy said that to avoid the 'suck factor,' Nintendo had to have a way of controlling the quality of software released for the AVS. Also, Judy pointed out, if the AVS could run the same games that ran on the Famicom, illegal Taiwanese games would flood the U.S. market. 'We need a security system,' he said, and Yamauchi and Hiroshi Imanishi set the NCL engineers on the task of creating one.

NCL's attempts to stop rip-offs in Japan, including the periodic system revisions, had been only partly effective. The licensing agreements also helped, but outfits that were going to counterfeit hardware or software didn't care about licensing agreements. Had NCL decided to put a security chip in the Famicom, it might not have lost some of the huge markets of the Pacific Rim. In addition, it might have been able to stop companies like Hacker International from releasing nonapproved games.

The security system the Japanese engineers devised was a complex implementation of a simple lock-and-key concept. The AVS wouldn't work unless a chip in the cartridges unlocked, or shook hands with, a chip in the AVS. The key was a kind of song the two chips sang to one another. If a cartridge was inserted into the machine that didn't know the song, the system would freeze.

Nintendo called the invention a 'security chip,' but it was referred to in the industry as a 'lock-out' chip; it stopped more than counterfeiters because no one could manufacture their own games for the AVS without Nintendo's approval. Only Nintendo had access to the technology, including the specific computer code at its heart. Lincoln had copyright and patent applications filed for the security system.

While the security system was being developed, Arakawa asked Don James to recommend the best NCL games for the AVS. James and Howard Phillips played hundreds of games and gave Arakawa a list of their favorites. Arakawa chose forty and sent instructions to Japan to prepare English-language versions.

The AVS was to debut at the January 1984 Consumer Electronics Show. Don James designed a booth for the occasion – more substantial than the one in which Nintendo had shown Game & Watch. Nervously, James, Arakawa, Lincoln, and Phillips traveled to Las Vegas with AVS demos and boxes full of brochures. 'The evolution of a species is now complete,' the brochure announced. On the cover was a picture of three televisions. Playing on one was 'Pong,' a few dreary white lines on a black screen. Playing on another was a color tennis game, roughly animated blue-and-yellow stick figures on either side of a net. The third screen was veiled in a red cloth. Inside the brochure the system, with its numerous peripherals, was introduced. 'Ninety percent of the

Japanese market won't play anything else. Welcome to the future of American home video entertainment.'

The show opened and Arakawa, James, and Lincoln excitedly manned the booth while Howard Phillips demonstrated games.

The AVS looked impressive, the Nintendo representatives were told. But almost all those who stopped by at the booth shook their heads when asked if they would consider placing an order. 'The memories of Atari were too recent,' Lincoln says.

Although Nintendo tried again at the industry's June show, it was clear that Arakawa had misjudged his ability to overcome skepticism. He hadn't been able to create the new category that combined computer power and entertainment. No one cared about the remote control, and they hated the keyboard – a turnoff to kids, industry executives believed (parents were irrelevant). The AVS had all the problems not only of the video-game business but of computers too. No one would touch it.

Back to the drawing board. Instead of attempting to improve on the video-game systems of the past, Arakawa decided that he should figure out a completely new way to sell it. He scrapped the computer peripherals. Kids wanted fun, not BASIC programming languages and cassette-tape storage drives. They tossed out the keyboard, the piano keyboard, and the remote-control unit as well as the name. R&D 1 was put in charge of a new peripheral that would make the system something other than a video-game machine.

In Japan, Gunpei Yokoi's team came up with ROB, or Robotic Operating Buddy. He was one foot high, gray, legless, and he really didn't do much. He was controlled by the video-game system. The flashing of the television screen activated a chip in ROB's head that caused him to move. Players controlled him at the same time they controlled action on the screen. In games designed for ROB, such as 'Gyromite' and 'Stack-Up,' players would cause the robot to pick up chips from one stack and drop them onto a pad that triggered a door in an on-screen game. More than anything, ROB looked cool. He would be used to sell the video-game machine.

James and Barr worked on a new design for the system – again high-tech gray, but boxier. Game cartridges slid into the front instead of the top, and revised controllers were attached by plastic cords. It wasn't toylike – it still looked like a consumer electronics product – but it was simpler than AVS. Nintendo de-emphasized the box in favor of ROB and the Zapper gun.

At the June 1985 Consumer Electronics Show, Nintendo debuted what Arakawa had renamed the Nintendo Entertainment System, or the NES. The operative word was entertainment. Everything Nintendo would do to sell the machine would emphasize this.

The reaction at the new show was somewhat better. Buyers liked ROB. Still, they were reluctant to place orders.

Arakawa stubbornly ignored the reaction. He said that the people in the industry were jaded. Kids would love it, he believed. To prove it, he commissioned focus-group studies in New Jersey. From behind a one-way mirror, he watched a random sampling of young boys play the NES and heard them say how much they hated it. Typical was the comment of an eight-year-old: 'This is shit!'

Depressed, Arakawa wondered if he should give up, and in a conversation with Hiroshi Yamauchi, he said as much. Yamauchi denounced such fatalism. The market in America wasn't that different from the Japanese market, he said. 'But the tests show . . .' Yamauchi interrupted him. 'Ignore them,' he said. 'Try to sell the system in one American city. Then, if it fails, it fails. But we must get it into the hands of the customer. That is the only test that matters.'

Arakawa, Ron Judy, Howard Lincoln, and Yamauchi considered the location of the test. Judy thought they should start a limited test in a small town, but Yamauchi shook his head. 'What is the most difficult town to start in?' he asked.

The answer was obvious: New York City.

Yamauchi asked why.

Besides the obvious hurdles of New York's competitive market, it also had been hit the hardest by the crash of the industry in 1983. What's more, much of the excess inventories had been dumped there – not to mention that New York had the most savvy and cynical buyers in the country.

Yamauchi said that New York was where they should go. He gave Arakawa a budget of $50 million.

* * *

In late summer 1985, Arakawa leased a warehouse in Hackensack, New Jersey, bordered by a railroad and a cemetery. There were no windows. The only light in the cavernous room was from a few dangling naked bulbs, and it was spooky and depressing.

Arakawa brought about thirty NOA employees East. Ron Judy and Bruce Lowry were the first to arrive. Then a deputation of twelve more – they called themselves the SWAT team – flew out and landed in Newark in the middle of a hurricane.

At the terminal, twelve rented cars awaited the team. They traveled in a shaky caravan to the warehouse, which was flooded. As the group surveyed the dreary headquarters, Arakawa cheered them on. 'If we can just get players to see it, it will be *really big*,' he said. 'I know we can do it. It's a big job, but everything worthwhile is difficult. We just have to get it to the players. If we do, it will be *really, really big*.'

He got through to them. An ebullient chorus came back: 'Yeah! It *will* be big.'

Arakawa said, 'It will be *really* big.'

They echoed, 'Really, *really* big.'

Other employees arrived over the next month. From Japan there was Shigeru Ota, who did the books, and a technician, Masahiro Ishizuka. Cindy Wilson was an executive assistant. Others included Rob Thompson, who became the service manager. Howard Phillips, who had become shipping-warehouse manager of coin-operated games, was flown in. 'We felt like the elite point team,' Phillips says.

Judy, Ota, and Ishizuka lived in a New Jersey house Nintendo had rented. Their furniture consisted of wooden boxes and suitcases that they never entirely unpacked. The house doubled as a place to store spare parts, and it also became Nintendo's after-sale service center.

Other employees lived in rented condos and apartments, two to five to a place, all furnished with junk-sale furniture and mattresses on the floor. Rob Thompson, Howard Phillips, and Don James lived together in a townhouse in Fort Lee. Howard Phillips woke up every morning at six and made his way to the shower, where he sang opera. Thompson and James threatened to murder him.

The various groups carpooled to the warehouse in the morning and worked all day, breaking in the evening for dinner at a neighborhood coffee shop. Then they returned to work and stayed late into the night. Howard Lincoln sent posters of Seattle for the SWAT team to put up in the warehouse so it wouldn't be so dreary. He and Arakawa, shuttling between Seattle and New York, made calls on retailers, as did Bruce Lowry. Judy met with advertising agencies and planned a promotion campaign. Other SWAT-team members manned the telephones, trying to convince buyers for large and small stores to see them. They pressed shopping-mall managers to allow them to demonstrate the NES. Arakawa used some of his budget to sign up professional athletes for the demonstrations. Mall managers were far more open to the idea of having famous ball players come by than businesspeople representing an unknown company with a strange Japanese name.

In October the push began in earnest. In pairs, the SWAT team hit the pavements, visiting department stores and large and small toy and electronics retailers. They worked to convince companies such as Toys 'R' Us, Sears, Circuit City, and Macy's. Although Charles Lazarus, founding chairman of Toys 'R' Us, and a very few others were receptive, most people could not pronounce *Nintendo* and were not interested in learning how.

Arakawa realized that the only way around the retailers' reluctance was to make it a risk-free proposition. Yamauchi, however, had trouble with this idea. He couldn't understand why he should offer a complete money back guarantee; Nintendo had never had to operate from a position of weakness. Arakawa argued that the ultimate sign of strength is to have so much confidence in your product that you would almost pay stores to carry it. Yamauchi didn't need to tell him how risky the tactic was.

Nintendo, Arakawa announced, would stock the stores and set up displays and windows. Nobody had to pay for anything for ninety days. After that period, stores would pay Nintendo for what they had sold and could return the rest. It was an offer store buyers couldn't refuse, although it was still greeted with skepticism. Then, one by one, companies agreed. 'It's your funeral,' one buyer said.

Many of the Nintendo team worked eighteen-hour days, seven days a week for the three months that preceded Christmas 1985.

Ron Judy would load up a couple of rented vans with Don James's displays and drive to Long Island or Westchester County or some other New York suburb. In malls the team set up colorful booths with twelve or so monitors, each one attached to an NES. They arrived in the middle of the night and worked until four o'clock in the morning setting up the displays, then drove home to sleep for a few hours. The next day they headed back to the malls, where they stood next to Mets stars who were signing autographs and tried to get passersby to listen to their spiel. Mookie Wilson and Ron Darling even played NES baseball, projected on a large-screen TV.

'The trick was to get people to come over,' Arakawa says. 'If we could get it in the hands of the consumers, they would be convinced.'

Howard Phillips turned out to be one of the team's best spokesmen; he had a knack for communicating his own enthusiasm, punctuating his sentences with words like *cool* and *neat*. He grabbed kids, old ladies – anyone – and before his victims realized what had hit them, he had them playing.

At one mall, the Nintendo team spent all night setting up its booth to be ready. Just as the crowds poured in, the mall's director came over and forbade them to turn on the games; 'They attract the wrong sort of crowd,' she said. She had only wanted to meet the baseball stars.

Days such as this made the Nintendo employees wonder what they were doing. 'We're overworked, underpaid, we don't see our families, nobody wants what we're selling – what's the point?' they whined. Ron Judy would buy them all dinner and reassure them. 'Just wait,' he said. Arakawa would pat them on the back and cajole them: 'It will be worthwhile. It will be . . .' They finished his sentence without enthusiasm – 'really big. We know.'

It was an uphill climb. Even with the guarantees, fancy in-store displays, and the promise of a $5 million advertising campaign, it took three sales calls to win over most stores. A buyer would finally be convinced, but then a merchandising manager would say a flat 'No way.' When he was convinced, a vice-president would say no. But the Nintendo team was persistent, and more stores agreed.

The advertising campaign and press relations were run by Gail Tilden, under the supervision of Ron Judy. Tilden had come on in

1983. She was a brunette with long hair, bangs down to her eyebrows, and gray-blue eyes. She was a combination of Annie Hall looks and self-confidence; she looked down, stumbled over words, and charmed almost everyone she met.

After a year at Britannia Sportswear, Tilden worked for a small Seattle advertising agency. When a former boss of hers left Nintendo to have a baby, she recommended Gail to replace her. Within a year she was Nintendo's ad manager. With input from Judy and Lowry, she hired an ad agency in early August 1985.

Although the Nintendo executives didn't know much about advertising a video-game system, they had learned from the company's botched effort to make commercials for Game & Watch to trust professionals: no employees were in ads.

Tilden instructed the agency in the rules of NES advertising, all designed to disassociate Nintendo from Atari. No-no's included the use of the term *video game*; this was an *entertainment system*. Software was never to be described as game *cartridges*, another word associated with Atari. At Nintendo they were game *packs*. The NES itself wasn't a *console* but a *control deck*.

The ads the agency came up with emphasized the variety of games and featured ROB and the Zapper. It wasn't easy to advertise video games on television, because watching kids play the games was about as exciting as watching someone read. The excitement was internal. They came up with ads that tried to convey the *feeling* of video games: energy, color, danger, irreverence. In the commercials, houses blasted off into space and kids explored a spaceship where the control panels were game screens. The voice-over asked: 'Will it be you? Will your family be the first to witness the birth of the incredible new Nintendo Entertainment System?' A light of the sort in *Close Encounters of the Third Kind* showed. 'Now,' the announcer exulted, 'you're playing with power.'

As promised, Arakawa began to blitz the New York area with television advertising. Meanwhile, Tilden met with members of the trade press, the reporters who covered the toy and consumer-electronics businesses. They were skeptical, even as they acknowledged that Nintendo's product had better graphics and games than the systems of the past; they simply didn't believe the company would be able to reignite consumer interest. Tilden tried to convince them that video games were an entertainment category, just like VCRs and stereos, but the reporters shook their heads; they had heard it all before. She explained the quality-control measures Nintendo had taken in order to prevent the market from becoming saturated with bad games that had plagued the industry in the past, but the journalists had stopped listening.

A second hurricane that swept through Hackensack one morning was a fitting metaphor. Through the warehouse door, the exhausted Nintendo staff watched the rain falling horizontally, from left to right. It became sunny for a while as the eye of the storm went over them. Then the rain poured down again, this time from right to left. Don James took photos.

Still, the extraordinary efforts began to pay off. A growing list of stores placed orders. But there was no time for the Nintendo staffers to congratulate themselves; success meant more work. Phillips, who managed the warehouse, received containers filled with systems from Japan and shipped them out to retailers. James had a team building window displays he designed for stores that had agreed to feature the NES for the holiday season. Everyone helped build them. One night, Arakawa and Lincoln raced Don James and Howard Phillips to see whose team could build more displays.

There was never a respite from the pressure, although there were some gratifying moments. When Howard Lincoln walked across Fifty-ninth Street in Manhattan and reached the FAO Schwartz store, he was stopped in his tracks when he saw the window display he and a few others had spent the previous night assembling. Midtown was crazy with holiday shoppers, and Lincoln got so excited he called Hackensack and insisted that the staff join him. Soon the members of the SWAT team were crowded together, standing in front of the toy store, staring at their window as if it were a barn they had just raised.

Howard Phillips, on the other hand, had a rather unexhilarating experience late one night while setting up a display at a Toys 'R' Us in New Jersey. A security guard on the graveyard shift came over and struck up a conversation. When he saw the video-game system, he asked, 'Are you from Atari?'

Phillips explained that he was from Nintendo with a new and better system.

The guard said, 'You're working for the Japs? I hope you fall flat on your ass.'

They worked until the day before Christmas. Between 500 and 600 stores were selling the NES. The team members were spent. A group of them summoned the energy to drag themselves to Newark Airport to fly back to Seattle to spend Christmas with their families, but their flight was canceled because Seattle was fogged in. Most of the SWAT team spent a lonely Christmas in New Jersey.

The advertising and mall tours succeeded in building interest in the NES, and stores were racking up sales. The New York test wasn't quite as successful as Nintendo had hoped, but half of the 100,000 systems shipped from Japan were sold. Most important, retailers had decided that Nintendo had a viable product. It was enough to justify going forward.

Los Angeles was next. It was a tougher sell there because of the time of the year. They hit stores in L.A. in February, a bad month for retailers, particularly for toys. Still, enough systems were sold to encourage Arakawa. The L.A. sales were slow but steady, and retailers were enthusiastic for the most part. The team continued – to Chicago, San Francisco, and several Texas cities before going national. By the end of the first year, a million systems had been sold in America.

It was still slow going. Stores remained reluctant to commit much to video games, and most people in the industry assumed that Nintendo's limited success was a temporary aberration. In the second year, however, the company sold another 3 million systems.

In 1982, Arakawa had ventured into the food business, opening a chain of Nintendo restaurants, and he got advice from Peter Main, his old friend from Vancouver, who had a wealth of experience in marketing and restaurant management. Nintendo's restaurants were making a profit, and Arakawa tried to convince Main to resign from his vice-presidency at General Foods and join Nintendo. He wanted Main to oversee the restaurants and help orchestrate what Main would later call Nintendo's 'Invasion of Normandy,' the NES launch.

Main, balding but with a trace of thinning gold hair on the sides of his head, wore big round glasses with thick root-beer-colored frames. Behind the glasses were dark eyes, jovial and frank. He worked in an office strewn with baseballs, a Hula-Hoop, and an electric train set.

A Canadian, Main had worked for years for Colgate-Palmolive. He headed their new-products group in Canada. He had spent years coming up with ways to convince people to buy Colgate toothpaste and various other products. In those businesses, a fraction of market share meant millions of dollars. 'You had to be a street fighter,' Main says. 'You had to beat them on the curbs.'

Main moved on to General Foods in Canada and managed its restaurants, including Kentucky Fried Chickens, steak houses, Burger Chefs, and White Spots. He also went into business for himself before returning to General Foods at about the time 'this neat young Japanese couple' bought the house across the street. 'It looked different from the other houses,' Main says. 'The shoes were outside the front door.' Soon he got to know the Arakawas – 'very, very warm people, even though their verbal skills were not considerable at the time.'

In 1980, Arakawa told the Mains that he was quitting his job and going to work for his father-in-law in America to set up in New Jersey something called Nintendo of America. Main thought it was a pinball factory. The Mains heard from the Arakawas through notes and Christmas cards and saw Minoru when he dropped by to check in on the property he still owned. Main later heard from Arakawa when he and Yoko had moved to Seattle after Nintendo returned West. In early 1982 Main advised Arakawa about the restaurant business. Five years later, when Nintendo was completing its market tests for the NES, Arakawa asked Main to come work at Nintendo. Ron Judy had been in charge of marketing, but he was going off to Europe to promote the NES there.

Main knew nothing about the video-game business, so he studied all the documentation he could find about the Atari crash. 'Nintendo,' he concluded, 'had a better mousetrap and a commitment to do this thing right.' He came on as vice-president of marketing, with responsibilities that included advertising, promotion, distribution, and merchandising.

Main first sought to improve Nintendo's relationship with the retail community. He also began an assault on Wall Street, meeting key analysts who follow the toy and electronics businesses. With the success of the tests behind them, sales could have been expected to at least slog along, but there was no guarantee of bigger numbers or market longevity. Large discount chains and department stores were still not convinced. Space in their stores was at a premium; to minimize risk, they put Nintendo in only a few stores and carried just a handful of games. The toy stores were coming aboard, but the retailing base was still tenuous.

A forceful salesman, Main met with analysts and gave them 'a hot tip.' Analysts were always on the lookout for the next big thing. They were also looking for companies with strong balance sheets that might employ their organizations when it came time to offer stock. Nothing was known about Nintendo when Main sat down with these people, one at a time, to pitch them. He presented them with background on NCL, its history, and its financial status – a balance sheet with no debt. This caught their attention, and so did the numbers: Nintendo had a lock on 90 percent of the thriving industry in Japan.

The analysts checked with their counterparts in Tokyo, and after corroborating the information, talked to retailers. Having the top analysts asking about Nintendo gave the company a credibility it had never had in the United States. When analysts heard that other analysts were talking about Nintendo, it confirmed that they were on to something. It was a chain reaction. When buyers at Circuit City, Babbages, or the other electronics retailers told analysts that they weren't carrying Nintendo – that the electronic-game business was not in video games but in computer software – they heard back, 'Are you *crazy*? These guys are already selling more of one title than you sell of all computer-game titles put together!' The buyers checked with other analysts and asked about the company. When Main went to Sears, a vice-president told him, 'Funny you should mention Nintendo. I was just at an investment-analysis meeting and there were people asking me what we were doing about Nintendo.' Sears was one of the toughest sells since it had been burned more than other companies by a huge investment in Atari.

The sleight-of-hand worked. Sears signed up, and Circuit City and Babbages (with its two hundred software stores) did too. Wall Street was inundated with stories about Nintendo. Kmart and Wal-Mart, conservative and cautious, expanded their commitment. To compete, the toy companies began buying more Nintendo products. 'It became a self-fulfilling prophecy that something would happen,' Main says.

In 1988, 7 million more NES units were sold, along with 33 million game cartridges. Two Nintendo games – 'The Legend of Zelda' and 'Mike Tyson's Punch-Out!' – sold 2 million apiece just as 'Super Mario Bros. 2' was released (the original 'Super Mario Bros.' was included with the NES).

By 1989, there would be an NES unit in one out of every four American homes. By 1990, one third of American homes would have one – more than 30 million of them. By 1992, the video-game industry would be thriving again – it passed $5 billion in retail sales that year – and, for all practical purposes, it had all been Nintendo's doing.

If Nintendo had been an American company playing by the rules such companies follow, it would have given up long before there was any indication of success – that is, after Arakawa's original market surveys, when the AVS failed, or when there was resistance at the first trade shows. Many American companies are so wedded to market research that the devastating results of focus groups have signaled death knells. Had Nintendo been American, the company would probably have retreated when retailers in New York declined to place orders, or when it took more than a year for big sales numbers to appear. But commitment to an idea and pure tenacity are inherent in Japanese business philosophy – and certainly to Japanese business successes.

Arakawa's perseverance was vital – 'I learned to set a goal and to do what is necessary to reach it' – but even more important was Yamauchi's commitment to back him. The money poured forth – more than the original $50 million Yamauchi had committed. He could afford to spend vast sums on the new product even if it meant fiscal quarter after fiscal quarter of weak profits or even losses. A CEO of a public company in America with stockholders to answer to four times a year would probably have withdrawn. Quarterly profit-and-loss statements do not tell the long-term story of a company, however. Heads of Japanese companies answer to investors, but they are not under pressure to deliver high dividends or dramatic short-term growth. The structure allows company heads to work toward long-term growth; they are not forced to abandon a strategy today because it didn't pay off yesterday.

Nintendo's success was proof of the superiority of a system that allows long-term commitment. This feature of Japanese business was one reason why Japanese companies ended up with almost 100 percent of the video-game hardware business, just as they had most of the television and VCR business and were on their way to having most of the business in products from flat-screen displays to certain high-capacity memory chips – all of them technologies pioneered in America.

As Arakawa succeeded in his conquest of the American market, he would be attacked by competitors and American politicians. Nintendo prevailed, they would charge, because of illegal practices, from price fixing to un-American monopolistic control to intimidation of retailers. But the companies (and the economy) that suffered because of Nintendo's success would have been better served if they had struck out against the American system which allowed Nintendo to stroll into a market that had been all but destroyed.

Still, Japan-bashers were correct in one sense. If the playing fields in Japan and America had been equal, Nintendo might never have destroyed the American competition. Even in its heyday, Atari never had much success in the Japanese consumer market. The Atari 2600 sold for about $120 in America, but by the time it reached Japanese consumers, after traveling through the trade barriers of middlemen and the many-tiered distribution system, it cost the equivalent of $380. At that price, few sold. Other American companies wrote Japan off, settling for small profits by licensing video-game systems to Japanese companies. Magnavox, for one, sold the rights to its Odyssey system to Nintendo. On the other hand, if the 2600 had been priced competitively in Japan, Atari might have become the standard there, as it had in America. Nintendo might not have been able to undersell Atari by so much, and so might never have tried to compete. The Famicom and NES might never have been developed.

After the Atari crash in America, almost nothing happened in the home video-game industry until Minoru Arakawa came along. Atari was in such bad shape (and had such a bad name) that its follow-ups to the 2600 sold a trivial number, and there remained no other American competition to speak of. The personal-computer companies could have come in at this point, but they weren't interested in that market. As a result of this miscalculation, Nintendo was soon making more money than Apple.

Arakawa also endured because he didn't care what anyone thought. Analysts rolled their eyes, but he refused to be dependent on the American industry's narrow view of the market. He kept slugging away because he believed, correctly, that kids in America were very much like kids in Japan. There were minor differences – gun games were popular in the United States, but not in Japan, while role-playing games did better in Japan – but the kids were similar enough to form a market that would buy more than 75 million Nintendo systems in the two countries by 1992.

The grumbling heard throughout the American industry could not diminish the fact that Nintendo did certain things better than companies in *any* industry. The company's products were good and the backing from its Japanese parent company was crucial, but Nintendo still would never have gained its enormous sales without phenomenal marketing – 'the kind that America had never seen before,' according to a competitor.

Peter Main and Arakawa led a multiphased assault that was meticulously planned and flawlessly carried out. Nothing was left to chance. Through the late 1980s, the company launched ad campaigns and the first organized merchandising program with interactive displays in stores throughout the United States. Anyone passing by a Nintendo display could stop and try it. TV commercials had piqued kids' curiosity, and soon anyone shopping with their children was dragged to Nintendo displays in stores. Once kids tried 'Super Mario,' Nintendo was put on Christmas lists. Peter Main wanted an even greater in-store presence. To get it he decided to bring in a professional merchandiser, John Sakaley, who knew the toy business inside out.

Sakaley had begun his career as a carpet buyer, then changed to become a toy buyer. He ended up working for Kenner, under Bernie Loomis, the company's well-known and respected president. Under Loomis, Sakaley formed Kenner's first merchandising department and introduced a series of innovations, including an approach begun by Mattel: stores within stores devoted to a single product (there was a *Star Wars* store in toy departments, with action figures, space vehicles, posters, and the like).

Eventually Sakaley left Kenner to become the group director of the retail sales force for the toy division at General Mills. Then Bruce Donaldson, the vice-president of sales for NOA, hired him.

When Sakaley was hired, he focused on developing a merchandising force that headed into the trenches and called on stores to make certain that the NES was prominently displayed. Eventually Toys 'R' Us would feature full rows of Nintendo merchandise, and Macy's would incorporate NOA's ambitious store-within-a-store, The World of Nintendo.

To get stores to invest in huge Nintendo displays, Sakaley initiated the 'merchandise-accrual fund.' For each piece of Nintendo hardware or software purchased, the retailer was credited with a specific amount in a fund – a quarter for an NES system, a dime for a game – that was used to purchase displays Sakaley's staff created. Retailers' credits toward their merchandising-accrual funds doubled when they agreed to have a World of Nintendo. Of course this benefited Nintendo at least as much as the stores.

Eventually, 10,000 retail outlets had Worlds of Nintendo, where they showcased a growing cornucopia of products, all of which carried the Nintendo Seal of Quality, an idea Ron Judy had come up with.

Nintendo displays were elaborate. At some locations, laser-light beams shot through the air. Silver-metallic and fluorescent-yellow pipes and tubes snaked over and around girders. It was as if you were *inside* a Nintendo game. The displays won awards from the Point of Purchase Advertising Institute (POPAI) several years in a row.

This mammoth effort resulted in strong NES sales, but Arakawa saw that they were still held back by an inadequate distribution system. Some chains had signed on but still ordered cautiously.

Others remained unconvinced. To get the holdouts, it seemed beneficial to hook up with a distribution network that already had a presence inside the stores.

Don Kingsborough was a legend in the toy business. He had been with Atari before founding Worlds of Wonder (WOW) to sell Teddy Ruxpin, a mechanical bear that told stories. Teddy's mouth moved when prerecorded tapes played on his built-in cassette player.

Teddy Ruxpin was the most popular toy around for a couple of Christmases; retailers wanted all they could get. To service them, Kingsborough developed a large, efficient distribution network.

Arakawa met with Kingsborough and made a deal that benefited both Worlds of Wonder and Nintendo. Joining forces with Kingsborough's group gave Nintendo immediate marketplace muscle. Teddy Ruxpin had brought in $93 million in revenues in 1985, its first year, and more than $300 million by the end of the next year. Overnight WOW was worth $550 million. By convincing Kingsborough to distribute Nintendo beginning in late 1986, Arakawa got presence and credibility. WOW had relationships with most toy, department, and discount stores. For its part, the Worlds of Wonder network gained a large new business servicing the Nintendo account. Revenues from the deal helped Kingsborough to expand.

Although the WOW operation did increase Nintendo's presence in the retailing world, Sakaley came to feel that Nintendo still wasn't getting enough 'bang for the buck.' He felt Nintendo could do a better job with reps committed *solely* to Nintendo, not to Teddy Ruxpin as well.

Sakaley discussed this with Arakawa, who gave him the go-ahead to start his own merchandising force. Sakaley had already started to organize it when, in the fall of 1987, Worlds of Wonder began to fall apart. The Teddy Ruxpin fad had run its course, and the company's costs were out of control. WOW had an assumed debt of $200 million and a tremendous inventory. 'Worlds of Wonder has been in a world all its own,' a toy-industry analyst said. Although a private investment group took over the company, Nintendo was told on a Friday in October that WOW would not be able to continue with its field-merchandising service.

Arakawa convinced Kingsborough not to lay off his field representatives for seventy-two hours. During that time he had Sakaley explore Nintendo's options. Sakaley and an assistant worked through the weekend, and on Sunday night he called Peter Main. In the morning, when the two men sat down with Arakawa, Sakaley told him that Nintendo should take over the WOW organization. After a call to Kingsborough, Arakawa had Sakaley hire the WOW reps as they were fired from WOW.

Sakaley had an instant force of 100 people and he hired fifty more. The new force carried cameras and photographed the Nintendo displays. Sakaley was able to send someone out almost immediately if a major store wasn't doing its part. The reps were also equipped with Panasonic hand-held computers with telephone modems that could relay sales information back to the main office. 'Back in the Colgate days, it used to take two months to get a report after the fact to find out the mistakes you made – which you were compounding and which were leading you down the wrong road,' Main says. 'We were getting it daily.'

Japanese companies in the automobile industry used efficient just-in-time inventory management systems. Essentially this meant that companies bought parts they needed only when they needed them. The merchandising feedback loop allowed Nintendo to instigate a kind of just-in-time inventory policy so that it ordered only what it needed as it needed it from NCL. Likewise, NCL could thus avoid over-or underproduction. Neither NCL nor NOA had to tie up money in inventory.

Main's and Arakawa's web sought not only to ensnare customers but to keep them. Nintendo encouraged customers to send in warranty cards with contests to win game cartridges. U.S. contest laws soon made it too complicated, so a new incentive was developed: anyone who sent in a warranty card became a member of the Fun Club, whose members got a four-, eight- and eventually a thirty-two-page newsletter. Seven hundred copies of the first issue were sent out free of charge, but the number grew as the data bank of names got longer.

From the success of the magazines in Japan, Nintendo knew that game tips were an incredibly valuable asset. The bimonthly newsletter's crossword puzzles and jokes were fine, but game secrets were the most valued. The Fun Club drew kids in by offering tips for the more complicated games, especially 'The Legend of Zelda,' which had all kinds of hidden rooms, secret keys, and passageways. In the newsletter a secret code was revealed that led players of 'Mike Tyson's Punch-Out!' to the last level – a bout with the champ. Without the code, it was extremely difficult to reach Tyson.

The Nintendo frenzy had now begun in earnest. Kids were competing with one another to finish games. When Nintendo's Redmond switchboard received telephone calls from players who wanted tips, they too were enrolled in the Fun Club.

The mailing list grew. By early 1988, there were over 1 million Fun Club members, and this led to Arakawa's decision to start *Nintendo Power* magazine. In Japan, Nintendo had allowed other companies to make fortunes from magazines devoted to the Famicom. In America, with its long list of potential subscribers, Nintendo would keep the money and the control itself.

Unilaterally Arakawa decided that the magazine would take no advertising. His colleagues told him he was crazy – he was turning his back on a potential gold mine. With that subscription base, Nintendo licensees and companies with products geared for kids would have paid top dollar.

Arakawa, however, was emphatic, insisting that the magazine would be purely editorial. Companies would not be able to advertise bad games, as they had in the Fun Club. Of course the 'editorial' content of *Nintendo Power* was really one long Nintendo advertisement – stories about game characters, lists of kids' high scores, and loads of maps and charts, as well as lots of game tips.

The company brought in a firm specializing in direct-response research to decide how to market the magazine, but after paying for a survey and a lengthy computer printout of advice, Arakawa threw the data away. 'All the kids really have to do is feel the magazine, look at it, touch it, and understand it,' he said, 'so what I want to do is mail the magazine free to the people whose names we have. *Then* they will buy it.' When he was told that this would cost $10 million, he was undeterred.

Gail Tilden had recently left the company to have a baby, but Arakawa wanted her back to run the magazine. Yoko said, 'There was so much male power there that he needed Gail to diffuse it.' Arakawa called and convinced her to come back to work, although her baby was just a few weeks old. She prepared the first issue in January 1989, and it was sent out to all the names on the data base, by that time 5 million of them.

There was something bordering on the insidious about *Nintendo Power*. Kids paid $15 for twelve monthly issues, which covered most of the costs of the magazine. The other costs, including mailing charges, were paid through the marketing budget. From the original mailing, 1.5 million people sent in $15 to subscribe. It was an audience that experts in the magazine business had almost written off: they didn't read and they had a million better things to do with $15. Nonetheless, *Nintendo Power* became the largest-circulation magazine for kids in America by the end of its first year.

Power had what Peter Main called an 'ability to pre-sell product.' It was as if Universal Studios owned *Premiere* magazine and other print media devoted to movies. Universal could then decide, well in advance, to trumpet a particular coming movie, building anticipation. As the movie neared completion, it could make grander and grander announcements. Just as the film was to hit the theaters, it could announce that it was the most incredible movie ever made, and that anyone who didn't see it immediately was missing the event of the season. The publications would then tell readers how much everyone loved the movie and push any hold-outs to see it, all the while creating enthusiasm for the *next* Universal movie.

Power meant that Nintendo didn't have to waste money developing hundreds of games. It could develop a select few each year and be all but guaranteed that the games would sell at least a set minimum amount. Any advertising beyond the magazine was gravy, since *Power* guaranteed that Nintendo was in touch with millions of its most dedicated customers, enough people to create word-of-mouth demand for a game.

Editor Tilden assembled materials for each issue with the help of Howard Phillips, the most enthusiastic in-house player, a contributing editor, and a character in a regular comic strip. Planning a new issue, the two went through games that were coming out to determine how much and what kind of coverage they merited.

There was no pretense of editorial independence; Arakawa, Main, and Lincoln approved the selections. The best games (or the ones Nintendo wanted most to sell) were covered in spread after glossy spread of maps, galleries of characters, and player tips.

'People sometimes just take kids for granted or act like they're really dumb,' Tilden says. Nintendo did its best to speak to kids as peers. The voice they devised was perfect. The prose was a cross between the dialogue in *Wayne's World* and a Pee-wee Herman routine. *Nintendo Power*, in 1990, was scripture for up to 6 million readers a month. 'Parents who complain that their kids don't read should pay attention – kids pore over every word of *Nintendo Power*,' according to Howard Phillips.

There was an unprecedented number of hungry consumers. Nintendomania was sweeping the United States. NOA's switchboard operators were deluged with calls from kids. They wanted more information than they could find in *Nintendo Power* magazine, things like how to set up their NES machines, so Peter Main came up with a way to take advantage of the calls. 'The phone system is really the closing of the loop in a fashion that no other consumer company in this country has been able to do,' he says. Phil Rogers, who oversees the consumer service department, says, 'When we started, what did we know about consumer service? Not a damn thing. We knew about service to distributors because we'd been doing that for arcade games, but we'd never even talked to a consumer.' When Main decided to set up the phone lines, Rogers figured that they needed four operators. They began with some six-button phones in January 1986.

Calls flooded in, so many of them that Rogers bought a $40,000 electronic call distributor in 1987. Within a year there were 550 people answering 150,000 calls a week on a new, $3 million phone system. Customers called an 800 number to reach consumer service representatives. If a store was out of a highly sought-after game, service representatives could advise a caller on its availability. Representatives took the callers' zip codes, and by accessing a data base, could tell the callers where games were available. Callers' names and addresses were added to the mailing list.

Many calls were from kids asking how to get past tricky villains in games. Consumer reps transferred the calls to Howard Phillips or other game players who worked for Don James. Some callers spoke Spanish and French, so bilingual representatives were hired.

The telephone company informed Rogers that their 800 number was backed up most of the time because half a million calls were coming in every week. Nintendo decided to initiate a 900 (pay-per-call) number for kids to reach the Captain Nintendo Hotline for tips and adventure stories about Nintendo games. More important, Nintendo initiated game counseling. Kids by the hundreds of thousands called a separate 800 number with questions about games. Counselors manned the phones from 4:00 A.M. till 10:00 P.M. – to catch the early-morning calls from New York and the late evening calls from California – seven days a week. Hundreds of game counselors huddled in partitioned work spaces, each equipped with a Nintendo system and stacks of games, a computer terminal, notes, and 'green bibles,' bound volumes of game maps and secrets.

Some of the callers had detailed questions, but others just wanted to talk. 'William, do you have a question about a game or what?' Sandoff finally asked a caller who wanted to talk about the problems he was having in school. A seven-minute rule was initiated; no call could exceed that time limit. Counselors developed ways to cut calls short when kids started asking about their favorite rock groups and movies. One caller sought marriage counseling. His wife, he said, was going to leave him if he didn't stop playing 'The Legend of Zelda.' Sandoff's advice to him was, 'Shut off the game.'

The phones were overloaded, and the 800-line service became so expensive that Nintendo discontinued it. Calls to game counselors became regular toll calls in 1990. Phil Rogers instructed the counselors not to speak with any child for more than three minutes without making certain that the parents knew that they were going to be billed for the call. After seven minutes, no matter what the child said, the counselors were told to gently get off the line. 'Parents were not going to blame themselves for not controlling their kids,' Rogers said. 'They were going to blame us.' Still the volume didn't slow down.

The game counselors did more than provide a customer service. First, they further bonded players to the company. The degree to which kids became obsessed with Nintendo amazed educators, psychologists, and parents. The magazine and counselors were part of the reason, encouraging kids to become immersed in it. Main says, 'For our more youthful players, many of whom come home from school and find neither Mom nor Dad there, Nintendo came to mean more to them. It filled a larger role in their lives.'

Second, Nintendo was gaining great insight into its customers: they were finding out which groups were excited by what games, and how games could be made better. Counselors gave pointers but also queried callers about their likes and dislikes. 'We used those calls as market research,' says Main.

The information about consumers – not from dated market research studies but from the daily input of diehard customers – gave Nintendo a living, breathing line to its customers every day, seven days a week, twelve hours a day. The feedback helped steer the company's product development and marketing strategies; the information went right back into the development process. Yamauchi had always boasted that he never let marketing people influence R&D, but this stuff was too precious to ignore. Best of all, since callers often asked Nintendo counselors what games were coming, demand was created for games months in advance through the phone network.

The counselors were some of the first people at Nintendo to realize that kids weren't the only Nintendo fanatics out there. Many of the early-morning callers were frustrated parents, some of whom had been up all night trying to beat a game. 'It kills them that their children are better at something than they are,' says Blaine Phelps. 'They're obsessed with beating their kids.' When Peter Main realized how many interested adults there were, he began directing marketing campaigns toward them. Similarly, calls from girls gave the company a better handle on what would make more girls buy systems and games.

Don James ran another operation that was part of the marketing loop. In addition to his work preparing Nintendo for trade shows (Nintendo's CES booths became the largest in the consumer industry, 60,000 square feet of light shows, lasers, rock music, and dancing girls) and overseeing design work done in-house, he headed product analysis, whose function was to monitor and maintain the quality of games. It was a way to be certain that the games the counselors and *Nintendo Power* recommended were good. More important, it could be used to direct customers to the better games.

When games were nearly completed in Japan, NCL sent them to Seattle, where James's crew reviewed them for the American market. Games had to be extraordinary on their own merits, and couldn't be dependent on characters that were well known in Japan but not in the United States. Eventually James initiated a formal evaluation process headed by himself, Howard Phillips, and Shigeru Ota, known collectively as the Big Three.

At first the evaluations were arbitrary and haphazard, but soon Ota (before he was tapped to go to Frankfurt to run Nintendo of Europe) adapted a system that had been used in Japan. He developed a forty-point scale on which each game was to be rated. The system had eight categories, each one worth up to five points. The Big Three played every new game until they got a feel for it. Then they evaluated it for attributes such as challenge, graphics, and fun. Some games were sent back for revision; some were killed. If there were doubts, a larger group of evaluators, mostly game counselors, gave their opinions. Phil Sandoff was part of the GC6 (which simply stood for 'six game counselors'). 'We're tough,' Sandoff says. 'First you think every game is the greatest. Then you get more critical.'

After the evaluations, Arakawa had a good idea of how a game would do in the marketplace. However, there were occasions when doubt persisted; for example, if the Big Three and GC6 disagreed. If Arakawa wanted more feedback, the toughest critics of all were called in. Hidden in a room behind a one-way mirror, Arakawa and James watched kids play the game. 'Sometimes you cannot get the honest answer by asking questions of children,' Arakawa says, remembering the failed focus groups back in New Jersey. 'But if you watch their faces while they are playing, you can tell very easily whether the game is good or not. We have more than 90 percent success in judging games.'

9
THE GRINCH WHO STOLE CHRISTMAS

The Nintendo marketing blitz had the biggest companies in America aiding and abetting (and, of course, cashing in on) the Nintendo invasion. Promotions were directed by Peter Main and Bill White, whom Main had hired in 1987.

White, who wore gold-framed John Lennon specs, brushed his fair hair back around a youthful face. Although he was always dressed in standard corporate attire, he looked like he would be more at ease behind a drum kit in a garage rock band than inside the high-pressure upper echelons of Nintendo.

White's father and sister were in advertising. After college, Bill got a job at Carnation while studying for an MBA in the evenings. Later he worked in the packaged-goods industry. When his boss convinced him to follow him from the 'stodgy' packaged-goods business to high technology, White moved to Seattle to work as director of marketing for a computer software company. Frustrated there, he picked up a copy of *Advertising Age* one day and saw that Nintendo was looking for a director of advertising and public relations. Two weeks later he was interviewed by Main, Arakawa, and Lincoln, and a week after that he had the job.

White found advertising at Nintendo similar to what it must be like at a movie studio. Arakawa made the decision that software, not hardware, should be the focus of most advertising. 'It is a software-driven business,' White says. 'The job is not so much to increase long-term brand equity as it is to build excitement around the next hit.'

One of the first commercials made under White was the market introduction for 'The Legend of Zelda,' which received a great deal of attention in the ad industry. A wiry-haired, nerdy guy walks through the dark screaming for Zelda. The next commercial, in November 1987, was for 'Mike Tyson's Punch-Out!' It had beefy Tyson walking into a room, sitting down, grabbing an NES with his mammoth hands, shoving in a cartridge, and facing a wall full of screens. Then he looks into the camera and breaks out laughing. In another, a Nintendo 'Ice Hockey' commercial, a kid is playing the game in front of a TV set when a puck comes crashing through the screen into his living room.

In early 1988, there were discussions at Nintendo about the benefits of broadening the company's message to an audience beyond six-to-fourteen-year-old boys (if nothing else, to gain some respectability from parents who were skeptical about video games). Bill White and Peter Main determined that there was no need to ante up the many millions of dollars necessary to 'buy another demographic target' with television advertising. Instead, they sought promotion partners who already targeted these broader audiences.

Pepsi had the right image and audience, so White went after it. Pepsi's promotion team was cautious. They studied Nintendo's market research and agreed to test an association with Nintendo with one of its smaller brands, Slice. The national TV promotion, which gave Nintendo systems and games away with Slice, worked so well that Pepsi executives said they wanted to plan a bigger tie-in for their enormous Christmas advertising campaign, this time with all the Pepsi products. Since Pepsi targeted the twelve-to-thirty-four-year-old audience, the key soft-drink consumers, Nintendo got vast amounts of exposure – and the credibility associated with Pepsi – for nothing. Commercials and in-store displays were only one way Nintendo benefited from the Pepsi tie-in. Pepsi bought nearly $10 million worth of Nintendo products at the same wholesale price Toys 'R' Us and other retailers paid, and Nintendo was advertised on the outside of 2 billion cans of Pepsi. In return, Pepsi got the cachet of being associated with Nintendo.

The promotion was so successful that Nintendo looked for other partners to increase its exposure to parents and other adults. Procter & Gamble approached Bill White and suggested a 'dealer loader' that retailers put up in stores throughout the country featuring Nintendo characters on Tide detergent displays. For Nintendo, the association with a product that was so well accepted in America brought more immediate credibility. Tens of millions of people were reached in the $20 million promotion.

The next partner Nintendo targeted was McDonald's. In 1989, White and Main sent a letter of introduction to the company's marketing division. The head of children's marketing at McDonald's was shown a preview of 'Super Mario Bros. 3.' After examining Nintendo's demographics and the results of the Pepsi and Tide promotions, she launched an entire campaign – including 'Mario' Happy Meals – around 'Super Mario Bros. 3.'

Another promotion for 'Super Mario Bros. 3' proved more valuable than any paid advertising ever could. Tom Pollack, the respected president of Universal Studios, met with Bill White and Peter Main and told them he wanted to make a movie around a video game. *The Jetsons*, a film that Universal had planned for a Christmas 1989 release, wasn't going to be ready and the studio needed a holiday film. When he heard about the various Nintendo competitions, Pollack came up with the idea of a *Tommy* for young kids that was called *The Wizard*.

Nintendo received a licensing fee from Universal, of course, and approval of both the script and the film's game footage. Bill White went to the film set in Reno to see how things were going, even though 'all we were really worried about was just making sure that the game footage was spectacular.'

It was. The 'video Armageddon' scene was filmed at the theater at Cal Arts, the college in Southern California. Universal spent

$100,000 on this set alone. As the movie's main character took the stage, the on-screen audience went wild when the feverish announcer told the contestants that the final, tie-breaking competition was to be on a game they had never seen before, the newest and best video game in the world. Dramatically, the curtains were drawn and a wall of monitors was fired up. 'Here it is, ladies and gentleman,' the announcer screamed, ' "*SUPER MARIO BROS. 3!!*" '

Nintendo itself could not have dreamed up a better promotion. The movie was ready by November, four months before the game was launched. The excitement in the theaters was far greater for 'SMB3' than for the movie itself. *The Wizard* made money even with its relatively small box-office gross, but the groundswell of anticipation it created for 'Super Mario Bros. 3' was enormous.

When the game finally arrived in stores, the hype had been so intensive that the resulting rush for the game shocked even Nintendo. Bill White's team oversaw the creation of a television commercial that showed no game footage at all, but simply thousands of kids chanting passionately, 'Mar-i-o, Mar-i-o, Mar-i-o . . .' The camera pulled back and the faces of impassioned boys and girls – decidedly white and clean-cut – became a sea of people calling out Mario's name. Then the camera zoomed back to a point out in space. Looking back toward earth, we see Mario's face in place of what should have been the North American continent.

Nintendo reaped the rewards when 'Super Mario Bros. 3' went on to outsell any video game in history, and gross more than $500 million.

The first Nintendo television show, *The Super Mario Bros. Super Show*, first aired in fall 1988, and soon went into syndication. In fall 1990, *Captain N: The Game Master* became a network show, and eventually there was a third show, *Super Mario World*. For several years running, Nintendo shows were numbers one and two on NBC's Saturday-morning schedule.

The television shows brought Nintendo licensing fees, but this wasn't the primary benefit. 'They're about trying to boost awareness of the characters,' White says. 'They're part of the endeavor to sell more Mario product by increasing the popularity and likability of the character, which, in turn, will help our character-licensing program – sales of T-shirts and all that – and of course the games themselves. There's really very little downside if the show is done in a quality manner.' The fact is that no one could have confused the television shows with anything approaching quality, but they were no worse than other Saturday-morning fare.

In addition to all the other licensing deals, Bill White also contemplated the idea of a feature film for Mario.

The movie went into production in May 1992 for a May 1993 release starring Bob Hoskins as Mario – an actor popular after his role in *Who Framed Roger Rabbit*. The bad guy, King Koopa, was played by Dennis Hopper.

There were a host of other promotions. In 1991 MCA released a record of 'Mario' songs that included a 'Mario' comic book. Among the musical numbers was the last song Roy Orbison recorded before he died. There was another feature movie in the works, too, an animated movie similar to (but hopefully better than) the TV cartoons.

Long before any talk about movies was heard in the halls and offices of Nintendo, Peter Main had told Arakawa that he felt it wise to market video games like movies – released cautiously, rationed so that demand outpaced availability, and then withdrawn from circulation as soon as interest began to wane. This rationing tactic, treating games like priceless objects, worked. After all the hype about a new game took hold, kids dragged their parents to stores, but outlets couldn't keep the games in stock. The rush to get games such as 'Super Mario Bros. 3' or 'Link,' the sequel to 'The Legend of Zelda,' caused near riots of excited game-buying.

The competition to acquire games rivaled that for tickets to Michael Jackson's last concert tour. Ultimately more product was sold. A kid who was absolutely dying to get 'Link' would arrive at a store, only to find it sold out. Maybe he would try a few other stores without success, but then he would buy another Nintendo game, so that his parents would end up paying $30, $40, or $50 for a second or third choice. Then, a week or month later, a new supply of 'Link' would come in. The kid wanted 'Link' more than ever then, and unless his were the most iron-willed of parents, they would succumb. Even the kids whose parents held out still managed to get games; in 1989, in a survey of what kids in Sandwich, Illinois, bought with their allowances and other money they earned, the near unanimous choice was Nintendo games.

The editor of one toy-industry journal noted that 'Nintendo has become a name like Disney or McDonald's. They've done it by doling out games like Godiva chocolates.' In 1988, *Fortune* observed that 'so far the strategy looks like a winner.'

'Inventory management' is what Peter Main called it. The Atari wave had floundered in large part because of a flooded market. Main made certain that scarcity whetted the public's appetite and sustained demand as Coleco had done in 1984, when there was a shortage of Cabbage Patch Kids. By design, Nintendo did not fill all of the retailers' orders, and it kept half or more of its library of games inactive. In 1988, for instance, it sold 33 million cartridges, but market surveys showed it could have sold 45 million. That year retailers had requested 110 million cartridges, or nearly 2.5 times the indicated demand. Main said that retailers exaggerated demand and Nintendo would rather have them pleading for more than have to worry about excess inventory.

In contrast to the prerecorded-video business, in which an average tape had the longevity of 90 to 120 days, some Nintendo games were popular for a year or more. If a game came through the evaluation process with a thirty-six or thirty-seven on the forty-point scale, Nintendo viewed it as 'a potential grand slam,' according to Main. A hugely successful game only had to sell 500,000 copies, and grand slams could sell millions.

When Nintendo released 'Dr. Mario' in 1991, Charles Lazarus, head of Toys 'R' Us, called Peter Main. 'It looks like we're going to be short on "Dr. Mario," ' he said. 'What are you going to do about it?'

Main made certain his largest customers got a healthy share of the games, but the company refused to cave in to their demands; *no* company had all of its orders filled all the time. By then, the toy and electronics as well as department stores were dependent on Nintendo, not the other way around. NOA accounted for an inordinate amount of the revenue of some companies. For Toys 'R' Us, it meant 17 percent of its sales and 22 percent of its profits. Nintendo called the shots even when it came to companies used to throwing their muscle around.

The fact that the parent company and the president of its American subsidiary were Japanese exacerbated NOA's problems when it played rough. Tactics that would have been called aggressive if used by an American company were viewed in some quarters as unscrupulous when the company was Japanese. In only thirty-six months Nintendo had gone from near anonymity to the point where it accounted for 20 percent of the toy industry and large percentages of other retailers' gross sales. It was felt that 'by definition we must be doing something illegal,' Peter Main says. No industry wanted to be so dependent on a single company, especially a Japanese company. In Main's view, 'Most of the criticism is from those who have decided not to join the club.' Some, however, hadn't been invited.

NOA's reputation began to be suspect around the time of the most severe game shortages. Although Nintendo orchestrated some of the shortages, they were worse than it had planned, and consumer demand was higher than the most ambitious forecasts. In 1990, retailers were furious when Nintendo couldn't deliver as many systems as they could have sold that year.

Nintendo had long since terminated its money-back-guarantee policy and replaced it with tough terms: order, receive shipment, and pay. The sales reps in the front lines made certain that retailers kept small inventories. By keeping customers on a short leash, Nintendo made enemies, but cash kept rolling in. This policy proved its worth in 1990 when the second largest toy-store chain in the United States, Child World, had serious financial difficulties and was on its way to bankruptcy. A listing of Child World's creditors was announced in December. Companies such as Hasbro and Mattel were owed up to $25 million, but though it had accounted for almost 20 percent of Child World's business, Nintendo wasn't on the list. 'These other guys were pumping all this product into a bottomless pit,' Peter Main said. 'They are still owed that money today.' Because Nintendo was working so closely with Child World and knew, from constant inspection of financial statements, that the company was in trouble, the retailer was told that it had to pay for its Nintendo product as much as a year in advance. 'We are not loved for that,' Main says.

In time, pandemonium ensued. One of the largest retailers in the country threatened to stop carrying Nintendo Systems and products. Nintendo refused to change the policy and the retailer refused the products. The retailer held out for three months; after that it crawled back and agreed to Nintendo's terms.

Piles of cash poured forth from America to Japan. NCL's net sales figures shot up, mostly because of its U.S. subsidiary. Arakawa became responsible for up to 60 percent of Yamauchi's business, according to Hiroshi Imanishi. NCL's net sales in 1987 were $1 billion. In 1988, they went to $1.5 billion. In 1989 and 1990 they topped $2 billion, and in 1991 they shot up to more than $3.3 billion. In 1992, Nintendo foresaw sales topping $4.5 billion. Pretax profits had risen from $186 million in 1987 to more than a billion dollars in 1991 and 1992.

Nintendo's stock soared. In 1991 the company reached number eighty-six on *Business Week*'s Global 1,000. In U.S. dollars, the company's market value was $14.56 billion, and it was ranked twenty-ninth among all Japanese companies.

Of the estimated $11.4 billion spent on toys in 1989, 23 percent was spent on Nintendo products. Of the thirty top-selling toys in America, twenty-five were Nintendo or Nintendo-related. NOA held every spot in the top ten – and this was during the greatest shortage of Nintendo products.

Arakawa couldn't fill orders. Before Christmas 1989, Peter Main was threatened with bodily harm and lawsuits by company managers and presidents who blamed him for single-handedly destroying their business. The only stores that had Nintendo products at Christmas that year were retailers that had sufficient cash reserves to allow them to begin hording systems and games that summer. Toys 'R' Us and a few other chains had invested heavily in Nintendo products for that Christmas and had a reasonable supply. Most companies, however, blamed Nintendo when their businesses plummeted. In one pre-Christmas month in 1989, toy-company stocks tumbled 42 percent, *Fortune* reported. *Financial*

World said, 'Nintendo . . . is once again sticking out its tongue at the rest of the U.S. toy industry.'

The toy industry *hated* the fact that Nintendo didn't play by its rules: it didn't use December 10 billing; it didn't belong to any toy manufacturers' associations; it didn't bother showing its products at most toy-industry trade shows. Charges began to surface that it was cutting into the toy industry, *taking over* the toy industry, manipulating it by illegally fixing prices and intimidating retailers, threatening to cut off their product supply if they carried competitors' products or dared to discount Nintendo machines and games.

Arakawa and Peter Main became the target of complaints – first from Nintendo's competitors, then from retailers, and eventually from members of Congress. Although Peter Main was named 1989 Marketer of the Year by *Adweek* magazine, a profile in *The New York Times* had this to say of him: 'To his admirers . . . he is a master seller of children's entertainment . . . To his critics he is an aspiring monopolist, squeezing supply and jacking up profits.'

Since the toy companies couldn't beat NOA, they tried to cash in on the Nintendo craze. Five major companies got licenses from Nintendo to release character-related toys such as Mario and Zelda board games and action figures. Mostly, however, other companies hoped that Nintendo's invasion of their territory was temporary. They prayed for (and in many cases, expected) Nintendo to go the way of Atari as they bided their time with old standbys: Slinky, Mr. Potato Head, Lincoln Logs, Barbie. But by 1991, Nintendo had become so well entrenched that the toy industry realized it wasn't about to disappear. Hasbro's chief acknowledged the troubles the country's economic recession had brought to his industry, but complained that 'the toy industry has been much more impacted by Nintendo.'

By 1991, Toys 'R' Us, which had a 22 percent market share of the toy business with its 450 stores (plus 100 more abroad), had sales of $5 billion, and Nintendo products represented almost one fifth of its total sales. Discounters became Toys 'R' Us's biggest competitors (Child World and Lionel Kiddie City shared 7 percent of the toy market). Kmart and Wal-Mart controlled up to 10 percent each. The largest, Wal-Mart, didn't even carry Nintendo's competitors. Although Wal-Mart had no World of Nintendo in its stores, Kmart, which had held out for years, agreed in 1991 to open five hundred of the stores-within-a-store.

The toy industry had been hurt by the recession as well as deep discounting of toys in pre-Christmas sales. Child World was on the brink of collapse (it finally went into it in 1992). The industry did better in 1992, but Nintendo still accounted for seven of the top ten toys of the year. It was, once more, the Grinch who stole Christmas.

10
FROM RUSSIA WITH LOVE

As Nintendo grew and its target audience, the classic audience for video games (young boys), was nearly saturated, the company went after new groups of customers. Peter Main says it was a strategic decision from early on. 'We wanted to break out from the historic video-game user, boys eight to thirteen, because the thirteen-year-old boy will soon be fourteen years old and pass from our grip. Our objective from day one was to move beyond that narrow base.'

Girls were an increasingly important market for Nintendo in mid to late 1991, when more powerful systems by competitors had distracted some of Nintendo's formerly loyal boys. A survey Peter Main commissioned revealed that girls from six to fourteen were the primary players in many households. Their level of satisfaction was 'intensifying,' according to the market researcher.

In Japan, adults had never been considered part of Nintendo's market. Inherent in the Japanese culture was *jyukyu*, a system of ethics dating from the seventeenth century, which held that the most important values were hard work, thriftiness, and seriousness, and that luxury and leisure were a waste of time. *Jyukyu* was behind Japan's phenomenal productivity, the high savings rate of its people, and, ultimately, its obsession with education and work. Vestiges of *jyukyu* made it unthinkable for many adults to sit in front of video-game machines.

Not in America. Adults in the West comprised many of the computer- and video-game players, and increasingly they wrestled controllers away from their children in order to play Nintendo.

NOA encouraged them. Arakawa had made a point of selling Nintendo products in electronics as well as toy stores. Peter Main says, 'We wanted to be in electronics outlets, department stores, and discount mass merchants in addition to toy stores because we knew there were varying signals that emanated from a product depending on where it was distributed.' Since the initial test in New York City, Arakawa had fought to get into Circuit City and Crazy Eddie – among the stereos and VCRs – as well as Toys 'R' Us.

A growing number of licensees came up with games for adults, alternatives to shoot-'em-ups and karate games, like 'Jeopardy,' 'Trivial Pursuit,' and sophisticated sports games. 'Bases Loaded,' made by a licensee named Jaleco, was particularly ingenious, even beyond its impressive graphics and sound, and serious baseball fans could obsess over its trivia and decision-making options. In 'Bases Loaded 2,' pitchers were guided by an ERA and batters by individual statistics. Programmed into the game were what Jaleco called 'a special player-performance system' that programmed players to have streaks and slumps. You decided if a player was having a bad day and if you ought to bench him. More than 4 million 'Bases Loaded' games were sold.

Adults played against each other, against their children, and in secret after the rest of the family had gone to bed. *Nintendo Power* featured celebrity adults who played, and the game counselors heard from parents who had devoted entire nights to practicing so they could trounce their kids. Still, nothing compared to the adults who flocked to Nintendo because of a new hardware product launched in 1989.

* * *

Gunpei Yokoi and his forty-five-man R&D 1 team of designers, programmers, and engineers came up with a device that married the NES and Game & Watch. Like the NES, it was a video-game system that played interchangeable cartridges, and like Game & Watch, it was quite small. Here was a video-game system that could be played anywhere – in planes, trains, and automobiles, or in the quiet of a bedroom. Inside its pretty package, Game Boy combined portability, miniaturization, and entertainment, three of the most important attributes of emerging technologies, according to Greg Zachary of *The Wall Street Journal*. Game Boy was so slick that a Sony engineering team was reportedly chastised by managers and executives in Japan for being beaten by Nintendo. 'This Game Boy should have been a Sony product,' a manager is said to have told the group, which worked on portable entertainment devices. Some of the engineers were shuffled to new departments, and one was so shamed that he left the company.

Game Boy, decidedly playful (Sony probably would have called it Game*man*), was housed in a gray plastic case the size of a transistor radio. On the face were buttons and a palm-sized, black-and-sallow-green liquid crystal display (manufactured by Sharp). Game Boy was released at a lower price than Yamauchi had aimed for, $100. He predicted Game Boy sales of 25 million units within three years. Once again, hardware sales were only the beginning. Game Boy was a tiny computer that could, if successful, create a viable software market all its own. Game Boy games, the size of a saltine cracker, would sell for $20 to $25, so a sizable sub-industry was possible.

When Game Boy was released, it was criticized because it didn't have a color screen. Yamauchi had decided to forgo color for cost and efficiency. A color display would have required the power of four or eight AA batteries instead of Game Boy's two. Color would also have drained the batteries too quickly. Low-priced color screens had other problems. They were difficult to see in bright light (Game Boy was difficult enough as it was). Competitors Sega, Atari Corp., and NEC released expensive hand-held systems with color screens that sold a small fraction of the number of Game Boys. Two hundred thousand Game Boys sold out in two weeks in Japan, and 40,000 units were sold the first day in the United States.

NCL sent 1.1 million Game Boys to the United States in its initial shipment, and Toys 'R' Us tried – unsuccessfully – to get them all.

Of course lots of kids played Game Boy – two could be connected for competitive play – but a remarkable aspect of its success was the number of adults who played it. Game Boys were frequently seen in first-class compartments on cross-country flights, in corporate lunchrooms, and in desk drawers and briefcases. President Bush, in hospital in May 1991, was pictured in newspapers commander-in-chiefing a Game Boy.

Nintendo unleashed Game Boy marketing campaigns that targeted adults. 'This Father's Day treat Dad like a kid,' read one of Bill White's ads. Another ad ran in an airline magazine to attract business travelers. 'If you're reading this ad, you're very bored,' the copy read. 'You've mastered the safety instructions in every language, and the flight attendant won't give you any more almonds. Now what?' The choices: 'Travel to another galaxy, golf . . . [all with Game Boy]. Game Boy won't ask you for your dessert, and fits just as neatly into the mouth of that screaming child beside you as it does into your briefcase . . .'

Minoru Arakawa first saw a prototype of Game Boy in Kyoto in 1987 and promptly topped Yamauchi's predictions. Before it was over, 100 million Game Boys would sell throughout the world, he said. To reach such astronomical levels, however, it would need a monster game, and Arakawa saw it at an arcade-industry trade show in June 1988, where Randy Broweleit of Atari Games was showing off a prototype of an arcade version of a game called 'Tetris.' At the convention with Howard Lincoln, Arakawa stood in front of the console and played, transfixed. Broweleit told Lincoln that Atari Games had the coin-op rights and that Atari's Tengen had the rights to produce a home video-game version. Broweleit said that 'Tetris' rights had also been sublicensed in Japan – coin-op rights to Sega and home-game rights to Henk Rogers's company, Bullet-Proof Software. Arakawa said he was pleased that 'Tetris' would be coming out on the NES. He did not say he was also pleased that there was no mention of the hand-held rights, which might still be available.

Back in Redmond, Arakawa's engineers created a test version of 'Tetris' that worked with a prototype Game Boy. When Arakawa plugged the tiny 'Tetris' into Game Boy and played it, it was as if they had been made for each other. The 'Tetris' pieces were large enough to be seen easily on the small screen, and the game was simple and hypnotic. Arakawa believed its appeal would cut across all age groups, as well as across the gender line, and said, 'We must have this game.'

Arakawa instructed Lynn Hvalsoe, the company's general counsel under Howard Lincoln, to track down the hand-held 'Tetris' rights, but she couldn't determine who held them. Apparently Atari Games had bought its rights from Mirrorsoft, the London-based software group owned by Maxwell Communications, and Mirrorsoft claimed it had secured all 'Tetris' rights from the creators in the Soviet Union.

'They were giving us all sorts of bullshit,' says Howard Lincoln. 'We weren't getting anywhere.' The reaction from Mirrorsoft made Hvalsoe suspicious, and she reported to Arakawa that Mirrorsoft's ownership of the rights appeared dubious. This led Arakawa to send an emissary to the Soviet Union to attempt to contact the inventor of 'Tetris.'

Alexey Pajitnov had the build of a medium-sized bear. His face was framed by auburn hair and a harshly clipped beard. He had grown up in Moscow, where his father was an art and theater critic, and his mother wrote for newspapers and for a weekly cinema magazine. As a child, Pajitnov's passions were mathematics and movies. As a rare privilege of his mother's occupation, he was given passes to the yearly Moscow Film Festival, where he watched five movies a day, fifty in ten days. 'It was the only window to the outside,' he says. His other love, math, was expressed in playing games that involved geometry, algebra, and other systems of logic.

When Alexey was eleven his parents divorced. He lived with his mother in a one-room state-owned apartment. He was seventeen when they were able to acquire a private apartment in a modern, fourteen-story building at 49 Gersten Street, in a fancy neighborhood of embassies and hotels not far from the Arbat, Moscow's far humbler Champs-Élysées.

Apartment 106 was, by Moscow's bleak standards, spacious and airy, with two bedrooms, a fair-size living room, and a small kitchen with a view of St. Basil's Cathedral in Red Square. Bookshelf-lined walls were crowded with scientific books, computer manuals, classic novels in Russian, French, and English, and books on art and film. On other walls were framed prints of paintings by Monet, Renoir, Matisse, and Modigliani.

Alexey was a good student, particularly in math; when he was fourteen, he was a finalist in a citywide mathematics competition, and he spent the last three years of school in a specialized math program. During that time, in the summer he turned fifteen, he sat down in front of a computer for the first time and created his first program, a number game.

'Mathematicians are usually very strange people,' Pajitnov says. 'They are fully in their abstract worlds, and I was there with them.' But he had other interests too. With friends he played cards, drank beer or vodka, and headed to the countryside for camping expeditions. He hung out with girls and was in every way, he says, a 'normal schoolboy.'

After his university studies, Pajitnov took a position at the Moscow Institute of Aviation, a technical university, in the department of math applications. He enjoyed teaching there, but one day he abruptly quit. His passion for math had been replaced by something new: by the universe he discovered in computers, where the exploration of numbers, games, programming languages, and mathematical logic had no limits. Thereafter computers consumed him. 'It doesn't matter to a hacker what he is working on – it could be a game or an abstract math problem, but if a computer is involved, he is a god and can do whatever he wants inside that world.'

This new interest led to Pajitnov's next job, at the Computer Center of the Moscow Academy of Science, one of the Soviet government's preeminent R&D labs. His office at the Computer Center was in a wood-paneled room crowded with a dozen metal desks separated by chest-high partitions. There he hunkered over the keyboard of an archaic Soviet microcomputer, an Electronica 60, spending long days and many nights drinking black coffee, smoking unfiltered cigarettes, and exploring artificial intelligence and the capability of the computer to recognize the human voice. Inevitably, he also created games and puzzles.

To most of us, puzzles are a diversion, but for Alexey Pajitnov they are metaphors and mirrors that reflect nature, emotion, and patterns of thought. The young mathematician had turned to computers with the belief that they could model consciousness. Where better did electronics and humanity collide than in computer games? At their best, games were sublime examples of the intersection of logic and humanity. They worked because of logic and mathematics, but also because of psychology and emotion. The best games held in them a challenge, but also a reward and certain elemental experiences: discovery, recognition, frustration, and completion.

Inspiration for Pajitnov's games came at unexpected moments. Visiting an aquarium one day, he wandered past tanks of eels and seahorses, a shallow pool of starfish and anemones, and a large pool of rays, salmon, and sharks. He stopped in front of a tank of flatfishes and became transfixed there, staring at the liquid world of the flounder, plaice, and sole. The fish were barely distinguishable from the rocks, sand, and sea grasses on which they rested. When a plaice glided over white gravel, it metamorphosed before his eyes, as if its orange spots had been bleached white. A brown-speckled flounder floated over a bed of kelp and turned a soft green. Pajitnov was mesmerized as he contemplated using nature's splendid invention in a puzzle; he envisioned chameleon pieces that hid by altering their colors or shapes.

Another time, walking along a quiet boulevard, Pajitnov stopped to peruse a sidewalk display of imported knickknacks – porcelain dolls, paper umbrellas, and brass incense burners. From a clay pot he withdrew a Chinese fan. As he unfolded the pleats, what had been obscured was revealed: a crimson crane surrounded by golden flames. Laughing aloud, he imagined how fantastic it would be to re-create in a game the essential emotion of the experience – recognition.

Pajitnov had read about Pentominoes, geometric puzzles designed by an American mathematician named Solomon Golomb. The puzzle pieces were formed out of different configurations of five squares (a line, a 'T,' and 'L' shape, and so on). The pieces could be fitted together into a perfect rectangle. In a small toy shop, Pajitnov found a Pentomino puzzle. When he removed the dozen pieces from the rectangular case and mixed them up, he discovered that 'it was a big problem' to put them back. He imagined a computerized version of the game in which randomly generated pieces would appear one at a time and with intensifying rapidity. An electronic version of Pentomino would require very quick thinking. He envisioned the puzzle pieces plummeting down from computer heaven and the frantic attempt to arrange them.

Sitting in front of his computer, Pajitnov experimented with permutations of Pentomino and finally settled on a simpler version, with each piece made out of four instead of five squares. From *tetra*, a form of the Greek word for four, he named the game 'Tetris.'

There is a theory in psychology that humans can process seven things (plus or minus two) at once: seven digits, seven shapes, seven concepts. It is the reason most people can remember seven-digit phone numbers but have difficulty beyond that. It so happened that seven different configurations of the four squares were possible. Seven 'Tetris' shapes, Pajitnov reasoned, could be memorized and instantly recognized, and the reaction to any one of them could be almost visceral, reflexive.

Since the Electronica 60 had no graphics capabilities, Pajitnov's puzzle pieces were actually spaces outlined by brackets. Generated by the computer and sent onto the screen, they would descend slowly at the easiest levels, fast and furiously at the most difficult. The player had until they reached the screen's bottom to turn them or move them so that they would fit snugly into a solid row when they landed. If the pieces did fit perfectly together and an unbroken row was formed, it disintegrated: success! If any spaces were left unfilled, however, that row became the beginning of a wall that would grow until it overtook the screen.

Pajitnov realized his game would be more fun if the computer code were translated into real-time graphics – that is, if the brackets delineating the 'Tetris' pieces were replaced by the real, moveable shapes they represented. A young hacker named Vadim Gerasimov set out to create a color version of 'Tetris' that would play on IBM-compatible computers.

Gerasimov was sixteen years old at the time and was still attending high school, but he was so far ahead of his peers that his teachers allowed him to drop in for classes a couple of times a semester. Raised by his mother, a nuclear physicist, Gerasimov had a revelation when he got his hands on a computer for the first time. 'He saw the computer and forgot about the other world,' Alexey Pajitnov says.

The wiry-haired Gerasimov, with enormous blue eyes behind thick-lensed glasses, was bean-thin and tall, with a slight stoop, and often wore the same shapeless gray wool sweater. Another programmer named Dmitri Pevlovsky introduced him to Pajitnov, who put the young boy to work. Gerasimov had a knack for finding glitches in programs, and had technical skills that neither Pevlovsky nor Pajitnov possessed. He had taught himself to program with Microsoft's DOS operating system from the West. He knew the BASIC and PASCAL languages, and how to perform miscellaneous feats on computers, breaking supposedly unbreakable copy protections and ferreting out viruses. Computer Center scientists twice his age asked for his help on programs, occasionally slipping the boy a few rubles.

Gerasimov worked with Pajitnov for two months to convert 'Tetris' to work on an IBM-compatible computer. In the end, the 'Tetris' pieces lit up in solid colors. Pevlovsky added a table that tracked high scores. When the program was bug-free, he copied it and distributed disks throughout the Computer Center. His colleagues congratulated him on his brilliant and addictive program. A friend who worked at a psychology institute gave the game to his staff, but soon realized that not much work was getting done because of it. One night, after everyone had gone home, the man went from desk to desk collecting the 'Tetris' disks and destroyed them all.

All across Moscow the game was catching on in computer circles – 'like a wildfire,' says Pajitnov. In a computer-game competition held in Zelenodolsk, in November 1985, 'Tetris' took second prize.

Pajitnov worked on other programs, including one called Biographer, a sort of therapist in a box. Information about someone's life was fed into the program, which revealed behavioural patterns and, in a crude way, drew conclusions. The program was a simple implementation of the idea that a computer could be more objective and more patient than a human psychologist. Through early

1986, Pajitnov continued to work on Biographer and other explorations of simple artificial intelligence. In the meantime, he suggested to one of his superiors that something should be done with 'Tetris' outside the U.S.S.R. 'We had no copyright laws at all,' he says. 'Certainly, by the spirit of our law we had no right to sell anything to anyone. We could do nothing for personal gain.' It would, however, be a significant accomplishment to have a program published.

Victor Brjabrin, who oversaw twenty researchers at the Computer Center, was particularly enthusiastic about 'Tetris,' and he sent an evaluation copy of the game to SZKI, the Institute of Computer Science in Budapest. Hungarian-born Robert Stein, who ran Andromeda, a software company in London, happened to be visiting SZKI at the time.

Born in 1934, Stein arrived in Britain in 1956 as a political refugee. He first got work as an instrument- and toolmaker in London. Later he worked for Olivetti, selling adding machines, then left that business to sell mechanical check-writing machines while studying marketing at night. In business school he discovered that he was as good at training as he was at selling, and he got a job teaching engineers how to communicate with clients. He consulted in this field for a while, serving such major clients as Texas Instruments. After that he set up a company to sell TI calculators, and eventually sold digital watches and the first television game, Atari's 'Pong.' When that company went bankrupt, Stein founded a new company to sell chess computers to Harrods and other department stores. The business grew when he started selling Commodore's Vic 20 computer. He soon realized the computer sold in direct proportion to the amount of software available for it, which led him to the software business.

When Commodore was preparing to introduce their C-64, a more powerful computer, they asked Stein to return to Hungary in search of innovative software. In 1982 he helped establish a software company there with Hungarian engineers. To sell their games and business programs, Stein founded Andromeda, which kept 25 percent of whatever the Hungarian programs brought in.

From his London office, Stein sold the rights to Hungarian products to Commodore and software companies in England such as Mirrorsoft, and he made a number of deals with Jim Mackonochie, the man who ran Mirrorsoft for the Maxwells.

In June 1986, Stein was at SZKI in Budapest to see Hungarian programs when, on a nearby computer, he noticed 'Tetris.' He sat down to try the game and couldn't stop playing. 'I was not a game player,' he said, 'so if *I* liked it, it must be a very good game.' He asked the director of the institute where the game had come from, and was told that it had been sent by a friend at the Computer Center of the Academy of Science in Moscow.

The same day, Stein claims, he was shown another 'Tetris,' this one on a Commodore 64 and Apple II. It was the same game, Stein says he was told, adapted by Hungarian programmers. Although they had obviously converted the Russian program to the other machines, Stein says he told the Hungarians he would license the original PC game from the Russians and the Commodore and Apple versions from the Hungarians.

Back in London, Stein sent a cable to the Moscow Computer Center indicating that he was interested in 'Tetris.' Victor Brjabrin saw the telex and delivered it to Pajitnov. 'It looks like someone is interested in your game,' he said.

Since there was no one else to do it, Pajitnov began the negotiations himself. 'We had no idea what to do,' Pajitnov says. 'It was an absolutely new experience for us.'

Answering the telex was comically difficult. Pajitnov's English was a little sketchy, so he composed an answer in Russian and showed it to the chief of the computer center, Professor Ju. G. Evtushenko, who had to sign an approval to have it translated. He then had to figure out how to send it.

Pajitnov had no access to a telex machine, but he learned that there was one in another division of the Academy of Science that he might be able to use if he could gather the required authorizations. His requisition had to be approved by his supervisors and half a dozen others at the Academy. It was weeks before he could send back the simple answer: 'Yes, we are interested. We would like to have this deal.'

Stein was already shopping the game around. He had showed it to representatives of British and American software companies. His plan was to determine if there was interest, and then, if it seemed worth his while, to secure the rights; he assumed it would be easy to convince the Soviets to make a deal. As it happened it took more than a year finally to secure the rights to Tetris. On reflection, Mr Stein thought that it would have been easier to use the Commodore 64 version produced by the Hungarians as a master source.

Stein pitched 'Tetris' to Jim Mackonochie at Mirrorsoft and to an American software company, Broderbund, but neither company showed much interest in it. Mackonochie wasn't convinced the game would sell, so he showed it to the two men who ran Mirrorsoft's sister company in America, Spectrum Holobyte, telling them he would license 'Tetris' for Europe if they would do so for the United States and Japan.

Phil Adam and Gilman Louie ran the California-based Spectrum Holobyte, 80 percent of which was owned by Robert Maxwell's Pergamon Foundation. Adam, with impeccably trimmed hair and fingernails and perfectly matched casual clothing (wool sweaters, khaki slacks, and oxford-cloth shirts), was a smart and well-liked manager of Spectrum Holobyte, which was known for its flight simulators.

'Falcon,' created by Gilman Louie, a computer whiz, was one of the best flight-simulation games available for PCs, and it sold more than half a million copies. Spectrum Holobyte went on to create a host of other computer games, in addition to simulators for the military.

His tortoiseshell glasses pushed up on his thin nose, Adam sat down at three o'clock one afternoon in front of a computer on which 'Tetris' had been booted. At seven, dinner companions who had been waiting for him for an hour came and literally had to unplug the computer in order to drag him away.

Louie, tall and slender, his jet-black hair untamed, had thick-framed glasses and, behind them, a curious, decisive expression. He too played 'Tetris' and loved it. After conferring with Adam, he told Mackonochie, 'Put it in a red box and get the rights.'

According to Robert Stein, Mirrorsoft and Spectrum Holobyte bought all the 'Tetris' rights except for the arcade and hand-held versions. From these companies, Stein got a small advance – about 3,000 pounds – against a fluctuating royalty of between 7.5 and 15 percent.

In his next telex to the Soviets, sent on November 5, 1986, Stein offered a firm deal: the Russians would get 75 percent of whatever he collected for 'Tetris.' This sum would be a percentage of gross sales. He also offered a $10,000 advance.

Pajitnov responded favorably to the offer in a telex on November 13. Signed by the Computer Center's Evtushenko, it said that the Academy of Science was ready to transfer the copyright to Andromeda. In another telex, Stein had offered to pay the Computer Center, in part, with Commodore computers, and the Soviets agreed to this as well. They also noted that the deal was for the IBM-compatible version of 'Tetris' only; they would consider non-IBM versions of 'Tetris' in the future.

Alexey Pajitnov now claims he indicated only that the deal sounded good. He did not mean to give Stein a firm go-ahead. 'I had no idea that this kind of polite telex can be a document,' Pajitnov says. 'I think of a document as something very serious which needs to be signed, changed, and signed again; then you shake hands and drink champagne.'

Stein paved the way for the signing of a contract in telexes to Evtushenko. The Academy of Science's licensing group, Licensnauka Prasolov/AcademySoft, took over negotiations and sent Stein a cable in late December, inviting him to come to Moscow.

When, much later, Stein did visit Moscow, he arrived with plans to talk to the people at the Computer Center about establishing a relationship similar to the one he had in Hungary: he would act as agent to sell Soviet-created software in the West. His immediate concern was to leave with a signed legal contract that confirmed his rights to 'Tetris.'

He met with a group of the Soviets in a hall at the Academy, a cavernous, poorly heated, ill-lit room, as grim as anti-Soviet propaganda in the West would have painted it. Down the center of the room was a massive wooden slab, a table that could have seated fifty, across which Stein faced six Russians. One of them was Alexey Pajitnov, the chain-smoking creator of the game.

Trying to ally himself with Pajitnov, Stein said, 'Gentlemen, in our country the most important person is the one who designs the game. I'm here to listen to his wishes, because if we don't sign a contract, it is he who will suffer.'

Stein also tried, unsuccessfully, to hide his eagerness. The contract he had drawn up was on the table in front of him, ready for the Russians to sign, so he was unprepared to be met with suspicion. The Soviets were swimming in uncharted waters – software licensing was baffling – yet they made up for their naïveté with caution and obstinacy. If Stein offered 75 percent, they pushed for 80; if he offered $10,000, they held out for $25,000. They asked for protections and limitations. The details were hammered out over several days of meetings, but Stein, although he caved in to their demands for a higher advance and royalty, left Moscow without a signed contract.

The Russians had tried Stein's patience, and he wondered whether the Mirrorsoft and Spectrum Holobyte people should abandon the PC version and use the Commodore 64 version created by the Hungarian programmers, which they had licensed simultaneously with the PC version from the Russians. Stein later said that the biggest mistake he made was that this did not happen.

But it was too late for that. Mirrorsoft and Spectrum Holobyte had seen great value in the fact that 'Tetris' was the first game to come from behind the Iron Curtain, which was still intact at the time. As Gilman Louie had suggested, they slickly packaged 'Tetris' in a red box, emphasizing that it was from Russia with love. Atop an illustration of St. Basil's Cathedral, 'Tetris' was written in Cyrillic, the final character taking the form of a hammer and sickle. Programmers at Spectrum Holobyte in the United States added battle scenes as background pictures and a simple animation that played at the start of the game: a Cessna flew across the screen and landed in Red Square. It was a homage to Matthias Rust, the young West German pilot who had flown his small plane from Helsinki to Moscow, past all the Soviet radar and air defenses, and landed in Red Square, embarrassing the Central Committee. Rust had been arrested, tried, and imprisoned.

Other modifications to the program were made. One was the addition of a 'boss button' to some versions of 'Tetris'; when a certain key was pushed, the game instantly disappeared and the computer would appear to be running a serious accounting program. Also added were high-quality graphics, and, for computers with sound-generation capabilities, music.

In April 1987, Stein informed the Soviets that the rights to 'Tetris' had been sold to Mirrorsoft, the Maxwell Communications software company, and to its American counterpart, Spectrum Holobyte. He specifically noted that the rights were only for the IBM PC (and compatible) versions of 'Tetris.' By then he had given up plans to license separate Apple and Commodore versions of the game from Hungary, and he noted that there would be separate advances for those versions when they were launched. He pressed for a contract to be signed.

In June, Stein signed the contract he had negotiated among Andromeda, Mirrorsoft, and Spectrum Holobyte. The contract designated that he was selling the 'Tetris' rights for the IBM PC, although the rights included 'any other computer system.' In addition to warranting that the work had no obscene or indecent material, Stein confirmed that he was the rightful owner of the copyright, free to grant the license, although there was still no contract with the Soviets.

In a letter sent to the Academy of Science in December, Stein pleaded with the Soviets to confirm his rights to 'Tetris,' and offered 'to travel anywhere and meet anybody' in order to get a signed contract. If nothing else, he wrote, 'we need a simple letter stating that you approve the terms under which we have signed this contract with Mirrorsoft.'

Mirrorsoft and Spectrum Holobyte, unaware of Stein's troubles, released 'Tetris' for personal computers in Europe and America in January 1988. It sold well in computer stores and received rave reviews. A reviewer for *The Times Educational Supplement* quoted from the Mirrorsoft press material and wrote, 'Another "remarkably simple, addictive, abstract puzzle game" doesn't fill me with excitement, but the provenance of this one is interesting. It was invented by a 30-year-old researcher at the USSR Academy of Sciences. Coding was done on an IBM personal computer by a teenage student at Moscow University.' Many British computer journals heaped on praise. 'I warn you. The addictive power of "Tetris" is frightening,' a reviewer wrote. 'It sounds so simple that you cannot believe your abysmal score, so you try again and again; only a manic lunge at the reset switch can save you.' Another reviewer called it, 'a stonking good game,' reporting that it had been banned from the PCs at Mirrorsoft's central office, 'and no doubt it will be banned elsewhere.' Yet another reviewer concluded, 'There are very few games that are so addictive you find yourself playing them in your sleep, but "Tetris" did exactly that for me . . . After a poor night watching shapes float down past my closed eyelids, I had to be firm with myself and refuse to play it again for at least 48 hours. I cannot give a higher recommendation.'

In Moscow, meanwhile, Pajitnov was busy with his day-to-day tasks at the Computer Center. A version of Biographer was working well; he wondered if it could be sold as educational software. In discussions about it, he met with a newly created Soviet organization called Elorg – short for Electronorgtechnica, the ministry for the import and export of hardware and software. In his meeting with an Elorg director named Alexander (Sasha) Alexinko, Pajitnov mentioned the difficulties he was having licensing 'Tetris.' Alexinko interrupted him. Licensnauka and the Academy of Science shouldn't be negotiating at all, he said. They were academic institutions, which were forbidden to indulge in commerce. This was Elorg's domain, and Alexinko said he would take over the 'Tetris' negotiations.

Examining the communications between Moscow and London, Alexinko concluded that Pajitnov had blundered in his negotiations, and that his telexes could have been misinterpreted. Now the inventor became the target of blame. 'You allowed this game to be published without our approval,' he was told. 'We must stop it now.'

Stein, further and further out on a limb, having sold the rights to a game he didn't own, now heard from Elorg. It was taking over 'Tetris' negotiations, and his deal was off. The Soviets were going to take over the international sale of 'Tetris' directly.

Backed into a corner, Stein composed a carefully worded memo to Moscow. He threatened to create a scandal for the Soviets. It would look very bad, he said, if the Soviet state stopped a commercial deal at this point; it would be extremely embarrassing in the international community. On the other hand, here was a chance, he pointed out, to begin an alliance that could be politically and economically significant. A deal had to be consummated.

Stein and Elorg tested one another with tentativeness, straining over minor points, but finally agreed that a deal could be made. Stein flew to Moscow to meet with Elorg's Alexinko in late February 1988. On February 24, a written contract was proposed that included a stipulation that Elorg had to approve any versions of 'Tetris' created in the West. It also gave Andromeda the right to adapt 'Tetris' to 'different types of computers.'

Stein and the Soviets negotiated for four days to finalize a contract. Even after this there was long-distance fine-tuning for several months until finally, after almost two years' worth of draft agreements, one was signed in May 1988. Stein breathed an enormous sigh of relief: he had successfully confirmed his exclusive rights to sell 'Tetris' for computers. In a memo, he told Mirrorsoft that the contract included 'TV games,' but excluded coin-op (arcade), hand-held games, and other concepts 'which we did not dream about yet.'

In the meantime, 'Tetris' had become the best-selling game in England and the United States, publicized by word of mouth and on computer networks. In the United States, in 1988 'Tetris' received the Software Publishers Association award in two categories: Best Original Game Achievement and Best Entertainment Program.

An article about 'Tetris' from a London computer magazine reached Elorg in Moscow. It described the version of 'Tetris' that was being sold in the West. It mentioned the graphics – the battle scenes and the image of Matthias Rust flying his plane across the Russian sky and into Red Square. Alexinko showed the article to Pajitnov, who was amused by the reference to Rust. He was not amused, however, by the battle scenes. Pajitnov had come to view 'Tetris' as a small but meaningful bridge between cultures at a time when the Cold War was thawing. 'Tetris' was a game of the intellect, completely nonviolent. He informed Stein that he wanted 'Tetris' to be 'a peaceful game heralding a new era in the relationship between superpowers and their attitude toward world peace.' The bureaucrats in Moscow were far more concerned about the reference to Rust. The Central Committee viewed the young pilot as a terrorist and did not consider the invasion of its air space a practical joke. Broadcast around the world, Rust's 'raid' had been a great humiliation.

The Soviets expressed their 'grave concerns' in their next meeting with Stein, who immediately contacted Jim Mackonochie. 'It would be useful if all battle scenes, as background pictures, would disappear,' he wrote, 'and planes flying across the title screen . . . would be omitted.' As a result, Mackonochie and Gilman Louie revised their games again.

Stein felt the Soviets had to be placated as much as possible if he was going to be able to obtain other 'Tetris' rights that Mirrorsoft wanted, particularly the coin-operated and hand-held rights. Atari Games was already preparing to release its own 'Tetris' arcade game in America, and it had sold the rights to Sega to release the arcade game in Japan. (Mirrorsoft had gone ahead and sold Atari Games the right to do this based on Stein's assurance that they were forthcoming.) Stein, however, was in the midst of another sluggish negotiation. He had made a firm offer for the coin-operated rights in July 1988 – a guarantee of $30,000 as an advance against royalties – but there had been no response.

Stein telexed a month later, noting that he was being 'pressurised' and needed an agreement by mid-August.

Alexinko met with Stein in Paris on July 5. While Stein pushed for more rights, especially the coin-op rights, the Russian had another agenda. He intended to register his dissatisfaction with the results of the deal that had already been signed because no checks were coming in from Andromeda.

Stein explained that it took time for money to be dispersed from company to company, but promised he would do what he could to expedite the royalty payment process. Alexinko wanted a penalty for late payments to be agreed upon, and threatened to withhold any new rights until the situation was remedied.

More telexes were fired back and forth between Stein and Alexinko after they had returned to their home bases. Stein implored the Russians to grant him the coin-op deal, while Alexinko, responding in a tersely worded telex, indicated that the existing deal was not satisfactory 'because no payment is effective yet,' even though 'Tetris' had been 'more than six months on the market.'

In another telex he asked Stein to add a clause to the original agreement that stated that a 5 percent fee would be charged monthly for late payments. Alexinko insisted that this clause was important 'to expedite the positive decision' regarding the 'Tetris' coin-op rights.

Stein sent word that he agreed, and once again begged Alexinko to sign a coin-op contract because 'someone will steal the product from under our noses.'

Typically, a company that licenses a game will exploit those rights as much as possible with sublicenses to other companies for other markets. Spectrum Holobyte and Mirrorsoft had a hit game on their hands, and it was not surprising that they set about to sell all the sub-rights they could. The chart of 'Tetris' licenses and sublicenses was beginning to look like a tangled family tree.

Henk Rogers, who had seen Spectrum Holobyte's computer game at an electronics trade show in January 1988, went after the rights to release the game in Japan on computers, video-game systems, and coin-op arcade machines. Since Spectrum Holobyte had been granted the rights for Japan in the deal with Stein, Rogers negotiated with Gilman Louie. Two separate deals – one for computer-game (floppy-disk) rights, another for video-game rights – were agreed upon. Rogers also wanted the coin-op game rights, but discussions for these were put on hold.

The day after Rogers signed a deal with Spectrum Holobyte for computer-game 'Tetris' rights for Japan, which was the day *before* he was to sign a deal for the Japanese home video-game rights, Gilman Louie called Jim Mackonochie in England to report on the deal. Mackonochie 'had a fit,' Louie remembers. The Mirrorsoft chief told Louie it was impossible for Spectrum to go ahead; he had already sold those rights to Atari Games. Hide Nakajima was getting 'Tetris' rights to North America and Japan in exchange for worldwide rights to an Atari game called 'Blastroids.'

Gilman Louie hit the roof. 'What are you talking about?' he shouted. 'Those are *my rights*!'

Louie argued that not only were all the Japanese and American 'Tetris' rights his, not Mirrorsoft's, but Mackonochie was making a terrible deal; 'Blastroids' was an atrocious game. Besides, he said, he had made a terrific deal with Henk Rogers.

Mackonochie explained that there was nothing Louie could do. The Maxwells had financial control of both Mirrorsoft and Spectrum Holobyte, but both men knew that the family had far greater interest in Mirrorsoft, which was personally overseen by Robert Maxwell's son Kevin. Kevin Maxwell supported Mackonochie's deal, so Louie was out of luck.

Louie insisted that he at least had to honor the deal he had already signed; Henk Rogers had to be able to have the sublicense for the floppy-disk game in Japan. Since it was the least valuable of the rights under discussion, Mackonochie agreed.

Atari Games' agreement with Mirrorsoft was not actually signed until May 30, 1988, only two weeks after Stein's initial deal with the Russians was signed. Hide Nakajima planned to exploit the 'Tetris' rights in as many ways as possible. In the United States he planned to release both a coin-op 'Tetris' and an NES version under the Tengen label, and he planned to sublicense these rights in Japan.

Gilman Louie called Henk Rogers to apologize; he explained that unbeknownst to him, Atari Games had been awarded the 'Tetris' video-game rights for Japan and the United States. Rogers's floppy-disk rights were secure, but if he wanted the other Japanese rights, he would have to negotiate with Atari Games.

Rogers tried, contacting Randy Broweleit and Hide Nakajima. Broweleit said the coin-op rights for Japan were gone; they had been sold to Sega. Dejected, Rogers said he would at least like to secure the rights for 'Tetris' on Japanese home video-game systems, including Nintendo's Famicom. What, he asked, would he have to do for these?

Broweleit was noncommittal, so Rogers went directly to Nakajima. The two men had dinner on August 16, 1988. It took until October to hammer out a deal. As far as he knew, Rogers had finally sewn up the rights to sell 'Tetris' in Japan, not only for computers but also for the far bigger market, Nintendo's Famicom and other home video-game systems.

Now Rogers headed to London for a meeting at Mirrorsoft. He brought videotape copies of versions of 'Tetris' for the Russians to approve. After the meeting, Rogers returned to Japan, where he received a faxed go-ahead to produce his game from a Mirrorsoft attorney.

Rogers's 'Tetris' for PCs was launched in Japan in November 1988. A month later he shipped his version for the Famicom. Tetrismania quickly swept Japan, just as it had the United States. Two million copies of the game were sold there.

By now Minoru Arakawa had decided that he wanted 'Tetris' for Game Boy. His lawyers had figured out that Mirrorsoft was probably tap-dancing around the fact that it didn't have the rights; indeed, it was possible that no one owned the hand-held rights. That is when Arakawa decided it might be beneficial to try other avenues to get the game. In a meeting with Henk Rogers, Arakawa made an offer. If Rogers could get the hand-held rights, NOA would take out a sublicense from him. Rogers was let in on the still-secret reason that Arakawa wanted 'Tetris': he was shown a prototype of Game Boy.

For all Rogers's impressive insight into game play, he was sharp about the business side of video games as well. When Arakawa challenged him to get the hand-held rights to 'Tetris,' the younger man viewed it for what it was: a potential fortune. 'If you've met Rogers, you know that he is capable of finding his way in the middle of any storm,' Howard Lincoln says. 'Telling him that we were ready to license from him was like showing red meat to a hungry lion.'

Henk Rogers faxed Robert Stein in London on November 15, 1988. He wanted to bid for the worldwide hand-held rights to 'Tetris.' Stein responded that he was trying to get the rights from Elorg, but the agency had not made a decision about them. He was close to pinning them down, however, and would get back to him.

Stein immediately wrote Jim Mackonochie. 'We must go for those rights immediately,' he said. But Stein had new worries. In late 1988 he received a telex that informed him that Sasha Alexinko had been replaced at Elorg. The reasons for his departure were unclear – he ended up leaving Elorg to found his own trading company, and there was speculation that he used his government work to set up the company – but there was nothing ambiguous about the character of his replacement, the vice-director of Elorg,

Evgeni Nikolaevich Belikov. Belikov, large-framed, slightly balding, and red-cheeked, was described by some who knew him as vicious, cutthroat, and bullheaded, and by others as savvy, amiable, and razor-sharp. All, however, agreed that he was a worthy adversary in any negotiation.

In late 1988 Belikov became the man to charm, outmaneuver, or otherwise win over in all future 'Tetris' deals. It was easier said than done. As Alexey Pajitnov discovered, 'He is an excellent actor.' Stein found him 'instantly dislikable; a creep.'

Rogers continued to try to push Stein to get him the hand-held 'Tetris' rights. Many calls, letters, and faxes later, however, he came to the conclusion that Stein was useless. His only chance to get the rights was to head directly to Moscow, which he did, in February. But he wasn't the only one to do so.

Kevin Maxwell helped run his father's empire, then thought to be the tenth-largest media concern in the world. In addition to newspapers with circulations that totaled in the tens of millions, he looked over such companies as Marquis, Thomas Cook Travel, Berlitz language schools, and MTV Europe. He also oversaw Maxwell's electronic-media companies – that is, on-line networks and the computer software company Mirrorsoft. This made him Jim Mackonochie's boss.

Kevin, a graduate of Balliol College at Oxford and a serious, morose workaholic, had spent his entire life working in the family companies. His brother Ian Maxwell had once lost his job with the Maxwell organization because he chose to meet a girlfriend in Paris rather than show up at the airport for a meeting with his father. That was a choice Kevin Maxwell would never have thought to make.

Like his father, Kevin tended to be inaccessible when his top executives needed his input, though he would meddle on a whim. And, like his father, he was short-fused and inclined to tantrums, tending to jump when it might have been prudent to think.

From the beginning, Kevin Maxwell had kept tabs on the 'Tetris' negotiations in consultation with Jim Mackonochie. When negotiations got so bogged down that Mackonochie decided to go to

Moscow himself, Maxwell stepped in. He was going to Moscow anyway, he said, and he could easily straighten things out with the Soviets.

Robert Stein, frustrated because he couldn't nail down the rights to 'Tetris' for hand-held or coin-operated games, worried because there were already coin-operated versions being sold in the United States and Japan, and under pressure from Henk Rogers, realized that he also had to head to Moscow again. Unbeknownst to one another, the three men flew to the U.S.S.R. at exactly the same time.

THE 'TETRIS' SONG

11

Alexey Pajitnov could tell instantly that Henk Rogers was a man after his own heart. Of all of those he had dealt with, from Stein to the bureaucrats at Elorg, Rogers was the only one who seemed to truly love 'Tetris.' He was a hacker, he spoke the language of games, and he understood the pure beauty of the 'Tetris' design.

Elorg and the Academy both hoped to establish a relationship with someone from the West other than Robert Stein. Of course they also wished to make as much money as they could, so when Rogers appeared in Moscow, after tracking down Pajitnov through chess players and computer hackers, the Russians had a second bidder and leverage against Stein.

For his part, Rogers was surprised by how naive the Soviets were about licensing deals. 'Whoever they had been doing business with obviously didn't explain what the world looked like,' he says. The jargon was unfamiliar to them, and he could have snowed them. At their first meeting at Elorg, he accepted the coffee the Soviets offered. Sounds echoed in the unadorned, chilly room. Rogers did most of the talking. Before he knew it, he was walking the Soviets through the video-game business as if he was teaching a course.

When the meeting ended, Pajitnov and Rogers struck up a conversation and ended up having dinner together at a restaurant. Then Pajitnov invited Rogers back to his apartment to show off other software he had been working on. It was an evening of frank discussion and good cheer. Pajitnov, suspicious of all the Westerners trying to get pieces of 'Tetris,' found that 'the most important thing about Henk was that he didn't ask for protection in the deal. He offered me nothing and asked for nothing.'

The following day, at Elorg, Rogers presented an offer for the hand-held rights to 'Tetris.' The deal was ironed out within a few days, and signatures confirmed it on February 21.

Delighted, Rogers promised an advance check right away. He also assured the Russians that the royalties would be significant; hand-held 'Tetris' would bring them a substantial amount of money.

In a celebratory mood, he mentioned that he had brought with him a copy of the home video-game version of 'Tetris' he was selling in Japan. The Russians looked at one another dumbfounded as he produced from his briefcase the brightly packaged Nintendo game cartridge and proudly passed it around the room.

Sitting on the edge of his seat, Nikolai Belikov spoke first. 'What is this game?' he asked.

Rogers explained that it was his 'Tetris' game for the Famicom, the video-game system made by Nintendo in Japan.

The Russians had never heard of Nintendo.

Rogers reminded the group that they had seen and approved a videotape of the game.

Belikov shook his head. 'We have approved nothing. We never licensed anybody to make this!' he snapped.

The mirth evaporated, and Rogers realized he was in trouble. Stammering, he told the Soviets, 'But I bought those rights from Tengen. I paid lots of money for them!'

Belikov's fists rested on the table. 'We don't know this company Tengen,' he said. 'We do not understand.'

It dawned on Rogers that the license he had bought from Atari Games/Tengen to market 'Tetris' for the Famicom was, as he said later, 'a sham.'

Rogers now recounted to the Soviets his negotiations for the home video-game rights that began with Spectrum Holobyte and ended when he was told that Atari held the rights. He said he had negotiated with Atari over the course of more than six months, and reported that Atari had announced that it was releasing a home video-game version of 'Tetris' for the Nintendo system in America. But there was more: Atari had also sold a company called Sega the rights to create an arcade version of 'Tetris' in Japan.

The Soviets were speechless. 'An arcade game has been sold?' Belikov asked. Rogers nodded.

Belikov finally spoke in Russian, uttering instructions to an assistant, who disappeared for a few minutes while Belikov told Rogers, 'We have not licensed anyone to make "Tetris" on home video-game systems or coin-operated games. I will show you.'

The assistant returned with a tall stack of documents, which he set on the table. Belikov flipped through the papers until he came to a copy of Elorg's contract with Robert Stein. He pored over the pages for a few minutes, and when he found what he had been looking for, set the document on the table and pointed with his forefinger to the paragraph explicitly stating that the rights granted to Robert Stein's Andromeda Software were for the IBM PC and other computer systems.

Rogers was as shocked as the Soviets were, but his immediate concern was to hold on to the video-game rights that he had just secured. He said he must have been lied to, and that he wanted to make things right with the Russians; pending negotiations, he would pay them directly for all the games he had sold so far.

Belikov indicated that this offer was acceptable, but that they would adjourn for the day. Rogers was to return in the morning, and an arrangement would be negotiated then.

When Rogers returned the next day, he came with exact calculations of the number of Famicom cartridges he had sold and offered to pay what amounted to a second royalty on the 130,000 cartridges. He immediately wrote a check for $40,712, representing a portion of that.

Meetings continued for the next few days, during which Rogers examined the Soviets' documents on the deal with Andromeda. He was convinced that the Russians had never – intentionally, at least – sold the video-game rights. The upshot of the meetings was an offer from Belikov: Rogers had three weeks to determine whether he wanted to make a proposal directly to them for *all* the home video-game rights to 'Tetris.'

Rogers warned, 'There will be trouble.' The companies that were selling 'Tetris' rights with abandon – Mirrorsoft and Atari Games – were heavyweights. He said he had a plan: he would return with a partner who not only had an enormous amount of money but clout enough to fight them. This partner, the company that had control of the largest market for video games in the world, was Nintendo.

Robert Stein had raced to the Elorg office that morning in a taxi from the Hotel Kosmos. Exhausted from travel and from the prospect of renewed negotiations, he waited obediently in a small room, where a rickety table held only a pitcher of water and a glass.

Finally Belikov, Elorg's new negotiator, stormed into the room. He refused to engage in small talk, but simply threw a document in front of Stein and told him to sign it.

Stein asked what it was. 'We already have a contract,' he pointed out.

Belikov explained that this was an amendment to the contract. Confused, Stein said he didn't understand; he was in Moscow to negotiate for the hand-held and coin-op rights to 'Tetris,' not to sign a new contract.

Belikov held firm; he would continue negotiations only if Stein signed the paper.

Stein examined it. It was an addendum that noted that it and the original contract were to be read as one. Concentrating on the payment schedules and fluctuating percentages, Stein's eye skipped over one line that defined computers, as referred to in the original contract, as 'PC computers which consist of a processor, monitor, disk drive(s), keyboard and operation system.' He was told that the one-page document – alteration no. 1 – was to amend the contract signed the previous May, which was why it had been backdated to May 10, 1988; it would be effective as of that date.

Stein returned to his hotel to study the amendment. It seemed to him that the most important item was about the assessment of penalties for late payments of royalties. He knew the Russians were concerned that money had not arrived frequently enough. The amendment was, in these circumstances, understandable. Though he read and reread the paper, he was unconcerned about the innocuous line clarifying the definition of computers. Later he deduced that everything in the document *other* than this line was 'a smoke screen.'

'Henk Rogers orchestrated it for Nintendo,' Stein believes. 'He advised the Russians.' The charade was all designed to take away most of his rights and offer them to Nintendo, which swooped in and snatched them.

Stein returned to the Elorg office the following day. He had no problem with the amendment, he announced, but said that he would not sign it unless the deals for the other rights were made. It was the only leverage he had. He had drawn up by hand an offer for the coin-operated and hand-held 'Tetris' rights, and he presented it to Belikov. In the document he included minimum guaranteed sales, advances, and percentages of royalties, but it was, Stein says, 'a mockery. They knew what they were going to do before I arrived.' He was told he could not secure hand-held rights at this moment, but he could have the coin-operated rights. He would have to pay dearly for them; within six weeks he had to come up with an advance of $150,000 or the deal would be off. He signed the contract and the amendment two days later, on February 24, 1989.

Oozing charm and self-importance, Kevin Maxwell was also at Elorg on February 22, meeting with the Soviets in a small room. He, Stein, and Rogers might well have run into one another in an Elorg hallway that day. After small talk, Maxwell asked Belikov why the deal for coin-operated and hand-held 'Tetris' rights was taking so long to settle. But Belikov had another agenda. Reaching into a sack, he withdrew, as a magician might reveal a rabbit from a hat, a video-game cartridge and placed it on the table. 'What is this, Mr. Maxwell?' he asked.

Maxwell reached for the cartridge – Henk Rogers's Japanese video-game version of 'Tetris' – and examined it. He had no idea that his own company had licensed the game via a sublicense to Atari Games, so he shrugged. Then the Russian asked him to look at the copyright notice on the cartridge. It read 'Elorg, Mirrorsoft, and Tengen.'

Maxwell said that Mirrorsoft had not licensed home video-game rights to 'Tetris,' so the cartridge must be a pirated game.

It was a crucial error. As a result, the Russians decided once and for all that they could maintain that Mirrorsoft had no right to the home video-game version of 'Tetris.'

Unaware of the gravity of the situation, Maxwell returned to his own agenda, the coin-op and hand-held 'Tetris' rights. Belikov excused himself and disappeared for a while. When he returned, he told Maxwell that he would sign a 'protocol agreement' promising Mirrorsoft the right of first refusal on ancillary rights to 'Tetris' – including coin-op, hand-held, and merchandising rights – contingent on Maxwell's assurance that he would make an offer for the video-game rights within one week. 'We must clear up the matter of this pirated cartridge,' Belikov said. 'Therefore we must have a deal within a week.'

A protocol agreement was signed guaranteeing Mirrorsoft the right to bid on all remaining 'Tetris' rights, even though the coin-op and hand-held rights were simultaneously being granted to Henk Rogers and Robert Stein. In exchange Elorg would get the rights to publish in the Soviet Union Maxwell Communications properties, such as *Collier's Encyclopedia* and other reference books. The Soviets may not have known much about the video-game business, but they demonstrated their uniquely effective method of negotiating. Their juggling of Rogers, Stein, and Maxwell had put them back in a position of complete control.

The upshot of Belikov's busy week was a deal for the hand-held rights for 'Tetris' with Henk Rogers, plus a chance for a new deal within three weeks on the home video-game rights with Nintendo. He had a signed deal for coin-operated 'Tetris' with Stein and the promise of a check for $150,000. Kevin Maxwell had given Elorg more than the rights to publish Maxwell Communications reference books: he had characterized the 'Tetris' game his company had licensed as a pirated game instead of insisting that Mirrorsoft had licensed the games from rights it held – thus supporting Elorg's position that it had never sold the video-game rights in the first place. If Mirrorsoft wanted those rights now, it would have to outbid Nintendo. It was not a bad week's work.

A letter was drafted to Henk Rogers on February 24 confirming that Elorg had not granted anyone the license 'to make, have made, duplicate, market, distribute, sell or in any way use' 'Tetris' for use on 'video games or TV games or game consoles, which are defined as computers which have no keyboard.'

Looking back on the week in Moscow after the fact, Robert Stein said that his only satisfaction was knowing he emerged from the meetings with the coin-op rights while Kevin Maxwell emerged with nothing but worthless paper. Otherwise, he said, the week was a disaster, the product of lying, cheating, and backstabbing. It was impossible, he said, for the Russians not to know about the BPS Nintendo game before Rogers showed it to them; he claimed he had provided Elorg with a copy of Rogers's videotape back in December 1988. He concluded that he had been set up, and that the amendment, the lies, and Kevin Maxwell's admission about the Japanese 'Tetris' cartridge all cleared a path for the Russians to double-deal him. 'I was set up because of stupidity,' he says, 'but also because I was under tremendous pressure to walk away with a contract for coin-operated games because Atari Games and Sega were already selling them all over the world without a contract.' He insists that Jim Mackonochie and Mirrorsoft had put him in the position of 'signing my life away' by knowingly selling rights they didn't own, and that he was forced to cover Mackonochie's tracks.

Bitterly, Stein says, 'I will never know if Jim Mackonochie is a good friend or if he knew he was screwing me. Maybe he was just a corporate animal. The fact is, he went right behind my back. I was fighting for my bloody life and he screwed me, acting as if the coin-op license was already theirs, so that if I didn't get it for them I would be sued out of existence. Then' – he shakes his head wearily – 'he concealed from me the fact that Kevin Maxwell was in the next room burying me, burying us all.' Now Stein finally understood why Belikov kept disappearing in the middle of their meetings.

* * *

Henk Rogers tied matters up in Moscow and quickly returned home, where he called Minoru Arakawa. His news was better than anyone could have hoped for. First, he had the hand-held rights to 'Tetris' for Game Boy. (He retained the rights to sell 'Tetris' on other electronic hand-held machines, such as the Sharp Wizard.) Reportedly he would receive $1 for every 'Tetris' sold with a Game Boy system, and more for games sold separately. This deal was worth between $5 million and $10 million to Rogers.

Best for Nintendo, however, was the news that the Russians claimed never to have sold the 'Tetris' home video-game rights to anyone. The rights that Robert Stein had sold to Mirrorsoft and that Mirrorsoft had sold to Atari Games and BPS were, according to the Russians, bogus.

Rogers was covered whatever happened – he had Japanese 'Tetris' rights from Atari Games or Nintendo, whoever ended up with them – but the beauty of the new development was that Nintendo could almost certainly have 'Tetris' for the rest of the world's home game machines.

There were no second thoughts: he and Arakawa would do whatever it took to get the home video-game rights.

Lincoln and Arakawa decided to send Rogers back to Moscow, this time with a lawyer. Lincoln called around and learned about John Huhs, a New York attorney who had worked in the Soviet Union. Huhs, who had been part of the Nixon White House, spoke fluent Russian, and, although he knew nothing about video games, was a talented international lawyer. Lincoln gave him a crash course on the phone before Huhs set out to meet Rogers, who was already en route back to Moscow.

After an initial meeting at Elorg, Rogers and Huhs made an offer for the home video-game rights to 'Tetris' on behalf of Nintendo. Included in the offer was an astronomical guarantee. The tough Soviet negotiators betrayed amazement over the figure. Arakawa wanted to be sure of clinching the deal; no one – not Atari Games, not even Robert Maxwell – was likely to touch the number he had authorized Huhs and Rogers to offer.

The same day, March 15, Elorg sent a telex to Mirrorsoft, noting that Mirrorsoft had promised to give Elorg its proposal for home video-game rights to 'Tetris' within a week of the meeting with

Kevin Maxwell in Moscow. As it was well past that week and Elorg had a competing proposal valid only until March 16, Mirrorsoft had one day to make an offer.

By design there was no chance for a Mirrorsoft bid. Elorg had elicited it in such a way as to address Maxwell's right of first refusal because it had been guaranteed in the protocol agreement. As planned, there was no response within that day, and so the path was cleared for Nintendo. Rogers and Huhs placed a call to Redmond. Huhs was convinced the deal could be signed and sealed if Lincoln and Arakawa could come to Moscow by Monday. He said they should head first to Washington, where their visas would be waiting at the Soviet consulate.

Arakawa and Lincoln told only Peter Main and Phil Rogers where they were going, for they were concerned that Atari Games would discover their destination. Everyone else at Nintendo thought they were going to Japan. To reach the consulate before it closed for the weekend, they had to fly to Los Angeles from Seattle and then take a red-eye to Washington. Arriving there at dawn, they checked into a hotel, showered, dressed, and hopped a cab for the office of the Russian consul general. There, in the visa office, the agent in charge had never heard of an Arakawa, or a Lincoln, or Nintendo. There had been no communication from Moscow, and without it a visa could not be given. All the Nintendo chiefs could do was wait. At 4:00 P.M. a telex finally arrived authorizing the issuance of visas.

There was just enough time to dash to the airport and catch the next flight to London, another red-eye. They passed out on the plane and awoke as it touched down at Heathrow, where it was now late afternoon. There was an evening to kill in London before the next flight to Moscow.

The two retired after dinner. Lincoln said he would ring Arakawa's room at 7:00 A.M. so they could catch the nine-thirty flight. But he slept through his wake-up call, stirring at about eight. When he realized the time, he frantically called Arakawa. The two threw their clothes in their bags and raced to the airport, where they sprinted through the terminal and tried to blast through the security checkpoint.

A bevy of security guards approached them. It was the first time they had paused to look at each other. They were unshaven, their hair was tousled, and Lincoln was wearing his pajama top under his suit jacket.

Fast talking got them past the security checkpoint and they got to the plane just as the door was about to be closed. The two looked as if they were on the lam from a madhouse.

They slept on the flight to Moscow that Sunday, March 19, 1989. Rogers and Huhs met them at the airport. Rogers, who had rented a black Mercedes 190, maneuvered the car through Moscow while Arakawa and Lincoln stared at the passing scenery, the heavy-coated pedestrians, and the surprisingly European architecture. It seemed like a film of New York in the 1940s.

Rogers told Arakawa and Lincoln that he had managed to find a Japanese exporter who had a fax machine they could use. He also had a portable computer and printer set up in his hotel room. He said he and Huhs would meet them the next morning at Elorg – he supplied the address on a piece of paper – and then dropped off his exhausted passengers.

At the front desk, Arakawa was informed that rooms were unavailable but that he and Lincoln needn't worry; the hotel would put them in an apartment in an adjacent building. It had a disconnected stove, a refrigerator missing a door, a ragged sofa, and, down a musty hallway, a small bedroom. They looked at the single bed and, without uttering a word, pulled out their wallets, slid out dollar bills, and played liar's poker. Arakawa lost and got the couch.

Despite their fatigue, the two men left the apartment in order to stock up on supplies and soon found what they were looking for: a liquor store with the crucial provisions. Their arms loaded with Heineken and cognac, they returned to their room, where they drank until Lincoln retired to the bedroom and Arakawa passed out on the couch.

In the morning, after rendezvousing with Huhs and Rogers, Lincoln and Arakawa were escorted into a conference room with high ceilings and shaded windows at Elorg's office. There they were introduced to the game's designer, Alexey Pajitnov, the Elorg chief, Nikolai Belikov, and some of his associates. Pajitnov attempted to size up Arakawa and Lincoln, but they were 'like people from another planet.' Lincoln was stoic, immune to Pajitnov's joking and teasing; Arakawa was introverted and inaccessible. But because of their alliance with Henk Rogers, Pajitnov was inclined to trust them and was their ally throughout the first meeting.

Although he had tried to talk fishing with Belikov and one of his assistants, once the major issues were on the table, Howard Lincoln was neither chatty nor amiable. Money was not the most important issue for the Nintendo team. They were more concerned with Stein's and Mirrorsoft's claims to the home video-game rights. Lincoln needed assurance that the Russians had never meant to sell those rights to Andromeda or anyone else. Satisfied with the answers, he said emphatically several times that he had to be absolutely certain that the Soviets would commit to the deal and stick with it to the end, and that the Russians had to be prepared for a variety of counterattacks from Andromeda, Mirrorsoft, and Atari Games. Arakawa sat by patiently, his hands folded on the table.

The Soviets had come prepared with copies of all the letters, telexes, and contract proposals, in addition to the signed contracts with Stein and Andromeda. Lincoln examined them. One document was worth all the others: the amendment Robert Stein had signed that defined a computer. The NES was without a 'monitor, disk drive(s), keyboard and operation system.' It was not a computer.

The Russians eagerly broached new business with Nintendo. Glasnost had begun, and partnerships with the West in the form of joint-venture companies were being encouraged by the government. Belikov said that they wished to form a partnership with Nintendo, a joint venture that would provide NOA with terrific new video games like 'Tetris.'

Lincoln suggested that they complete one negotiation at a time.

Next the Soviets asked why they couldn't manufacture the 'Tetris' cartridges themselves.

'That's not what we had in mind,' said Lincoln. 'Nintendo manufactures all the cartridges.'

The Russians then said they wanted to make Nintendo systems themselves and sell them in the U.S.S.R.

'We make them in Japan, thank you.'

To impress the men from Nintendo with Russia's engineering prowess, an Elorg representative brought out a small box. 'Our people made this,' he said.

Arakawa opened it. Inside was a Game & Watch that played 'Donkey Kong.' There was no sign of Nintendo's name or trademark on the watch. Arakawa politely complimented the Soviets on the product.

After the initial meeting, Arakawa and Lincoln took Huhs, Rogers, and Alexey Pajitnov out for dinner at the only Japanese restaurant in Moscow. It had no liquor license, so a waitress was dispatched to a store and returned with several large bottles of beer.

When a plate of sushi arrived, Pajitnov's first, he tried a small bite. Arakawa explained that sushi should be eaten a whole piece at a time. Bravely Pajitnov tried some *toro*, the fatty tuna belly set on a tiny brick of rice, carefully balancing it on his chopsticks and maneuvering it into his mouth. The taste was surprisingly pleasant, he found. He got more proficient with the utensils as he tried yellowtail, eel, crab, and *tamago*, a miniature omelette set on rice. Then he attacked a gluey green ball on his plate and popped it into his mouth as his companions, in a chorus, shrieked, '*No!*' They were too late; Pajitnov had downed a mound of *wasabi*, the wildly hot horseradish meant to be used in small amounts to spice the soy sauce for dipping. He felt a stinging explosion in his nostrils and behind his eyeballs, which vibrated as if they were ready to launch from his head. He tried to drown out the burning with beer, but in vain.

Arakawa couldn't hold back his laughter. Rogers joined him, and soon the others did too while Pajitnov wiped the tears that streamed from his eyes. He had better luck managing the courses that followed: *shabu shabu*, ginger fish, and vinegared seaweed, all washed down with beer.

After dinner, the party shifted to Pajitnov's apartment to see a new game he had created which he planned to sell through a joint-venture company in Moscow. Lincoln was concerned that the game, 'Welltris,' might be derivative of 'Tetris,' and that perhaps he should sew up the rights to it as well. Arakawa was more interested in seeing a Russian apartment; he had come equipped with a Game Boy for Alexey's children.

When they all entered the Gersten Street building and got into the elevator, Arakawa and Lincoln exchanged glances as it began its creaking, unstable ascent. Below them, the elevator shaft could be seen between the floorboards, and Lincoln pressed himself against a wall in an effort to keep his weight off the elevator floor. When they reached their destination, the elevator doors opened three or so precarious feet below the landing, and everyone had to climb up to reach the floor.

Inside the cheery apartment, Pajitnov's wife, Nina, served icy vodka and Russian brandy. Both Arakawa and Lincoln had questions to ask about life in Moscow, and the Pajitnovs were happy to answer them while their eldest child, Peter, played his father's game on Game Boy. Peter was told he was the only child in the Soviet Union with a Nintendo system.

The following day, the Nintendo representatives returned to Elorg ready to iron out the deal. Howard Lincoln outlined his plan to prove that the video-game rights to 'Tetris' had never been sold, then confirmed Nintendo's offer. The negotiations continued for three days. Lincoln was determined not to leave Moscow without a signed contract, and with Henk Rogers on the word processor, they knocked one out, paragraph by paragraph, in Rogers's hotel room. In morning meetings with the Soviets, the details were spelled out, and in the afternoon the changes were typed out and printed.

In one meeting, Lincoln said he wanted it to be clear what the game's author's rights were. The Elorg people answered that since Pajitnov worked for the Computer Center and had created the game on company time, the copyright was owned by the Academy of Science, and that as the trade organization, Elorg was authorized by the Academy to license 'Tetris.' Pajitnov nodded his confirmation. He was resigned to a small degree of glory, perhaps some opportunities for the future, but no money.

Lincoln insisted on a clause in the contract that committed the Soviets to cooperate in any litigation that might ensue; they would have to come to the United States to testify if it became necessary. Then, at the last minute, the Soviets began to squabble over the royalty Nintendo had offered, but Lincoln said the deal was no longer negotiable. Nintendo was going to be responsible for the legal expenses, which would probably be sizable because many people would be upset about the agreement they were about to sign. These included, he noted, Stein, Atari Games, the Mirrorsoft people, and Mirrorsoft's owner, Robert Maxwell. The mention of Maxwell dampened the discord, particularly since Belikov was all too aware of the latest telex from Mirrorsoft that had arrived that morning: Jim Mackonochie, responding to the last Soviet communiqué, had written to insist that Mirrorsoft didn't have to offer anything for the video-game 'Tetris' rights since it already owned them.

By way of reply, Elorg sent a telex informing Mackonochie that neither Andromeda, Mirrorsoft, nor Tengen had been authorized to distribute 'Tetris' on home video-game systems, and that the rights were no longer available since they had been granted to Nintendo of America. The telex was sent on March 22, the same day the Nintendo contract was finalized. Arakawa signed for Nintendo, Pajitnov signed as the author, and Belikov signed for Elorg.

The signing ceremony was attended by representatives of Nintendo and Elorg, as well as two senior officials of the Soviet government, Edward A. Maksakov, deputy chairman of the State Committee for Computer Systems and Informatics, and Dr. Stanislov I. Gusev, head of the Department of Scientific-Technical Information at the Computer Center of the Academy of Sciences. The advance guarantee was kept confidential, but rumors had it at $3 to $5 million. Lincoln says it was less, but will not divulge the amount.

Dennis Wood, Atari Game's counsel, says the amount 'would entice anybody to double-license.'

An attempt to derail the Nintendo deal arrived on March 23, addressed to Belikov. Kevin Maxwell wrote: 'I give you formal notice that you are now in grave breach twice over of our agreements with you.' He added that the matter would be raised during the forthcoming visit to London of President Gorbachev and stated flatly, 'We already hold the worldwide rights to "Tetris" on the Nintendo family computer. Indeed, we have been marketing it accordingly, both directly and through Tengen in the United States and Bullet-Proof Software in Japan since January 1989 . . .'

Maxwell said he was coming to Moscow and was willing, 'in the spirit of reconciliation,' to meet Belikov to 'hear how you intend to remedy your double breach of our agreement.'

He concluded by threatening that if the Russians didn't make good, he would carry the matter to the highest legal and political levels.

It was too late. That evening, Arakawa, Lincoln, Rogers, and Huhs celebrated at the Japanese restaurant with Alexey Pajitnov. Sitting at the Teppan Yaki bar, they asked the Japanese waitress if she would go to the liquor store for beer.

'Finnish beer?' they heard her say.

Fine, they responded, and she scurried off.

Arakawa tried to contain his elation, but his smile was enormous. 'We've got it,' he said exultantly to Lincoln. Spirits were so high that the table almost levitated.

The waitress hadn't returned with the beer and it was time for a toast. Lincoln saw the waitress and called her over. 'Where is the beer?' he asked her.

'Finish beer,' she repeated. 'Finish beer.'

'Fine,' Lincoln said, 'but . . .'

With her delicate hands, the woman made an X. '*Finish beer!*' she said firmly.

Roaring with laughter, they toasted instead with soft drinks. (Later Henk Rogers sent Howard Lincoln a case of Finnish beer as a present.)

They all exchanged warm hugs after dinner and said good night. Rogers was particularly happy. Not only did he have the hand-held rights to 'Tetris,' sublicensed to Nintendo for Game Boy, but as a reward he had also been given a sublicense to distribute 'Tetris' for home video-game systems in Japan, the rights he thought he had bought from Atari. This time, though, he got the game at Nintendo's cost. This meant his profit would be $5 to $8 more per cartridge than what other licensees made on games manufactured by Nintendo. Combined, he was about to make perhaps $30 to $40 million on 'Tetris.'

That difference was pocket change for Arakawa and Lincoln, who, back at their squalid apartment, finished off the warm

Heineken they had bought earlier. They were too excited to sleep and sat up all night talking.

Heading to the airport the next morning to fly home, Arakawa said, 'I'm never coming back to this place again.'

'Not so fast!' Lincoln interrupted. 'We promised we'd be back with a bunch of Game Boys for their hospitals and orphanages.'

Arakawa shook his head and grinned. 'We did,' he said, 'and they'll be very grateful for them when *you* deliver them.'

'We knew we had those bastards by the balls,' Howard Lincoln says. 'We knew we were going to make a fortune on this product and they, in turn, were going to get kicked in the head.' He worried only about what Robert Maxwell would do when he heard that Nintendo had snatched 'Tetris.'

In late March, Belikov sent telexes to Mirrorsoft and to Stein at his London office. Hand-held 'Tetris' rights were no longer available. The telex stated, 'It is a pity that we were forced to conclude the contract concerning "Tetris" for hand-held with another firm.'

Stein sublicensed his hard-won coin-op rights to Mirrorsoft, but Maxwell's company was unable to secure the most valuable rights, in particular the home video-game rights that it had already sublicensed to Atari Games. Mirrorsoft was in trouble because Atari Games had already invested millions in the Tengen version of 'Tetris.'

Back in Redmond, Lincoln relished the moment he sent a fax on March 31 to Hide Nakajima and Atari Games in California. It informed Nakajima and company that they must 'cease and desist from any further manufacture, advertisement, promotion, offer for sale or sale of "Tetris" for the NES or any other home system' because the rights belonged to Nintendo.

An attorney from Dennis Wood's office ripped the fax from the machine and read it quickly, stared at the paper, shocked, and rushed to Dennis Wood's office. Wood read and reread the fax before walking, stony-faced, into Hide Nakajima's office.

Tengen quickly called Mirrorsoft to find out what was going on. The initial response from Mirrorsoft was not to worry; the rights were theirs. Whatever Nintendo and the Russians were up to would not work, Dennis Wood was told.

It took until April 7 for Tengen to respond to Nintendo. 'We are in receipt of your letter . . . and quite frankly are quite confused. As Nintendo has known since last year, Tengen received all NES rights to the game "Tetris" in early 1988. These rights are, in Tengen's view, clear and unequivocal . . .'

Howard Lincoln offered to discuss things further, but by then, on April 13, Atari Games had filed an application for a copyright on the 'audiovisual work, the underlying computer code and the soundtrack' for 'Tetris' for the Nintendo system. Atari did not inform the Copyright Office that its version of 'Tetris' was simply a spruced-up version of Alexey Pajitnov's game, or that Nintendo had informed Atari that it held the exclusive rights to the game.

In a conference in London, Jim Mackonochie told Kevin Maxwell about Nintendo's frontal attack. Maxwell decided it was time to inform his father, and the senior Maxwell 'went berserk,' as an associate put it. 'He went ape shit.'

When told that the Soviets had broken the protocol agreement, Robert Maxwell had Kevin explain the details of the 'Tetris' negotiations. A protocol agreement is not a legal document, but it is, the elder Maxwell insisted, the equivalent of a gentlemen's agreement. To break it was, according to Robert Maxwell, tantamount to a slap in the face. The ultimatums Mirrorsoft had been given by the Russians were clearly for show; the legal right of first refusal had been mocked.

At that time, Robert Maxwell was steadfastly building a global media empire that would span more territory than Her Majesty's empire ever did. 'Information is growing at 20 percent a year,' Maxwell said in the early 1960s. 'Communications is where oil was ten years ago. There will be seven to ten global communications corporations. My ambition is to be one of them.' He had pursued this ambition tenaciously, gobbling up or founding communications-related companies from Britain to China, the Soviet Union, and Brazil.

Maxwell not only had a formidable world presence as a businessman, but used his position to gain remarkable influence in world politics. He was a trusted adviser of leaders in Israel and Canada and a powerful force in opposition to the Conservative governments of Margaret Thatcher and John Major in Britain. He spoke nine languages fluently, and his phone rang incessantly with calls from world leaders. When a secretary told him that the prime minister was on the phone, he asked, 'Which one?'

Maxwell was trusted by Soviet president Mikhail Gorbachev, but he had been a familiar face in the Kremlin even earlier. He had known and published books by four former Soviet leaders – Brezhnev, Andropov, Gromyko, and Khrushchev – so there was every reason to believe his boasts about his influence in the U.S.S.R.

Although Maxwell's son Kevin was in charge of Mirrorsoft over Mackonochie, the elder Maxwell had a twenty-four-hour-a-day watch on all aspects of his parent companies, Maxwell Communications Corporation and the Mirror Group. It was a way to be certain that no one, not even his sons, knew exactly what he was up to. He was a general who kept his commanding officers in the dark on most important operations, informing them on a need-to-know basis and playing them off against each other. He staged surprise troop inspections to keep his top brass on their toes.

Kevin Maxwell tried to avoid going to his father for anything, but big guns were required in the 'Tetris' deal. When he was told that the Soviets had double-dealt them, Robert Maxwell punished his desk with his fist. 'They won't get away with it,' he bellowed. 'Rest assured of that.' He promptly wrote letters to his friends in the Kremlin, including the minister of foreign economic relations, who catered to him when he visited Moscow. 'We attach high importance to our excellent commercial relations with the Soviet government and many leading agencies in the fields of information, communications, publishing and, indeed, pulp and paper production,' Maxwell wrote. 'We face the prospect of all this being jeopardized by the unilateral action of one particular agency.'

That agency, Elorg, was concerned when there were rumblings from above. However, this was perestroika and, as Jim Mackonochie put it, the Elorg bureaucrats were 'feeling their oats.' Still, when the foreign economic relations minister began to pry into the agency's affairs, Belikov realized trouble was brewing.

Next Maxwell contacted his own government and asked Lord Young, secretary of state for trade and industry in Britain, to intervene; he wanted 'Tetris' to be discussed between the heads of state during a forthcoming visit by Gorbachev.

Word filtered back to the Moscow Academy of Science that Maxwell was throwing his substantial weight around, and people there and at Elorg worried that their authority might be undermined. At the same time, they were also delighted. In a strategy meeting with Belikov, the Academy chiefs debated how to respond to the Central Committee of the Communist Party, which was certain to react to an inquiry from the secretary general.

Belikov felt justified in having made the deal with Nintendo, and he planned to stand up for it. For all his dinner parties with the Gorbachevs, Maxwell had offered the Academy, via their dealings with Elorg, only a fraction of what Nintendo would bring to the country's coffers. In addition, Mirrorsoft was continually behind in its payments. Most of all, Belikov was convinced that Mirrorsoft had willfully stolen the Russians' game, and that Gorbachev himself would understand that Elorg had made the correct decision. Elorg, Belikov decided, would defend its decision whatever the pressures.

The infighting was epic as Elorg and the factions of the Party loyal to Maxwell exchanged urgent messages. There were threats of prosecution, and that the KGB would be used against individuals who refused to cooperate. The pressure on the Russians peaked when Robert Maxwell flew to Moscow to meet Gorbachev directly. He was prepared to discuss his planned printing ventures and the newspapers he wanted to launch, but first on his list was 'Tetris.'

Maxwell arrived in Moscow on his private jet and was whisked to the Octoberskaya, the government's elite hotel, by police motorcade. The meeting that afternoon was friendly, and he brought 'Tetris' up only after initial small talk and joking. Maxwell later claimed that after the discussion, Gorbachev promised him the matter would be resolved to his satisfaction; 'He said I should no longer worry about the Japanese company.'

Lincoln returned to Moscow in late April and was joined by his New York lawyers, Huhs and John Kirby, as well as one of Kirby's associates, Bob Gunther. For the New York attorneys, the trip began with a comedy of errors. Gunther dropped and broke a printer he had lugged from New York, and then left his wallet, which contained $1,000, in a Moscow taxi. Kirby had all his shirts stolen at Kennedy Airport, and as a result he had to shop for clothing in Moscow before he could begin the series of meetings. He found a stack of pitiful polyester shirts at a concession stand on a street near his hotel.

The Nintendo team showed up for a meeting in the main Elorg conference room, where Belikov, Pajitnov, and half a dozen other Russians were waiting, visibly shaken. They were not unfriendly, just burdened; increasing pressure was descending on them from the top. The meeting progressed with no mention that there was anything wrong, but Howard Lincoln sensed trouble. 'What is it?' he asked Belikov. 'What has happened?'

Belikov shook his head vigorously. 'Nothing has changed,' he said, but during a break in the meeting he pulled Lincoln aside. 'You do not understand,' Belikov said under his breath. 'We have done the right thing with you, but the Maxwells have threatened us. We have said, "No, we will not be threatened by you. A contract is a contract and we will honor it and Nintendo is our licensee." ' Whispering, he continued, 'But I must tell you, Mr. Lincoln, we are getting calls from the Kremlin, calls from people who never before knew we existed. Many of them have shown up to examine our records and to question us on this deal. We have told them we have done the right thing. We have stood up to them, but we do not know what will happen.'

The meeting resumed with a hint of counterespionage in the air. There were worries about spies in Elorg and KGB surveillance, not only of the meetings but everywhere twenty-four hours a day – tapped hotel telephones, monitored strolls, and bugged restaurant tables.

Preparing for the worst, the Nintendo attorneys interviewed Pajitnov the next day, as well as people at the Academy of Science, the Computer Center, and Elorg, and examined every scrap of paper that dealt with 'Tetris.' Belikov also wrote a lengthy letter to John Kirby recounting his version of the 'Tetris' history, and this was later included in the court record as Belikov's declaration.

In the meantime, on his jet winging its way from London to Jerusalem for a meeting with Israel's Prime Minister Yitzhak Shamir and Defense Minister Moshe Arens, Robert Maxwell was asked by a reporter why his intervention with Gorbachev had apparently been futile. He snapped, 'How do you know about that deal? How do you know about the meeting?' Then he shrugged it off as if it had been inconsequential. 'So much money was involved, his people convinced Gorbachev to work with the Japanese company,' he said. 'I did what I could.' He blamed his losing the fight to Gorbachev's tenuous hold on power. 'He said other people in the government felt strongly that it should go the other way, so we were stopped.' Maxwell insisted that the principle was what had goaded him. 'I am an honorable man and I expect honorable treatment, but you take your lumps along the way.' It was not the last lump Maxwell would take.

In the middle of the night, Howard Lincoln was awakened in his Moscow hotel room by the telephone. The operator said she had a call from America.

The time in Redmond, eleven hours behind Moscow, was two in the afternoon, and the caller was one of his associates at NOA; 'Tengen has sued us,' she said.

At Elorg the next morning, Lincoln announced this news with a bit of glee. The Soviets were in for a taste of the American legal system, as sluggish and inefficient as the leviathan Soviet bureaucracy.

To begin to prepare, Lincoln, together with Huhs, Kirby, and Gunther, continued to interrogate each of the principals involved in the 'Tetris' negotiations, wanting to be certain their case was airtight. Before it was all over, Alexey Pajitnov would tell his story a few dozen times. When he was satisfied, Lincoln flew to Japan to confer with Yamauchi and Hiroshi Imanishi before leading home. Yamauchi was delighted with everything that had happened, unconcerned about the lawsuit. It was the kind of wheeling and dealing he admired. 'You and Arakawa-son have done well,' he said.

Back home, Lincoln filed a countersuit against Tengen, and lawyers on both sides girded for battle. Evidence was gathered and depositions were taken in the United States, England, and then, in June, in Moscow.

John Kirby's staff continued to investigate on Nintendo's behalf in the United States. Kirby found that Tengen had filed applications for trademark registration of 'Tetris' in the United States, Japan, Australia, Canada, the United Kingdom, West Germany, Italy, and Spain. Pajitnov sat for still another interview, this one four hours long. Huhs had Pajitnov reconstruct, in ponderous detail, the story of 'Tetris,' from its inception to the first letter from Stein and up to the present.

Tengen shipped its first batch of 'Tetris' cartridges in May 1989, despite the notice it had received from Nintendo and the pending litigation. Setting out to sell what the company felt would be Tengen's hottest game ever, Randy Broweleit and Dan Van Elderen placed a full-page ad in *USA Today* announcing 'Tetris': 'It's like Siberia, only harder,' the ad read. 'It's here, America . . . The nerve-wrackingest mind game since Russian Roulette . . . So round up a few of your high-IQ pals, okay? You know, macho men with the first-strike capability to beat the Russian programmers who invented it . . . But there's one little catch. If you can't make the pieces fit together an avalanche of blocks thunders down and buries you weaklings!' This was hardly in tune with Pajitnov's vision of 'Tetris' as a peacemaker.

Tengen held a grand reception for retailers, trade reps, and the press at the Russian Tea Room in New York on May 17. The place was packed, and there was free-flowing vodka and Russian hors d'oeuvres amid the Tea Room's year-round Christmas motif. Russian music played in the background, and Tengen 'Tetris' games were set up for play.

Beginning in June, the case was heard in San Francisco in the courtroom of Judge Fern Smith, who also was trying the Nintendo-Atari Games antitrust and breach-of-contract cases. Ultimately the 'Tetris' suit hinged on personalities, semantics, and two lines buried in the pounds of documents. Stein's contract with the Russians stipulated that he was being given the rights for computers, and no one argued this point. But Atari Games contended that the Nintendo system was a computer, a microprocessor-based machine that ran software. To prove that there was no valid distinction between the NES and other computers, Atari Games' attorneys noted that Nintendo itself viewed its machine as a computer, with planned hookups that would connect to the expansion portal. The anticipated peripherals – such as a modem, keyboard, and, ultimately, a CD – were proof that the NES was a computer. In Japan, the NES was even called the Famicom, or Family Computer. As one Tengen spokesman observed, 'In court Nintendo went to great lengths to say that the NES was a toy and its cartridges were the equivalent of Barbie's arms and legs, but at the same time they were signing up AT&T to use its machine for stock reports. There was a Nintendo computer network in Japan and one planned in the U.S. Sounds like a computer to me,' he said.

The Atari contingent echoed the charges made by Robert Maxwell that the Soviets saw they could make a lot more money from Nintendo, so they found a loophole and pleaded ignorance. This was in spite of Alexey Pajitnov's insistence that the deal never was meant to include more than PCs; Pajitnov, the Atari contingent charged, was Nintendo's dupe, instructed on exactly what to tell the court.

Dan Van Elderen believes the Russians were less innocent than they pretended to be. 'Whether the language was ambiguous or not, they knew they had sold all those rights until they figured out, counseled by Henk Rogers and Nintendo, that there was a loophole. They realized they could have gotten a lot more money, so they double-dealt us all.'

Tengen's Randy Broweleit revealed in his deposition how much was on the line for Atari Games. In 1988 his company had devoted more than three personnel years to 'Tetris,' and more than $250,000. By January 1989, Tengen had committed to manufacture 300,000 'Tetris' cartridges and spent $3 million on them, plus millions on packaging, engineering, and marketing. One hundred thousand units had been shipped, and there were initial orders for 150,000 before the game was released in May 1989.

Atari's Hide Nakajima insisted that Nintendo had colluded to steal his game. 'Something went on between the Russian author and Nintendo,' he charged. 'Nintendo knew we had the license, and it urged us to go forward with the game. Nintendo only cared once we filed the antitrust suit against them. They went after us. Howard Lincoln and Arakawa wanted to stop us. It was revenge.' Howard Lincoln has affirmed this last point. 'It *was* revenge,' he says. 'And you know what they say about how sweet revenge can be.'

Nintendo's argument was straightforward: in spite of their innocence about international software licensing, the Soviets knew exactly what they were doing when they assigned the rights to Stein Computers were computers. Just as the Soviets' contract with Stein excluded the rights to hand-held and arcade games, the Russians had had no intention of selling home video-game rights. Two lines in the contract proved it: the line stipulating computers in the main body of the final contract, and also a line in the amendment – alteration no. 1 – which specified that a computer had a keyboard, monitor, and floppy-disk drives. The NES machine had none of those; ergo, it was excluded.

Nintendo held fast to the position that it had bought the 'Tetris' rights fair and square, giving the Russians a fair deal, while Tengen's rights were part of a faulty chain. The weak link was the original one with the West, Robert Stein's contract, which covered PCs clearly and explicitly. Assumptions made beyond that, whether by Stein, Mirrorsoft, or Tengen, were nothing short of thievery.

Nintendo and Tengen were trying to stop each other from selling 'Tetris' with cross motions that they filed for preliminary injunctions to prohibit the other from selling the game. A hearing about this was held on June 15, 1989.

After reviewing the depositions and mass of documents, Judge Smith decided that there was no evidence that Tengen (and the licensing chain that awarded it the rights) had ever been granted the video-game rights. She said she believed that Nintendo was likely to prevail in court, and therefore she granted Nintendo's request for a preliminary injunction. Tengen was enjoined and restrained from manufacturing and selling the home video-game 'Tetris' as of June 21.

At this point, Hide Nakajima, Dennis Wood, and Dan Van Elderen (Randy Broweleit had left Atari Games to start an independent software licensing company) could only hope that the court ultimately would reverse this opinion, although it seemed unlikely (and no trial was scheduled at the time of writing). Tengen's production of 'Tetris' cartridges ground to a halt. Although it claimed that its version of 'Tetris' was superior to the one Nintendo released, Tengen had to lock its games away in a warehouse pending a final verdict, and its 'Tetris' soon became a collector's item, selling for as much as $150.

Nintendo released its NES version of 'Tetris' – slickly redesigned, with a score of Russian music – and it sold rapidly, remaining on the Nintendo top-ten most-popular game list (behind 'Super Mario Bros. 3') for over a year. Pajitnov laughed when he heard that when millions of American children watched the evening news and saw a shot of St. Basil's Cathedral in Red Square, they shouted excitedly, 'Look, the "Tetris" towers!' Similarly, Tchaikovsky lost credit for his 'Dance of the Sugarplum Fairy'; kids knew it only as 'the "Tetris" song.' On a modest level, Pajitnov's dream that his game would be a bridge between cultures was realized. 'Tetris' contest winners were awarded a ten-day tour of Kiev, Leningrad, and Moscow, 'home of Alexey Pajitnov.' *Nintendo Power* ran features about his homeland, and kids who played the game saw that something wonderful had come from the former 'evil empire.'

Grown-ups flocked to 'Tetris' too. Arakawa had predicted correctly: feedback from its customers told NOA that a third to a half of the 'Tetris' players were adults, and Nintendo's presence in the adult market increased to such a degree that almost half (46 percent) of the Game Boy players in the West were adults.

Arakawa was also right about another thing: 'Tetris' sold millions of Game Boys. A total of 32 million of them sold worldwide through 1992, more than Hiroshi Yamauchi had predicted. A U.S. senator, a 'Tetris' addict, joked that the game was a Soviet plot to distract and hypnotize Americans.

The game also did things for Nintendo that Arakawa hadn't anticipated. When the company was attacked by educators and psychologists for the mindless violence and lack of redeeming value of its games, Nintendo now had fodder for counterarguments. Some theories claimed that 'Tetris' play increased intelligence scores (at least in the area of spatial relationships). Also, a study in Moscow showed that 'Tetris' helped improve driving skills because it trained players to make decisions extremely quickly, shortening drivers' reaction time.

Kids were getting Tetrisized and played compulsively. After they stopped playing, however, they complained that 'Tetris' shapes remained impaled somewhere in their consciousness. Grown-ups became Tetrisized as much as kids. A reader wrote in to a national women's magazine; '["Tetris"] led me to beg my coworkers not to leave me behind in the office when they left, for fear I'd stay [there] all night playing. I removed the game from my computer at home and threw it away, but I passed a Game Boy in a store and couldn't stop. I went in and bought it.' A Russian cosmonaut even took one into space. (The Russian had been given the game by Howard Lincoln, who had returned to Moscow with his sixteen-year-old son, Brad, on what was, for the most part, a social visit. He brought with him the one hundred Game Boys that Arakawa had promised. Arakawa kept the other part of his promise by staying home.)

The journey of Alexey Pajitnov's program from Moscow to most places on the globe – and to space and back – left a number of casualties in its wake. Robert Stein says, ' "Tetris" made enemies out of friends and corrupted people left, right, and center.' Andromeda, Mirrorsoft, and Atari Games, he says, felt that every penny Nintendo earned on 'Tetris' should be theirs. 'So why don't we all get together instead of fighting like lunatics?' he asks. But fight like lunatics they did, so infighting tied up most of the profits earned by the versions of the game not controlled by Nintendo and BPS. Mirrorsoft saw modest profits on its floppy-disk 'Tetris,' but almost nothing from the licenses it sold to Atari Games, which refused to pay Mirrorsoft anything pending the outcome of the litigation with Nintendo.

Atari Games released a coin-op game and sold 15,000 to 20,000 units, according to Dan Van Elderen. It also earned a royalty on the arcade games Sega sold in Japan, but Atari's sublicense to Henk Rogers was useless and it would probably have to return Rogers's advance for the home video-game rights in the original deal.

Robert Stein admitted that over the years he had made about $200,000 on 'Tetris' but said he could have made millions. Instead, he watched as the Soviets severed all of his ties to the game, citing nonpayment of royalties. Stein lost his rights to the computer versions of 'Tetris' in 1990. Spectrum Holobyte had been paying royalties to Mirrorsoft, which refused to pay Stein. The Russians'

75 percent of Stein's nothing was nothing, so Elorg finally revoked his license. In order to retain the rights to 'Tetris' on PCs (and to retain the rights to sell 'Tetris 2'), Spectrum Holobyte had to negotiate a new deal directly with the Soviets. Gilman Louie found that the Soviets had learned a great deal from the 'Tetris' experience, and he had to pay a far higher royalty than in his deal with Mirrorsoft for the license he already had.

At this point Stein still held the coin-operated 'Tetris' rights, but he received nothing for them as long as Atari Games didn't pay Mirrorsoft. Since he didn't pay, Elorg announced in February 1992 that it was terminating the coin-op deal as well. Stein vowed to fight, but it would be an uphill battle. The man who had discovered 'Tetris' for the West lost all his rights to the game.

The lawsuit remained unsettled well into 1992, although rumor had it that Atari Games would settle. If this happened (or if Nintendo prevailed in court), Atari Games would probably go after Andromeda, Mirrorsoft, and, ultimately, Maxwell. Maxwell and Stein had warranted that they owned the rights they had sold, and probably would be held responsible. Stein wouldn't be worth going after, but Mirrorsoft, with Maxwell's deep pockets, would have been – that is, until it turned out that those pockets were actually black holes. The upshot of the scandalous collapse of the Maxwell organization was the dissolution of Mirrorsoft (its meager assets were bought by Acclaim Entertainment) following Robert Maxwell's suspicious death.

Other 'Tetris' players fared better, although Kevin Maxwell was left to suffer for his father's corrupt business practices. Not only was he left with no assets or income, but there was a good chance he would be indicted, despite the fact that he had been kept in the dark about Maxwell senior's illegal maneuverings.

Jim Mackonochie had been forced out of Mirrorsoft well before it collapsed, back when Kevin Maxwell restructured the company in 1991. Mackonochie ended up working as a consultant in the industry before being hired to work on CDTV software by Commodore International in London.

As their country transformed, the Russians at Elorg and the Academy of Science scattered, although Nikolai Belikov remained at Elorg long after the Communist Party fell from power. A freer country meant increased opportunities for trade, and Belikov, no longer saddled by the pressures of the Party's interests, saw abundant possibilities for exporting Russian technological achievements. His first Yeltsin-era task was negotiating the tough deal with Gilman Louie for 'Tetris 2' – designed along with Pajitnov and others.

The Academy's Sasha Alexinko wound up in Vienna, where he formed a trading company. Victor Brjabrin also left Russia and found challenging work in Western Europe with a nuclear-regulatory commission run by the United Nations. Young Vadim Gerasimov left Russia too. At only twenty, he moved to Tokyo, where he studied Japanese and worked with a software developer, who then advertised that the codeveloper of 'Tetris' was on his staff.

In America, Phil Adam left Spectrum Holobyte in the hands of his partner, Louie, who took Spectrum on to new ventures, from new combat simulators to other Nintendo games. In 1992, Louie debuted a futuristic video-game system for arcades and shopping malls. Kids climbed into a slick pod or stood inside a device that looked like a gyroscope, strapped on binocular-like goggles, and entered computer-generated virtual realities. In one multicontestant game, players stalked each other in a surreal cybernetic environment of multicolored platforms and stairways. Armed with a missile-lobbing blaster, they 'flew' around and attempted to nail enemies (who broke into pieces if hit) before being shot themselves, though occasionally a pterodactyl swooped down from the sky and carried them off.

In his modest office in London, Robert Stein continued to struggle to keep Andromeda afloat. He distributed Atari Corp.'s computers in England and attempted to take advantage of the post-Communist revolution in Eastern Europe, particularly in Hungary. He also kept trying to sell Hungarian games in the West; perhaps there was another 'Tetris' out there. But he had learned his lesson: if he found a great game, he would sew up all the rights *before* selling it.

Henk Rogers made more from 'Tetris' than any individual save, ultimately, Hiroshi Yamauchi. The Russian bureaucrats at Elorg and the Academy made almost nothing, although the Russian government made millions from the game, mostly from the Nintendo deal. They also took in roughly $150,000, all told, from Andromeda, plus advances and royalties directly from Spectrum Holobyte.

As always, Nintendo did best of all, though it is impossible to calculate exactly how much it made from 'Tetris,' since there is no way to measure accurately how much 'Tetris' contributed to the success of Game Boy. Three million 'Tetris' cartridges for the NES were sold, plus all those Game Boy units. Once a customer bought one, Nintendo could sell more games, an average of three a year, at $35 a pop. Not counting Game Boy, 'Tetris' brought Nintendo at least $80 million. Counting Game Boy, the figure is in the billions of dollars (in both 1991 and 1992, Game Boy earned nearly $2 billion).

Alexey Pajitnov made very little money directly from 'Tetris' royalties or advances. Elorg had made and then canceled a side deal that would have granted him the 'Tetris' merchandising rights (Nintendo eventually got them, too), so he ended up getting nothing on the 'Tetris' watches, clocks, board games, and the like.

Westerners criticized the Soviet system that robbed Pajitnov of a stake in the game that made so much money for so many people, but Belikov defended it. 'If "Tetris" had been made by a Boeing employee on Boeing time and Boeing sold the license, would the designer have received any more than Pajitnov?'

On the other hand, if Pajitnov had retained the 'Tetris' rights and signed a deal typical of those in the United States, he would have earned up to 15 percent of net revenues. Pajitnov would have seen at least $3 million if he was earning this standard percentage of the Soviet government's share. If he had licensed it directly, the number would have been as high as $20 million, perhaps more. Instead, the Computer Center awarded Pajitnov his own personal computer, an IBM AT clone, for which he was grateful since it would have taken him sixteen years to be able to buy one on his Academy of Science salary.

Henk Rogers, who came out of the deal with a good relationship with Elorg, appealed to Belikov on Pajitnov's behalf in a letter. He wrote, 'If someone plants an apple tree and it brings you many, many apples, you ought to give them some apples – it would encourage them to plant more trees.'

There was no response. The Elorg team was not particularly sympathetic. Pajitnov's apartment was nicer than the homes of most of his Academy superiors and the Elorg bureaucrats, and in addition he had gained recognition throughout the world, far more than any Soviet citizen dared hope for.

It amazed Pajitnov that Americans couldn't believe he wasn't bitter. This, he came to realize, was one of the key differences between him and most of the people he met in the West, where financial reward was the measure of accomplishment. 'For me, to have my game played everywhere is the greatest thing to know,' he says. In 1989, he was called to the telephone at the Computer Center to talk to a reporter who was writing a story about 'Tetris.' Every question was slanted to make Pajitnov admit that he was resentful, but he told the reporter, 'I will make my games and send them to you. *You* can fight over them.'

The Soviet Union thawed, and as trade opportunities increased, Pajitnov was able to take advantage of the success of his creations by licensing games and other programs through several joint-venture trading companies that paid small advances and royalties on his designs. With the income that trickled in, he bought a car – his first, a used Jugoli, a Russian clone of an outdated Fiat. The Pajitnov family had something more: Peter and Dmitri, Alexey's sons, had one of the only two Nintendo Entertainment Systems in the U.S.S.R., which had been sent by Henk Rogers (the children of his friend Vladimir Pokhilko had the other).

SONIC BOOM

12

Between them, Hiroshi Yamauchi and Minoru Arakawa had created a new mammoth industry and, with it, a field for competition. Seven American and Japanese companies were marketing video-game systems by 1988. But the contenders had little success in damaging Nintendo's share of the market, which was 85 to 90 percent on both sides of the Pacific. Atari sold a handful of its 5200s and 7800s, and Sega sold a total of 2 million Master Systems. Other companies sold too few to count.

Having failed to break Nintendo's lock on the NES generation of video-game systems, the would-be Davids attempted to topple Nintendo's Goliath in the next generation with more powerful hardware. They took aim at Nintendo's single vulnerability: its success. Nintendo was dominant, and such companies tend to stagnate by sticking with old technology. The problem for Nintendo, which was raking in a large part of its fortune from licensees, was that it had so much invested in the NES-Famicom technology.

If the company planned to release a new system, the game-designing companies would worry that the NES was obsolete, and the shift could precipitate an early crash of its bread-and-butter NES business.

Nintendo also suffered from a malaise typical of industry leaders. Fat and happy, it had been lulled into a sense of invulnerability. Yamauchi and Arakawa felt they didn't have to react to competitors simply because they were Nintendo. This could have been a fatal mistake.

If there was any threat, according to Yamauchi, it was when NEC, the Japanese computer and communications giant, entered the video-game business. If NEC was a termite, it was a voracious one. With $22 billion in net annual sales, the company was sound and well run. Each year it invested a hefty 16 percent of its net sales in R&D and engineering programs – $3.7 billion in 1988 – more than any of Nintendo's annual net sales until 1992.

To push its first video-game system, NEC formed a home-entertainment group and released PC Engine in Japan in October 1987. A more expensive system (at $200) was released to the American market in 1989. The TurboGrafx-16 was an expandable system, with 16 bits of power.

For a long time, to the kids who comprised the primary video-game players, bits and bytes were only slightly more relevant than Latin. Then NEC fired the first shot in the battle of the bits. The TurboGrafx-16 had twice as many bits as Nintendo, and kids learned that more bits meant more realistic games, with more and brighter colors and awesome sound effects – arcade-quality games.

When NEC launched the TurboGrafx-16, video-game players were impressed with the meatier, more textured feeling of the first games. There was, however, a flaw in the more-is-better logic behind the new technology, and NEC learned the lesson the hard way. While its powerful system played games with better graphics and sound, NEC hadn't improved its video games. They were not as much fun. In the end, NEC's 16 bits could not compete with 'Tetris,' 'Super Mario Bros.,' 'The Legend of Zelda,' and hundreds of other great Nintendo games. In spite of its clout, less than 1 million TurboGrafx units were sold. For all their technical prowess, NEC's machines could be no better than the software that ran on them, and NEC had limited access to good games. 'Bonk's Adventure,' in which a bantam-weight caveman bounces his way through a Paleolithic paradise, was a good game that accounted for many TurboGrafx sales, but most of the credit-card-size cartridges NEC released were unexceptional. Since it had no experience making games, it depended on third-party developers to build a library. But the best entertainment-software companies were too busy making Nintendo games to bother making ones for Turbo-Grafx.

Sega never was a threat as far as Yamauchi was concerned. The $700 million Japanese company – founded, curiously enough, by an American – had a reasonably successful history in the video-arcade business in Japan and the United States, but it seemed too small and too specialized to make inroads into Nintendo's vast consumer business. Sega had released the Master System as a competitor to the Famicom and NES but never gained more than 5 percent of the market. Although it, unlike NEC, was an able software company, it never seemed to be playing in the same league as Nintendo.

Yamauchi underestimated Sega, whose executives understood the importance of software to drive hardware sales. This philosophy was built into the company's 16-bit contender, the Genesis, which it launched in 1989 in Japan (1990 in the United States). Genesis was the first dedicated video-game system powered by a true 16-bit processor; it had the same 6800 processor that ran the Macintosh computer. Sega had simply taken the design of its 16-bit arcade machines and adapted it for Genesis. It could therefore boast not only such 16-bit features as high-definition graphics and animation, a full spectrum of colors (more than 500), two independently scrolling backgrounds that created impressive depth-of-field, the illusion of three dimensions, and near CD-quality sound, but also a proven software catalogue: Sega's arcade hits. As a peripheral to the Genesis, Sega also released a unit called the Power Base Converter. For $35 it allowed Master System games to be played on the Genesis.

Sega got a reputable distributor in America (Tonka), spent $10 million in advertising, and set out to fell Goliath. The machine, priced originally at $199, was launched on the strength of software titles that kids who hung out in arcades already knew. One was 'Altered Beast,' a brutal game in which a hero metamorphoses into a werewolf, weredragon, and werebear, gaining the powers of the revolting creatures he kills. Sega attacked Nintendo head-on. 'Sega Genesis does what Nintendon't,' its slogan read.

Competition was exactly what Nintendo and the video-game industry needed, though Nintendo was unlikely to acknowledge this. 'We listen to our players,' Bill White told the press. 'They tell us they are extremely happy with the existing system and are totally involved with the games. We haven't maxed out our 8-bit system yet.' This attitude left the company in the dust of the 16-bit war.

At first the market reinforced Nintendo's confidence. During the first two years Genesis was on the market, Nintendo sold 18 million 8-bit systems in America. Sega's arguments for 16 bits weren't supportable. The first Genesis games, even the knock-offs of the arcade hits, were not as much fun as the best Nintendo games. In many cases, the Sega programmers were so intent on exploiting the possibilities of detailed graphics and exciting sound that they forgot what made great video games.

The Genesis continued to flounder through its first couple of years on the market, although Sega showed Sisyphean resolve. It sold machines to anyone it could, mostly to older boys who were diehard video-game buffs. They were the kids who insisted on having (and could afford to have) both the NES and the cutting-edge machine. Sega released some better games and sold more systems – a hundred thousand here, a hundred thousand there. The savvier kids extolled the virtues of 16 bits and scoffed at the dweebs still playing Nintendo. The result was that Sega began to embody cool. NOA commissioned a study that confirmed it: younger kids and girls liked Nintendo, but the trendsetters in the video-game world, young teenage boys, were talking Genesis.

Working with sports celebrities such as Arnold Palmer and Tommy Lasorda, the Sega designers figured out ways to take advantage of the Genesis's 16 bits for 'deeper' – more complex – games. The resulting games were superior to the ones on the NES. Joe Montana signed on for a reported $8 million, and Sega released a great football game. Its sequel, 'Joe Montana 2: Sports Talk Football,' had running commentary by a semirealistic-sounding announcer who screams, '*Montana drops back. He's got a man open . . . He passes. It's – no good. Incomplete.*' Behind him is the sound of a wall of cheering fans.

Sports games and arcade knockoffs remained Sega's strong suits. Yet by and large, its designers came up with great-*looking* games – better than any that had been seen to date – but not great-*playing* games. Examples were those that came out of Sega's licensing agreement with Disney, such as 'Fantasia' and 'Castle of Illusion,' both featuring Mickey Mouse. 'Fantasia' had rousing classical music from the film and great-looking Sorcerer's Apprentice brooms that danced. In 'Castle of Illusion,' the expressiveness in Mickey's face set a new standard for video games. However, they weren't that much fun to play. Sega was missing what Hiroshi Yamauchi had long before acknowledged to be the most important single asset of a video-game company: 'one true genius.' It needed a Sigeru Miyamoto or an Alexey Pajitnov.

While Sega hoped for a 'genius' to emerge, it got an enormous boost from its first third-party licensee. Although its base of 1 million systems paled in comparison to Nintendo's, Trip Hawkins of Electronic Arts calculated that Sega had created a promising market, one for which the price of admission was far less than Nintendo's. There was little competition – the software companies in the video-game business were all after Nintendo's 70 million players – and the million people who had invested in the Genesis were dying for good games; indeed, they were demanding more games than were owners of personal computers.

Hawkins met with the Sega chiefs, who planned to initiate a licensing agreement with similar restrictions and fees as Nintendo's. Hawkins refused – Sega wasn't big enough to throw that kind of weight around. EA engineers had succeeded in reverse-engineering the Genesis without using any confidential information, and Hawkins maintained that he would release games for Sega with or without a license.

Determined to maintain a stake in the Genesis software market, Sega said it would sue. To avoid 'a pissing contest,' Hawkins says, particularly since both companies had a common goal – to advance the Genesis marketplace – he agreed to enter into a licensing agreement under terms he found acceptable, far less restrictive (and costing less) than those for a Nintendo licensee.

EA's stock crept up as it shipped its first Genesis games in 1990. The next year it shipped nine more, four of which shot onto the list of the top-ten bestsellers. Having hedged his bets – he had also become a Nintendo licensee – Hawkins thrived in the Genesis market and made a killing. A quarter of EA's sales in 1990 were from Genesis games.

The Genesis's 16 bits meant that EA could convert some of its floppy-disk bestsellers to the Sega system. EA released 'John Madden Football,' which went up against Sega's 'Joe Montana Football,' and an impressive list of other games, from an award-winning martial-arts game called 'Budokan' to a gory version of Will Harvey's 'Immortal,' in which 16-bit graphics allowed some particularly repulsive blood and guts.

Other software companies signed on (reportedly with less liberal licensing deals than EA's but still preferable to the Nintendo straitjacket), though many Nintendo licensees feared retribution by Nintendo. EA took the risk, gambling (successfully, it seemed) on the Sega technology, and some other software companies went to Sega because they had nothing to lose. Tengen, for one, out of the Nintendo business pending its litigation, jumped in with a series of Genesis games (licensed this time; it could afford no new lawsuits).

With each new convert Sega was more and more legitimized. Fueled by games released by licensees, the list of Genesis software grew – good software, to be sure, but no 'Super Mario Bros.' Sales of the Genesis hardware also grew, so that by mid 1991, there were well over 1 million in use. By then NOA had sold 31.7 million units in the United States, but Sega had established itself as the market leader of the next generation. Mighty Nintendo, which had announced that it would enter the 16-bit market only when it was good and ready, was in trouble.

Hiroshi Yamauchi had had a 16-bit system in the works for years. Masayuki Uemura, in charge of the top-secret project, had been experimenting with a follow-up to the Famicom-NES since the late 1980s. Yamauchi left the technical specifications to the engineers, but he did insist that his company must be poised to jump into the 16-bit market by 1990. There was no perceived urgency, however; the NES was flying so high that Nintendo felt no pressure to rush.

One issue that Yamauchi made the engineers consider was the compatibility of a new system with the hundreds of millions of Nintendo games in circulation. New-generation hardware was always resisted if it made old software obsolete. Yamauchi correctly anticipated a backlash against Nintendo, particularly from parents, if its new machine couldn't play the libraries of games collected for its 8-bit technology.

Uemura accomplished many feats in his design of the new Super Family Computer (dubbed the Super NES, or SNES, in the West), but one of them was not compatibility. The cost would have been too high – at least $75 would have been added to the price of each unit. Uemura found that a major leap in technology was, almost by definition, *not* compatible with old technology.

Arakawa and Yamauchi discussed the problem and decided they could deal with backlash generated by the compatibility issue. After all, consumers were buying CD players even though the new technology wasn't compatible with their libraries of tapes and records. Arakawa insisted that video-game customers would do the same.

Uemura had better luck with other features of the new system. Around the central processor were special chips for sound and extremely high-resolution graphics and video. The new SNES could generate many more colors than the Genesis's 512 – 32,000 in fact, many of them barely distinguishable (especially on most televisions). This would be important, however, when video games began to incorporate real film footage. There was also a math coprocessor that allowed the hardware to do some of the work normally done by software and would make it easier to create games for the new system. Like the Genesis, the SNES could display several layers of backgrounds so that it could create the illusion of three dimensions. It also had the capability to generate (and move) large objects on the screen, and many more things could happen simultaneously in a game. It also had one other key feature: an improved version of the patented Nintendo security chip.

The Japanese version of the Super system was made to look somewhat like the original Famicom, but Arakawa had a different version designed for the United States. Don James and product designer Lance Barr sought a balance so that it would be sleek enough – Arakawa said it had to fit in next to a VCR – and accessible. The Genesis was housed in a black box with rounded edges. James and Barr came up with a far more elegant gray with right angles. Their colors represented the images of the respective machines. The Genesis, in black, was the outsider, the heavy metal of video-game machines. The SNES, sleekly styled in gray, was commercial and pop.

As 'Super Mario' had sold the NES and 'Tetris' had sold Game Boy, Yamauchi and Arakawa had to decide what game would be used to spark sales of the SNES. In the end there was no real debate. 'Super Mario Bros. 3' had been the most successful video game in history. What would convince more buyers to cough up $200 for a new system than 'Super Mario Bros. 4'? Sigeru Miyamoto was assigned to create it.

After the exhausting months of completing 'SMB3,' Miyamoto's team had taken fifteen months off to do nothing but conduct technology experiments to explore the outer reaches of the SNES. He and his thirty-person team were still scratching the surface of the machine's potentials when he was asked to press forward on a game that would show off the 16-bit bells and whistles and improve on 'Super Mario Bros. 3.' It was an onerous assignment, made more difficult by the undisguised pressure to succeed. 'Super Mario Bros. 4,' renamed 'Super Mario World,' was supposed to be so great that there would be no question when it came to choosing a 16-bit platform.

'There's no emotion in a game,' Tony Harman says. 'It's all ones and zeros; we're creating illusions. The magic comes from inspiration . . . The best of the rest of the efforts can be no better than second best.'

Miyamoto set to work to create sleight of hand beyond any he had managed before, and he did manage some great innovations. Still, when it was completed, 'Super Mario World' was disappointingly similar to its antecedents. Mario had new skills, and the game offered some fascinating innovations. There were opportunities throughout it for players to hone new skills – first in nonlethal, then in semilethal, and finally in dangerous situations. To encourage players to enjoy Mario's ability to fly, for example, Miyamoto designed a world with no enemies where players could practice in a sky filled with coins. Every hundred coins were good for a free life, so there was plenty of incentive to wallow there, take a running start, pump the A button, and take off.

Miyamoto also made the game nonlinear – a player could return to different worlds at any time – and there were other touches that seemed as if they would lead to future developments. However, 'Super Mario World' wasn't a sufficient departure from its predecessor. 'People don't know how to write 16-bit software yet,' Greg Fischbach said at the time. 'It will be revolutionary, but it will take some time to understand.' There would be more lifelike and emotion-filled games because of 16-bit processors. Miyamoto says, 'Wait, and I will learn more about the limits of this machine.' In the meantime, 'Super Mario World' was a disappointment, particularly when it was compared to a new game that was released for Sega's 16-bit system.

An independent development team contracted to Sega came up with 'Sonic the Hedgehog,' a game featuring a cute creature who impatiently tapped his foot – er, paw – when the player took too long to act. Impatience was Sonic's essential characteristic: he had places to go – and quickly. He zipped along, collecting brass rings when he could find them, before rolling up into a ball and flying down slides with loops and underground tunnels. For the player, it was like a roller-coaster ride. Sega pronounced 'Sonic' the fastest video game in history. It had finally found its Mario.

'Sonic' was not a great game, but it was novel, the character was likable, and it had good graphics and a bouncy musical score. Like so many games, it was plagued by repetition, but with not much competition at that time from Nintendo or any licensees, 'Sonic' took off and sold hundreds of thousands of Genesis systems. Best of all for Sega, 'Sonic' was there to mock Nintendo's launch of its Super system.

* * *

In spite of Sega's growth, Nintendo believed it would release its Super systems in Japan and America and easily do away with the Genesis, 'Sonic' and all. Sega may have stockpiled cash ($400 million) and earned a cooler-than-Mario reputation, but this was only because Nintendo hadn't yet entered the field. Finally it announced plans to release its 16-bit machine. The announcement was, in large part, a warning to would-be Genesis buyers not to make a mistake they would regret.

The actual launch began a year later in Japan, where anticipation of the new system was rabid. In late October 1990, there were rumors that the Super Family Computer was coming, and stores were inundated with calls. As soon as Hiroshi Imanishi informed his sales team that a shipping date was forthcoming, some stores began taking orders. The Hankyu department store in Osaka announced that it would accept 'reservations' beginning on November 3. A week later it had accepted more than it would be able to fill and stopped accepting orders. Other stores announced lotteries, and some had customers pay the 32,000 yen (about $200) for the system plus 'Super Mario World' in advance.

Yamauchi and Imanishi jointly directed Operation Midnight Shipping, which commenced in the wee hours of November 20, 1990. Kenji Takahashi, in his recent book on Nintendo (*Light and Shadow of an Enterprise That Surpassed Matsushita and Sony*), described the secret transport: 'On a night in the fall . . . with the wind blowing through the Kyoto Basin, adding a considerable chill, an unusually large number of over-sized ten-ton trucks congregated at a warehouse in the city. Workmen quietly loaded the trucks, which then disappeared, one by one, into the darkness of the sleeping town and onto the state highway . . .

'At the same time, other trucks departed from warehouses throughout Japan. The last truck left the last warehouse as dawn was breaking.'

All the secrecy was to head off thievery, Hiroshi Yamauchi subsequently revealed. A *yakuza* ring was rumored to be planning to hijack some of the trucks. Worth their weight in gold, the goods would have ended up in mob warehouses, from which they would have been parceled out to special customers. Fearing leaks, the Nintendo executives informed their staff about the details of

Midnight Shipping only on a need-to-know basis. Similarly, only the key people expecting shipments were told when the trucks would arrive. When they did appear, carefully predetermined allotments of systems and software were parceled out.

The hundred trucks, each loaded with three thousand Super Family Computers and boxes of the first two Super Famicom games, 'Super Mario World' and 'F-Zero' (a racing game), had dropped off their secret cargo by the end of the business day on the twentieth. The next morning, store managers braced themselves before announcing that the next Nintendo generation had arrived. If high drama was part of the marketing plan, it worked. One department store closed down its toy department by 11:30 A.M. because it feared a riot. A small toy store on the main street near the Shakujii Koen train station in Tokyo received only six units. 'It was not enough to meet even the request from our neighbors and the children of our friends,' the elderly store owner reported. 'As we would have been embarrassed to turn down our friends, we closed the store and posted a notice saying that we had taken a trip.'

Three hundred thousand Super Famicoms were delivered that night, though the orders numbered 1.5 million. Four out of five customers were disappointed, including some who had paid in advance. It was a mess, although Hiroshi Yamauchi enjoyed hearing that the full supply was gone by the third day. A total of 2 million Famicoms were sold within six months, and over 4 million within a year.

The U.S. launch was trickier. The NES market had already peaked for a number of reasons, among them the fact that the United States was in an economic recession. But what was even more relevant was that Nintendo had reached relative saturation of its largest group of buyers, households with young boys. The arrival of the 16-bit generation of technology diverted some potential customers and deterred others who decided to wait and see what happened before choosing a system to buy. Another factor was that neither Nintendo nor any licensee had released any superhot, must-have game since 'Super Mario Bros. 3' and 'Teenage Mutant Ninja Turtles' (although 'The Simpsons,' released by Acclaim, designed in collaboration with Matt Groening, was one of several big sellers during this period). For all these reasons, there was to be no Operation Midnight Shipping in the United States. Nintendo had its work cut out for it if customers, en masse, were to be convinced to shell out $200 for the new system.

Peter Main and Bill White stepped in with a marketing blitz. Twenty-five million dollars was spent on TV commercials for the September 1991 launch, and Gail Tilden at *Nintendo Power* – which then had about 1.2 million subscribers and 4 million readers – hyped the SNES shamelessly. There were also SNES promotions with Pepsi ($8 million worth), Kool-Aid, and other companies.

For the previous year (1990), the average amount of money spent on toys per child in America was about $225, according to Jodi Levin, a spokeswoman for the Toy Manufacturers of America. Since the year of the SNES launch, 1991, was a recession year, the figure wasn't likely to go up. The question was whether parents would spend almost all of their kid's Christmas budget on one toy. But by October 1991, despite predictions of an extremely bleak Christmas, Nintendo had decided it was going to make its goals for the SNES debut. It claimed it would sell all the SNES units it shipped in those first four months – 2.2 million, according to the company. Peter Main was claiming he could sell twice as many if NCL were able to meet the demand.

At the January 1992 Consumer Electronics Show, Nintendo boasted that it had already blown Sega out of the water, and, as Peter Main put it, 'You ain't seen nothin' yet.' He announced sales predictions for the year: 6 million SNES units in the United States. According to the company's calculations, this would bring total sales to 8 million, not a bad start considering that the original NES had sold only 1 million in that amount of time. Most industry watchers believed these figures were slightly optimistic, an attempt to jump-start sales by creating a bandwagon mentality. The fact was that SNES had little chance of approaching the NES's success since Sega had already assured that Nintendo wouldn't have the market to itself.

Sega lowered the price of the Genesis to $149 and the system was packaged with 'Sonic the Hedgehog,' which continued to propel sales. The game's immense popularity took Sega by surprise, but the company ran with it. It didn't quite stop the SNES in its tracks, but it gave both Nintendo and customers pause. Sega boasted that in a test conducted by a market-research firm, seven out of ten kids preferred 'Sonic' to 'Super Mario World.'

A Sega press release was headlined SEGA CONFRONTS NINTENDO IN $1 MILLION AD ROADBLOCK. Their television commercials, which vied for airtime with Nintendo's massive ad blitz, showed a kid resisting a pushy salesman's attempt to sell him the more expensive SNES. 'Super Mario World' looked timeworn compared to 'Sonic the Hedgehog,' the game playing on a nearby monitor. The ads ran with *Beverly Hills 90210, Cosby*, and *The Simpsons*.

'This is war,' boomed Sega's Al Nilsen, who steered and cheered the battle. It was the company's first and probably only chance against Nintendo. Sixty percent of his customers had defected from Nintendo, and Nilsen planned to keep them. His ads featured the 'Sega advantage,' 100 software titles for Genesis (made by Sega and twenty third-party developers) as compared to a mere handful for the SNES.

The close of 1992 through 1993 would have a great deal to say about the disputed figures released by both companies. Analysts and retailers predicted that a total of some 10 million Genesis and SNES systems would be sold by the end of 1992, with the two companies in a virtual dead heat. If this occurred, it would be a rousing victory for Sega, which could then continue a head-to-head battle. If Nintendo ended up way ahead, the status would remain quo. Nintendo would still control perhaps 75 to 80 percent of the market, and Sega would be a modest number two (though certainly stronger than before).

Choosing sides or attempting to play both against the middle, the licensees had a major stake in the competition. Nintendo's licensees continued to release NES titles – the market had weakened, but 35 million games for the NES and another 25 million games for Game Boy would sell in 1992, according to the company's predictions – and most signed up to make SNES games. Nintendo planned to sign up 100 SNES licensees so that the SNES – Genesis game gap would cease to be an issue.

In the United States NOA sought to control the quality of its new licensees' product in a unique way. There was no longer an exclusivity clause (in part, at least, because of the FTC and the antitrust cases pending). Instead, Nintendo would allow licensees to make three games a year. But it also built in a strong motivation for companies to make excellent games: games that earned thirty or more points in the Nintendo rating system didn't count as one of the three games. Also, a more objective method for choosing what games would be covered in *Nintendo Power* was initiated: only those games with thirty or more points would be featured.

Most Nintendo licensees liked the idea of competition between Nintendo and Sega, even though it meant they had to make choices about which system to support – or whether to support both. The attitude of some licensees was that anything that weakened Nintendo was good news. Part of this was resentment – it was always good to see a tyrant fall – but part was that it strengthened their positions. Whereas they had originally come to Nintendo hat in hand when they wanted to become NES licensees, now Nintendo needed them. Nintendo had to have a strong library of games to beat Sega, and the licensees were key.

In spite of their discreet rooting for Genesis, the licensees found neither openness nor benevolence at Sega, whose own licensing terms got tougher until they appeared to be nearly as strict as NOA's. The only thing some licensees had going for them was that they were being wooed by both Nintendo and Sega, which gave them some negotiating power. 'As often happens, a revolutionary accomplishes a coup and becomes the next despot,' a licensee said. 'Sega was as bad as Nintendo because Sega wanted to *be* Nintendo.'

As the early months of the contest rolled by, SNES sales remained healthy, though nowhere near as strong as NES sales had been at their peak. The trade press remarked upon it as if they had found a chink in Nintendo's armor, and indeed, the first round of the 16-bit war proved that NOA was no longer infallible. The future was up for grabs, although there was one certainty: it would be a mistake to discount prematurely the Arakawa-main marketing force and the resolve of Hiroshi Yamauchi.

In a lapse of his ability to foresee the long-term future, Yamauchi had realized too late the importance of sewing up the 16-bit market, even at the expense of some 8-bit sales. At stake was more than the $10 billion-plus that consumers would spend on video games in

1992 and the escalating amounts predicted for the following years. The video-game industry was changing. It had found itself at the center of a new industry, fast emerging as *the* consumer-electronics and home-computer industry of the future.

SELECTED BIBLIOGRAPHY

Adlum, Ed, 'The Replay Years,' *Replay*, November 1985: 121–172.
Brand, Stewart, *The Media Lab* (New York: Penguin, 1987).
Burstein, Daniel, *Yen! Japan's New Financial Empire and Its Threat to America* (New York: Ballantine, 1988).
Bylinsky, Gene, 'The Marvels of Virtual Reality,' *Fortune*, June 3, 1991: 146–150.
Carse, James P., *Finite and Infinite Games* (New York: Ballantine, 1987).
Choate, Pat, *Agents of Influence* (New York: Knopf, 1990).
Cohen, Scott, *Zap! The Rise and Fall of Atari* (New York: McGraw-Hill, 1984).
Corr, O. Casey, and Jimi Lott, 'Nintendo Power: Bigger Than Mickey Mouse,' *Pacific Magazine*, December 16, 1990: 10–14.
Crichton, Michael, *Rising Sun* (New York: Knopf, 1992).
Dertouzos, Michael L., Richard K. Lester, and Robert M. Solow, 'Made in America: Regaining the Productive Edge,' *The Report of the MIT Commission on Industrial Productivity* (Cambridge, Mass.: MIT Press, 1989).
Ditlea, Steve, 'Inside Artificial Reality,' *PC/Computing*, November 1989: 91–102.
Dvorak, John C., 'Is the CD-ROM Rip-off About to End? Ask Nintendo,' *PC/Computing*, September 1991: 66.

SELECTED BIBLIOGRAPHY

Fuller, Buckminster, *Education Automation* (Carbondale, Ill.: Southern Illinois University Press, 1961).

Garver, Lloyd, 'No, You Can't Have Nintendo,' *Newsweek*, June 11, 1990: 8.

Gibson, William, *Neuromancer* (New York: Berkley, 1984).

Greenfield, Patricia Marks, *Mind and Media: The Effects of Television, Video Games, and Computers* (Cambridge, Mass.: Harvard University Press, 1984).

Ishihara, Shintaro, and Akio Morita, *No to ieru Nihon* [*The Japan That Can Say No*] (Tokyo: Kobunsha, 1990).

'Japan Goes Hollywood,' *Newsweek*, October 9, 1989: 62–72.

Japan Publications (ed.), *Hanafuda: The Flower Card Game* (Tokyo: Nichibo Shuppan-sho, 1970).

Katz, Donald R., 'The new Generation Gap,' *Esquire*, February 1990: 49–50.

Kidder, Tracy, *The Soul of a New Machine* (Boston: Little, Brown, 1981).

'Less Fun, Few Games? Toy Industry Analyst Is Bearish on Nintendo,' *Barron's*, December 3, 1990: 16–63.

Levine, David, 'Special Effects: Broadcast Arts Has Created a New Genre in the World of Television,' *Continental Profiles*, April 1991: 23–40.

Levy, Richard C., and Ronald O. Weingartner, *Inside Santa's Workshop: How Toy Inventors Develop, Sell, and Cash In on Their Ideas* (New York: Henry Holt, 1990).

Levy, Steven, *Hackers: Heroes of the Computer Revolution* (New York: Bantam Doubleday Dell, 1984).

Loftus, Geoffrey R., and Elizabeth F. Loftus, *Mind at Play: The Psychology of Video Games* (New York: Basic, 1983).

McLuhan, Marshall, *Understanding Media: The Extensions of Man* (New York: McGraw-Hill, 1964).

Moritz, Michael, *The Little Kingdom: The Private Story of Apple Computer* (New York: William Morrow, 1984), p. 13.

Nakata, Hiroyuki, *Success Legend in the Semiconductor Era: Nintendo's Great Strategy (The Day Mario Exceeded Toyota)* (Tokyo: JICC, 1990).

Okimoto, Daniel I., *Between MITI and the Market: Japanese Industrial Policy for High Technology* (Stanford: Stanford University Press, 1989).

Orey, Michael, 'Godzilla in Toyland: Why Nobody Beats Nintendo of America at Its Own Game,' *The American Lawyer*, April 1990: 62–69.

Papert, Seymour, *Mindstorms: Children, Computers and Powerful Ideas* (New York: Basic, 1980).

Perry, J. Nancy, 'Will Sony Make It in Hollywood?' *Fortune*, September 9, 1991: 158–166.

Provenzo, Eugene F., Jr., *Video Kids: Making Sense of Nintendo* (Cambridge, Mass.: Harvard University Press, 1991).

Rayl, A.J.S., 'The New, Improved Reality,' *Los Angeles Times Magazine*, July 21, 1991: 17.

Reischauer, Edwin O., *The Japanese Today* (Cambridge, Mass: Harvard University Press, 1977).

Rosenberg, Scott, 'Condemned to Be Mario: The Video-game Plumber as Existential Hero,' *Image*, September 1, 1991: 22–25.

Schlender, Brenton R., 'The Future of the PC,' *Fortune*, August 26, 1991: 40.

Schwartz, John, 'The Next Revolution,' *Newsweek*, April 6, 1992: 42–48.

Selnow, Gary W., 'Playing Videogames: The Electronic Friend,' *Journal of Communications*, Spring 1984: 140–148.

Sheff, David, 'How Nintendo Did It,' *Men's Life*, Fall 1990: 84.

—— 'Interview: Pat Choate,' *Upside*, February 1991.

—— 'Interview: Trip Hawkins,' *Upside*, August/September, 1990: 46.

—— 'Mario's Big Brother,' *Rolling Stone*, January 9, 1992: 45.

—— '*Playboy* Interview: Shintaro Ishihara,' *Playboy*, October 1990.

—— '*Playboy* Interview: Steve Jobs,' *Playboy*, February 1985.

—— '*Playboy* Interview: Robert Maxwell.' *Playboy*, October 1991.

—— 'Reversal of Fortune,' San Francisco *Focus*, May 1991: 54.

Skow, John, 'Games That People Play,' *Time*, January 18, 1982: 50–58.

Takahashi, Kenji, *Super Famicom: The Intrigue of Nintendo (Light and Shadow of an Enterprise That Surpassed Matsushita and Sony)* (Tokyo: Kobunsha, 1990).

Tatsuno, Sheridan M., *Created in Japan* (New York: Ballinger, 1990).

'Teaching Japan to Say No,' *Time*, November 20, 1989: 81–82.

Tiley, Ed, *Tricks of the Nintendo Masters* (Carmel, Ind.: Hayden, 1990).

Turkle, Sherry, *The Second Self: Computers and the Human Spirit* (New York: Simon & Schuster, 1984).

Utsumi, Ichiro, *Secrets of Nintendo's Gulliverian Oligopoly* (Tokyo: Nihon Bungei-sha, 1989).

'Videogames: Fun or Serious Threat?' *U.S. News & World Report*, February 22, 1982: 7.

Warshofsky, Fred, *The Chip War* (New York: Scribner's, 1989).

Webb, Marcus, 'Into the Unknown!: New Decade Brings Promises and Pitfalls for Hopeful Coin-op Tradesters,' *Replay*, January 1990: 41–66.